The Nature of History

The Explosion of British Society 1914–1962 (1963)
Clifford Allen: The Open Conspirator (1964)
*The Deluge: British Society and
the First World War* (1965)
*Britain in the Century of Total War:
War, Peace and Social Change, 1900–1967* (1968)

The Nature of History

ARTHUR MARWICK

MACMILLAN

First published 1970 by
MACMILLAN AND CO LTD
Little Essex Street London WC2
and also at Bombay Calcutta and Madras
Macmillan South Africa (Publishers) Pty Ltd Johannesburg
The Macmillan Company of Australia Pty Ltd Melbourne
The Macmillan Company of Canada Ltd Toronto
Gill and Macmillan Ltd Dublin

Printed in Great Britain by
WESTERN PRINTING SERVICES LTD
Bristol

Contents

∞∞

'Puritan Revolution' 4. The American Revolution 5. The
Industrial Revolution 6. Imperialism 7. The Origins of the
Second World War

Preface

~~~~~~

THIS book is aimed at the general reader and at the student who is just embarking upon the serious study of history. It follows that my learned colleagues will find little in it that is new, and, very probably, much that is irritating; certainly they would be well-advised to skip the simple historiographical account given in chapters 2 and 3.

Nonetheless this book only became possible through the willingness of academic colleagues to discuss with me the many problems involved in a study of the nature of history. First of all I wish to thank Mr Alan Bullock who, from the moment he knew that I proposed to attempt a book of this sort, gave me every encouragement in what, at the time, seemed a most dubious enterprise. Alan Bullock, despite many other infinitely more important and pressing claims upon his time, read the entire typescript; thanks to him I was guided away from many serious errors of commission and omission. Professor Denys Hay read the early chapters and saved me from some grave mistakes in medieval and Renaissance historiography. Mr Owen Dudley Edwards read the whole book; his sparkling discussions of its inadequacies were both helpful and enjoyable.

Among those who went out of their way to share with me their understanding of the nature of history were: Mr A. J. P. Taylor; Professor Max Beloff; Dr Henry Pelling; Professor Harry Hanham; Professor John Bromley; Professor James Joll; Mr Christopher Hill; Dr Eric Hobsbawm; Professor Raymond O. Rockwood; and Professor John T. Halstead.

Many other colleagues found a convivial pint soured by my persistent questioning. On sociological topics I have for many years been picking the brains of Professor Tom Burns; my guidance on the history of science came mainly from Dr Eric Forbes. Most of the references for 'video-history' I owe to Dr Paul Smith.

Such a list is, of course, no insurance against my own ignorance and lack of understanding; of both, no doubt, plenty remains. Yet I like to think that this book is in some sense a memorial to my years as a student and teacher at the University of Edinburgh. Whether that university would like to think so too is another matter. In any case I should add that the final stimulus towards undertaking this exploration came from an invigorating year's teaching in the United States where I was forced to re-examine many long-held assumptions.

This book is intended for use. I have therefore tried as far as possible to illustrate my text with references to books which are easy to obtain: in particular I have made frequent recourse to that invaluable collection of readings *The Varieties of History*, edited by Fritz Stern. Publication dates cited in the text and footnotes refer to first publication in country or origin – full information on American and British publications is given in the bibliography.

Among the many obvious omissions the one I feel saddest about is History of Art. The interested reader is directed to the excellent chapter by Professor David Talbot Rice in *Approaches to History*, edited by H. P. R. Finberg. I fear the other omissions may not be so easily remedied.

My standpoint is that of a working historian practising in the third quarter of the twentieth century. To many readers it will seem that I have done poorly by such philosophical writers as Hegel and Croce. Frankly, neither of these famous philosophers mean much to me as a historian, and I have thought it best to admit this openly. That Marx influenced all subsequent historical writing seems to me very important; that Hegel influenced Marx does not, for my purposes, seem to me at all important. The word 'dialectic' does not appear once in my text. Nor is there any mention of the German philosopher Wilhelm Dilthey. Again the reader must seek guidance from among the illustrious books cited in the bibliography. I have not sought to compete with them.

Finally my warmest thanks to Mr C. T. Harvie and Mr Neil Wynn of the Open University, who not only read the proofs but suggested valuable last-ditch improvements.

1 *Justifications and Definitions*

∽∽

1 First Things First

Attend an introductory course in economics or philosophy or sociology, or, for that matter, in chemistry, and you will first learn something of the aims, methods and history of the discipline you are studying. Up till the present the tendency in historical studies – the odd course in historiography apart – has been to take such matters for granted. Any fool, it seemed, could tell at once what history was, and what it was about; and many fools, certain critics implied, were suitably employed in the practice of this ill-defined profession. This book has been written in the belief that, for the intelligent layman as well as the serious student, the value of any historical reading that he may do will be greatly enhanced if he first has a grasp of the nature and basic principles of historical study. I would myself go so far as to argue that the survey courses which at present form the usual introduction to history at university or college level ought to be scrapped in favour of courses which treat of the nature and purposes of history. Although there are a number of valuable books in print which deal in various ways with these matters, they do not seem to me to quite meet the present need, being either entirely professional, in that they aim at one or other of two very different levels within the historical profession, or so amateur that in effect they are personal statements, offering little guidance to the reader who seeks insight into the standards generally acceptable to most historians. Of the professional works the vast majority are aimed at the advanced student balanced fearfully on the verge of that dark and (often) bottomless pit, research. The comment of the *American Historical Review* on Fritz Stern's collection of readings *The Varieties of History* (1956) was that 'his paperbound book ought to be in the hands of all graduate students and many of their teachers'; why not in the hands of all students, all interested laymen? Professional works on the lower level, which aim 'to develop explicitly the awareness and approach the instructor usually assumes his students to have',[1] serve a valuable purpose in remedying the deficiencies of high-school education, but make rather tedious reading for the informed reader. Clearly distinctions must be made between different levels of intellectual activity, but the barriers are already too high between 'scholars', 'researchers', 'senior students', 'junior students' and the lay public, leaving aside the barriers between those involved in the pursuit of different academic disciplines. The physicist who is friendly towards historical study should be given the basic tenets of that study; the physicist who is hostile has the right to demand that the historian stand up and be identified. The reader of the *Sunday Times* book review who occasionally dips into one of the historical works which so dominate its pages can well ask for some more extensive rationale of what is good and what is bad history – even if he goes on preferring the latter. If history is worth studying at all, such study should be firmly integrated with teaching in the nature, methods and purposes of history, regarded not simply as a set of background assumptions, but as something fundamental to any intelligent discussion of history at any level.

It is still on the whole true, as Professor Richard Pares put it, that 'these things are more discussed by philosophers than by historians', that 'the philosophers are much readier to say what the historian ought to be doing than the historians are to say what they are doing'.[2] Among themselves historians today are not always too confident about just what it is they are doing. In a world increasingly dominated by science and technology they share in the sense of diminished importance experienced by all practitioners of the humanities; more critically, they are finding that many of their brighter potential students are turning their backs on history in favour of sociology or political science. In public historians talk of the complexities and subtleties of their craft; in private they lament that their subject has little in the way of basic entrance requirements and that anyone with a gift of the gab can flannel his way through a history course. History is often the subject of the students whose real interest is in athletics or dramatics: academically what they want is a soft option. Or, conversely, history is the subject of the dullards who merely wish to continue the familiar book-learning they have acquired at school. In August 1968 the London *Sunday Times* published an intriguing gossipy item which must have confirmed many prejudices about the nature of history:

> His Serene Highness Prince Michael Grousinski insists he learned nothing at Cambridge, in a formal sense at least. 'I was as capable of distinguishing myself in Tripos on the day I arrived as in the weeks before I left', he says. In the weeks before he left in 1966 he achieved a most distinguished honours degree in history – 'history being the supreme discipline that trains dynasts, a fact of which the University of Cambridge appears unaware. I derived absolutely no benefit, intellectual or political, from the time I spent there, and the sole redeeming feature of undergraduate existence was certain social pleasures.'

Maddened perhaps by the public arrogance of the historian, critics have accused his profession of having no clear aims, no special methodology, no sense of its place and purpose. A distinguished social scientist places historians in a 'private world inhabited exclusively by penetrating but unfathomable insights and ineffable understandings'.[3] History is attacked, from the intellectual heights, as being vague, cliché-ridden and devoid of basic standards, and, from the popular lowlands, as being pedantic and over-concerned with the detailed pursuit of the insignificant. Even to those innocent of any interest in the maintenance of intellectual standards and unfamiliar with the pedantries, the very name of history often smells of rank boredom. The Duke of Cumberland's dismissive words to the eighteenth-century historian Edward Gibbon have been quoted in various forms: 'So, I suppose you are at the old trade again – scribble, scribble, scribble', is one version. Alexander Pope addressed a scornful couplet to historians:

> To future ages may thy dulness last,
> As thou preserv'st the dulness of the past.

Most crushing of all, and weighty evidence that distrust of the historian far antedates the rise of modern scholarship, are the remarks of the sixteenth-century Englishman, Sir Philip Sidney:

> The historian . . . loaden with old mouse-eaten records, authorising himselfe for the most part upon other histories, whose greatest authorities are built uppon the notable foundation heresay, having much ado to accord differing writers, and to prick truth out of partiality: better acquainted with a 1,000 yeres ago, than with the present age, and yet better knowing how this world goeth, than how his owne wit runneth; curious for antiquities, and inquisitive of novelties; a wonder to young folkes, and a tyrant in table talk.[4]

Henry Ford's 'History is bunk' was actually a casual and unpremeditated aside: the significance of the remark lies in the fact that it is so often quoted with so much approval.

One very real problem is that the only history with which most people are familiar is the history taught to them at a very elementary level; and the history taught at an elementary level is often not very good history. Dates and boring facts of course. And also, in the recollection of many, a terrible tub-thumping jingoism, glorifying the United States, Britain, France or whatever the country may be (but, naturally, never all three), which strains the credulity of the more intelligent child. History is not synonymous with propaganda, but it has to be admitted that it often seems to be. Then also there are the 'history' questions on those ubiquitous and interminable television quizzes: 'Who were Queen Victoria's uncles?' Who cares? Certainly not the historian, but that, nonetheless, for many is history.

Already it will be clear from these rather scattered instances that criticism of history takes two distinct forms: there are those who see no virtue, only dullness, in the very subject itself; more important, there are those who feel that however immense and important the possibilities of the subject, as in the past and at present practised it has grievous flaws. The first criticism cannot be dealt with absolutely: though a man can see with his own eyes the pleasure afforded to countless thousands by the company of the dog, he may personally be aware only of the animal's odour and stupidity. The second criticism will take at least the whole of this book to answer. It arises in part from an understandable failure to comprehend the special character of history and the strangely assorted claims it has to meet: in one sense a soft option, history is also one of the most taxing of intellectual disciplines. Central to the difficulties of history are two very different problems, which will be elaborated at later stages in this book: although the historian is concerned with many of the same materials as are handled by the social scientist, his work must at all times be conceived within the fourth dimension of *time*; if history approaches sociology, it is sociology *in motion*. Secondly, at the core of the historian's activities there lies the problem not simply of establishing what happened, but of *communicating* his discoveries.

2 The Necessity for History

History, it has been said, is a 'major industry' in contemporary society, an industry encompassing the white-collar men of pure research, the black-coated professors and academic administrators, and the black-collar workers in the schools and in journalism. Also included, according to Professor Conyers Read, is anyone else who 'undertakes to interpret the past to the present', novelists, playwrights 'and above all radio commentators' (Professor Read was writing before the days of television). The image of an industry, though usually used in a hostile manner by embattled social scientists, is a good one, and illuminates with startling clarity the very nature of history. Quite simply, human society *needs* history; the sophisticated societies of our own day need a lot of history. We are all constantly calling upon history, constantly making historical judgements, as when we contrast President Richard Nixon with President Franklin D. Roosevelt, or liken Prime Minister Harold Wilson to Prime Minister David Lloyd George, or declare current economic problems to be 'unprecedented', or seek the origins of the mini-skirt among the 'flappers' of the 1920s. During the period of rioting in Northern Ireland in October 1968 the British intellectual weekly, the *New Statesman*, published a leading article entitled 'Ulster will be Wrong'. The allusion was a historical one, Lord Randolph Churchill in the previous century having coined the slogan: 'Ulster will fight, and Ulster will be right'. To those who pose the question, 'What is the use of history?' the crispest and most enlightening reply is to suggest that they try to imagine what everyday life would be like in a society in which no one knew any history. Imagination boggles, because it is only through knowledge of its history that a society can have knowledge of itself. As a man without memory and self-knowledge is a man adrift, so a society without memory (or more correctly, without recollection) and self-knowledge would be a society adrift. Leaving aside the notion of the collective subconscious, human society, unlike the individual, has no organic memory: so every society must have some functionary, whether priest, bard, or Keeper of the Public Records, responsible for preserving and communicating such knowledge. Those who ignore history, said Professor Lévi-Strauss, condemn themselves to not knowing the present, because historical development alone permits us to weigh and to evaluate in their respective relations the elements of the present. Frederic Harrison invited us to 'suppose a race of men whose minds, by a paralytic stroke of fate, had suddenly been deadened to every recollection, to whom the whole world was new'. Can we, he asked, 'imagine a condition of such helplessness, confusion, and misery'? Cicero put it even more neatly: 'Not to know what took place before you were born is to remain forever a child.' Effectively we do not even make a choice: we eschew perpetual childhood and grab, however erratically, at history. The primitive tribe, living in relative isolation, requires knowledge only of its own traditions, of great heroic deeds, and of the way things have always been done. A more complex society will still require a knowledge of its own past: here is the rudimentary justification for the much-criticised state of affairs in which French children learn mainly French history, American children American history, English children English history (ignoring even Scottish and Welsh history). If there is to be any possibility of changing 'the way things have always been done' there must be reasoned appraisal of how and why they came to be done in this way. But in a developed society the need arises too for an understanding of the relationship of one's own society to other societies, of the place of one's own culture relative to a wider civilisation and to all civilisations.

'When I enlisted as a private in the Grenadier Guards during the last war,' the historian Maurice Ashley tells us, 'the first thing our sergeant taught us was the history of the regiment'. When the allied landings on Italy began during the Second World War, Mussolini's plaintive ejaculation was: 'History has seized us by the throat.' Our own Western civilisation has inherited from Judaeo-Christianity a particularly strong sense of history. But interest in, and dependence upon, history is no occidental monopoly: both the Muslim school and the great Chinese school of history have been central elements in their own civilisations.

The fundamental justification for historical study, then, is that history is necessary: it meets a basic instinct and need of men living in society.

The necessity for history has two aspects. History is *functional* in the sense of meeting the need which society has to know itself and to understand its relationship with the past and with other societies and cultures. It is also *poetic*, in the sense that there is inborn in almost every individual (leaving aside our spiritual dog-haters) a curiosity and sense of wonder about the past, an awareness as G. M. Trevelyan has put it, of 'the quasi-miraculous fact that once, on this earth . . . walked other men and women, as actual as we are today, thinking their own thoughts, swayed by their own passions, but now all gone, one generation vanishing after another, gone as utterly as we ourselves shall shortly be gone like ghosts at cockcrow'. There exists in the human imagination an 'instinctive wish to break down the barriers of time and mortality and so to extend the limits of human consciousness beyond the span of a single life'.[5] The instinct is akin to that aroused in those autumnal days when there is wood smoke on the air and a strange disordered nostalgia pervades the mind; or to the emotions inspired by distant church bells on a calm Sunday morning.[6] Whether he stresses the poetic or the functional element, the historian is ministering to a human need: if he says, as many historians still do, that he is studying the past 'for its own sake', he is either such a good historian that he has long since taken the explicit justifications for his craft for granted, or else he is a specially bad historian. As with the artist, it is often true that the less overt attention the historian pays to his social role, the better in fact does he fulfil that role. The historian, like the artist, is quite justified in apparently neglecting the social purposes of his work. It is history rather than the historian which society requires: the historian who is too conscious of social needs may well produce bad history. For although history has this peculiarly strong social element which is its special justification, it is also, alongside the humanities, the social sciences, and the natural sciences, a part of man's broad attack upon what is not yet known, a participant in man's struggle to understand his environment, physical, temporal and social. As well as its peculiar and basic justification, then, (not necessarily, of course, greater than those that can be advanced on behalf of other areas of human endeavour), history shares in the general justification which attaches to all intellectual activity designed to further human knowledge.

What is here presented is a very elementary justification for the study of history. It is not the justification that is always, or even most often, put forward; but before attempting to demonstrate that all other explanations are essentially corollaries of the basic justification, it would be helpful to offer one or two definitions. 'History' as commonly used has three levels of meaning. First it can connote the entire human past as it actually happened. Life, doubtless, would be simpler if this usage could be abandoned in favour of the unambiguous locution 'the past'. Language however is a common property, ill-defined, often badly cultivated, but not subject to enclosure by precious academics. Even those scholars who have publicly renounced this usage of the word will be found at some stage to betray themselves, for it is very hard to avoid such plump pronouncements as 'History is not the handiwork of hero-figures', or 'Now is the time to take stock of human history'. History, secondly and more usefully, connotes man's attempt to describe and interpret that past: it is, in the words of Professor Barraclough, 'the attempt to discover on the basis of fragmentary evidence the significant things about the past'.[7] This is the history with which we are concerned when we talk of history as a social necessity, of history being an 'industry'; and this is the sense which comes nearest to the original Greek meaning, 'Inquiry'. Some ventures in discovery or inquiry are clearly more successful than others: some ages have regarded as 'significant' matters which we would now relegate to the realms of superstition, myth or polemic. We can enjoy and profit from historical works spread across the entire timespan of human literary activity,' such as those of Thucydides, Ssŭ-ma Chi'en, Bede or Machiavelli: but we must note that the systematic study of history, history as a *discipline* (the third meaning), is a very recent phenomenon, becoming established in West European and North American universities only in the nineteenth century, far in arrears of philosophy, classical languages, mathematics and natural sciences. In this book we shall be specially concerned with the development of modern historical studies; but an important theme will be the difficult, but highly exciting tensions generated between history as an academic and sometimes pedantic discipline, and history as an essential facet of human experience.

The threefold usage of the word 'history', once we have identified the three meanings, is not as absurd as it may sound, though it may at times be confusing. Even where terms have been coined for such new disciplines as sociology there always remains the possibility of confusion between sociology as the structures and processes studied, and the study itself. 'Chemistry' or 'biology' or 'physics' are words we use in a variety of ways – almost poetically when we explain a friendship as due to 'chemistry' or say we can't attend an interview at the other end of the earth as a sheer matter of 'physics'. More obviously, such social sciences as 'economics' and 'politics' cover a range of meaning almost as wide as that of history itself. To geography there attaches meanings exactly analogous to the three which attach to history. True, there does exist the clumsy but useful word 'historiography' which, on the principle of reserving to history the sense of the entire human past, has sometimes been used to cover the second and third meanings given above. However, so pedantic a word is better reserved for a more precise task: not the writing of history, but the study of the writing of history (analogous to the procedure by which history means not the past, but the study of the past). If I study American history I attempt within the limits of my capabilities and of the time at my disposal to get as close as I can to the objective reality of the American past (history in our first sense), by means of ordinary conversation, high-school instruction, works of popularisation, textbooks, secondary authorities, scholarly monographs, documents and other primary relics of that objective past. If I study American historiography I am unlikely to be interested in the more elementary works of exposition (though I might be); I will not be studying documents or relics; I will be studying the writings of significant historians, with an interest in what they said and why they said it, rather than in the what and why of the objective past; I will, at the least, be interested in their interpretations rather than in my interpretation. Historiography is thus a narrower and much less interesting study than history itself: it is a part of historical study, and, in rudimentary and perhaps unconscious form, a preliminary to any important historical endeavour: most of us realise that the content of a casual conversation is likely to be less reliable than the content of a textbook.

If this book must be categorised I suppose it would have to be called historiography: certainly it is intended as a preliminary to the real pleasures and purposes of history. Further difficulties of definition arise with 'philosophy of history', a phrase which again can have three main meanings. In its first sense philosophy of history is concerned with high-level theorising about the underlying currents or essential forces of history as objective reality ('the past'). Less grandly it may be used to describe the basic outlook and fundamental assumptions which a historian brings, or a school of historians bring, to bear on the particular historical problems they deal with, involving theories of causation, concepts of progress, and so on. Finally it can be roughly synonymous with historical 'methodology', the actual processes which the historian at work goes through. Since we cannot in practice say 'this word shall have this meaning and no other', it is important always to be sure which of various possible meanings is intended. Unhappily many of the terms employed in historiography or in the various forms of philosophy of history are even more ambiguous. A flagrant example is the bastard noun 'historicism', born of the German *Historismus* (formerly translated into English as 'historism') out of the Italian *storicismo*. Various alternative definitions will be offered later; for the moment it is sufficient to note that the best thing to do with this word is to avoid it.

A few historians maintain that historical study should be pursued

purely and simply for the pleasure it gives: nothing surprising about this
– mathematicians, biochemists, sculptors have said the same thing of
their own activities. In part the pleasure aspect of historical study is a
corollary of the basic point about man's instinctive craving for history
which, naturally, is likely to be felt most strongly by the committed
student of history (professional or lay). In part it relates to the principle
that something that is pleasurable to the individual is not thereby precluded from being socially useful. Very few historians, on being
pressed, have denied all utility to the study of history. To maintain that
history is self-justifying as the pursuit of knowledge is to say everything
or nothing: if the knowledge is not communicated the pursuit of
history has scarcely left the shelter of the kennels; if it is communicated
a human and social goal is thereby served. The task is to compare and
contrast this service with that performed by other branches of intellectual activity. In doing this historians have most usually stressed the
'educational' value of their subject, as a 'training of the mind' or as a
practical guide to the problems of human society and politics. The
trouble with the training of the mind argument is that it depends
very much upon the rigour and intensity of the historical studies pursued, and is scarcely applicable to those who have little more than a
casual acquaintanceship with one or two of the major works of history.
He who pursues an intensive course in historical studies will undoubtedly find his mind greatly improved thereby – as will anyone who
undertakes any rigorous intellectual discipline. On behalf of the special
case of history it is declared the best form of 'liberal education'.
In so far as this phrase now has overtones of dilettantism and literary
froth it is no justification at all; in so far as it implies comprehension of
man in all his variousness it is essentially a corollary of the basic
justification that history is the necessary recollection of the past
activities of men and societies which makes it possible for the individual
and the society to orientate themselves amid the bewildering currents of
human diversity. The point has been made in various ways. Drawing
an analogy between the study of history and foreign travel, Professor
W. H. Walsh has declared it a major function of history to 'make men
aware of the character of their own time by seeing it in comparison and
contrast with another'. The nineteenth-century French historians
Langlois and Seignobos said of history that 'it familiarises us with
variation in social forms, and cures us of a morbid dread of change'.

The 'practical guide' argument, too, is essentially an extension of my
main thesis: if society needs to know and understand its past, so, even
more, must its leaders and administrators. Great historians often make
absurd pronouncements, especially in the heat of historical controversy.
Just as there have been extreme denials of any possible utility in
historical study, so more recently the social function of history has

been rather crudely overemphasised – making it easy for the ostriches
to score debating points. The careful modern historian does not venture
beyond the belief voiced by Professor Strayer, that 'his learning is useful in meeting new situations, not because it provides a basis for
prediction but because a full understanding of human behaviour in
the past makes it possible to find familiar elements in present problems
and thus makes it possible to solve them more intelligently'.[8] This does
not mean, as some great historians seem to have thought, that only
recent history has this practical value. Though not taught in the
medieval universities, history was always considered an important topic
in the tuition of princes and prelates – Bishop Bossuet's *Universal History*
of 1679 was written with just such a purpose in mind. Abstracted and
left to stand on its own this justification for historical study has two
weaknesses: it suggests that history is for an élite only, 'a sacred
science reserved for the future rulers of states, a science for princes, not
for subjects'; and it has, in practice, served to reinforce the idea of
history as mere common sense applied to the past, to foster a history
palatable to budding politicians, but lacking in conceptual or methodological rigour.

One other familiar justification for the study of history merits attention. History, Professor C. N. L. Brooke has said,

> unfolds not one but many different forms of thought. At one extreme
> historians amass and analyse evidence, very much like a descriptive
> science – and so gain an uneasy respectability from the kindlier logical
> positivists; at the other extreme we analyse the play of human person-
> ality and all the subtleties of the human mind, and so mingle with
> literary criticism. History is not a separate mode of thought, but the
> common home of many interests and techniques and traditions, de-
> vised by those who have dedicated their best energies to the study of
> the past.

Or, in the words of Professor Stuart Hughes, history has always thought
of itself as 'an inclusive, a mediating discipline'.[9] Having formerly
linked philosophy with poetry, it now links literature with social science.
Sometimes, perhaps, historians have alienated potential allies by making too much of the synthesising role of their subject: but whether
capably fulfilled or not, there can be no doubt as to the inescapability
of history's mediating purpose. Because everything has a history, history
as a discipline covers everything. The young clerk studying the principles
of insurance will in part be studying the *history* of insurance; part of
the work of the literary critic, part of the work of the scientist who
studies the development of his subject, must be historical. History
therefore does become a meeting ground for different disciplines, which
is why, at its best, history is such a fascinating subject. Yet again all
we are really doing is elaborating the fundamental justification for

the study of history: man must know his past, and so he must know the infinite richness and variety – in art and science as well as social organisation and politics – of his past. That richness and variety is the subject-matter of history.

3 THE DIALOGUE

It is often said, though I believe the idea is not always well understood, that each age writes its own history, for each age will make a different evaluation of what is 'significant' in its own past, will tend to see the past in the light of its own preoccupations and prejudices. History, in E. H. Carr's striking phrase, is a dialogue between the present and the past. At the one extreme this simple fact has strengthened the elbows of the 'history is bunk' school; at the other it has flattered the self-indulgence of those historians who rejoice in the fascinating uselessness of their subject. Because of its peculiarly strong social affiliations and obligations history necessarily is particularly affected by the material and moral circumstances of the age and society in which it is written. But it is too easily forgotten that all intellectual activities, being the activities of men, are inevitably affected in some degree by the environment in which men work. The famous eighteenth-century chemist Priestley, despite his great discoveries, could never free himself from his belief in the existence of 'phlogiston'. The apparent statistical precision of the pioneer demographer Thomas Malthus was mere top-dressing for an instinctive response to the evidence of expanding population which he saw all around him; it was Malthus's concept of the 'struggle for survival' which precipitated the final crystallisation of the evolutionary doctrine of Charles Darwin with its emphasis on the 'survival of the fittest'. Science in the war-scarred sceptical twentieth century is much more subtle and much less brashly positivistic than the science produced by the rapidly expanding economies of the nineteenth century. It would be a bold man who would argue that scientists and social scientists today are totally free from all prejudices and misconceptions derived from the age in which they live and work. However there can be no doubt that the point is a specially valid one in regard to historical study.

Nineteenth-century historians (in Western Europe and North America) dealt largely with governments and great men, and with the development of national consciousness and the growth of political liberalism; twentieth-century historians, more interested in economic and social democracy, have turned towards economic and social history, towards peoples and away from individuals. Traditionally, historians in the western countries were interested only in their own civilisation, seeing the rest of the world, if at all, in terms of interaction with Western culture. Now that many new nationalities compete for attention on the world stage there has been a boom in African history, in Latin-American history, and, above all, in Chinese and East Asian history. In these days when colonisation is in sad disrepute the attempt is made to study the various civilisations involved from the standpoint of their indigenous development, rather than from that of their contact and conflict with the West. The shape and content of history, too, vary according to the methods and materials available to different generations. The explosion in historical studies at the beginning of the nineteenth century was in part touched off by the opening at that time of the major European archives. Heavy emphasis today is placed on those problems, such as population growth or the social stratification of small communities, which are amenable to today's sophisticated techniques of quantification. The entire spirit in which history is written, the philosophy of history (in the second of its three meanings) varies according to the prevailing beliefs at the time of writing. Lord Acton, at the end of the nineteenth century, believed it his duty to make overt moral judgements; Mr A. J. P. Taylor, writing in the middle of the twentieth century, does not. The two most powerful currents in nineteenth-century historical writing, objective empiricism (with its conviction that the facts could be established 'as they really were') and the 'genetic' (or, by one definition of that troublesome word, 'historicist') view of history as an unfolding process, implying a faith in progress from age to age, were both products of nineteenth-century self-confidence; so too was the 'positivist' view which sought to reduce history to a series of general laws. Historians of the twentieth century, working in the shade of Freud and Einstein, developed, as a counterpoise to the earlier belief in objectivity, an attitude described by its leading exponents in the United States as 'historical relativism'. Historians more recent yet, having lived through great wars and social upheavals, have tended to discount the notion of 'continuity' in history, and to examine closely the tensions between individuals and groups which so often issue in violence and bloodshed.

Since the historian is himself concerned with understanding how one age differs from another, he above all should be aware of these problems, though for a time they did in fact remain hidden from the nineteenth-century objective empiricists. Ranke, one of the German pioneers of this style of history, felt able to designate his American contemporary Bancroft a 'great democratic historian' while apparently quite unaware of the way in which his own work was coloured by his ultra-conservative sentiments. Bishop Stubbs, Ranke's foremost disciple in England, was so dedicated to, and blinded by, his painstaking search for documentary materials that he did not realise how far his study of medieval England was governed by a basic Victorian faith in evolutionary liberalism and parliamentary institutions. However, T. H. Buckle, who aspired to the formulation of general laws of historical development, shrewdly noted in the first volume of his *History of Civilization in England*, published between 1856 and 1861, that 'there will always be a connection between the way in which men contemplate the past and the way in which they contemplate the present'. Today all historians would accept that they are in some sense prisoners of the age and society in which they live. And this very self-awareness is the saving grace of the historians of our own time. As a servant of human society he must write his history in a manner which has meaning and significance for his readers. But since history is so important to society, it must be the best possible history – it must be as 'true' as possible. The historian who is aware of the limitations imposed upon him by his stance in space and time can strive more successfully to counteract distortions caused by these limitations.

A great deal of nonsense was talked at the height of the American 'historical relativist' movement (itself a most salutary reaction against the German school of Ranke) which came close to suggesting that since there were no objective standards one historian was as good as another, and that older historians, as they fell out of fashion, should be scrapped: they move, Conyers Read said wittily, if not wisely, 'in never-ending march from our studies to our attics and from our attics to our dustbins'. Actually one historian is not as good as another; and a good historian writing in the nineteenth century is still far more worthy of the attention of today's reader than a bad historian writing in the twentieth century. If history is a constant rewriting and reinterpretation, it is also a cumulative development. Seeing where our predecessors were entrapped by the fallacies of their age, we are that little bit better equipped to avert the fallacies of our own age. Only the ignorant or the very lazy among historians refuse to read the work of their illustrious predecessors, spurning the insights and the glimpses both of achievement and of potential error to be gained thereby; they are only a degree less naïve than the unsophisticated student who believes everything he sees in print, just because it is in print, and believes the more if the print is fading, the style a shade archaic, the binding leather. History is a dialogue. Each age must reinterpret its own past. Nonetheless with advances in technique, with advances in self-awareness, and with the powerful shoulders of our illustrious predecessors bowed for us to stand on, there is also absolute advance in the quality, the 'truthfulness' of history.

As well as a dialogue between present and past, history should also be a dialogue between the historian and his reader. The definitive historical work on any topic has not been written and never will be. The reader may accept four-fifths of a book and reject the other fifth as inconsistent with the rest, clearly reflective of personal or national bias, or perhaps as sheer rhetorical fancy. He may, while finding the book stimulating, reject its findings *in toto*. He may derive glimmerings of perception which the historian himself, too immersed perhaps in his factual material, had not overtly intended. The more the reader knows of the fundamental nature and methods of history, the better will he be able to perform this fruitful critical function (which brings us again to one of the purposes of this book). The historian will try to present his interpretation in as persuasive a fashion as possible: but he must also play fair with his reader (the science-minded critic who feels a rush of saliva at this point might recollect that the cooking of scientific experiments is not unknown). Correctly used, the critical apparatus of bibliography and references is intended, not as an over-weening demonstration of the historian's self-important pedantry, but as an aid to the reader in playing his part in the dialogue. By using a recondite language of their own, the social scientists often seem to get away with murder: the historian uses the ordinary language of every-day life, with all the dangers of imprecision this involves, because it is his duty to share his discoveries with his readers, exposing himself as necessary to intelligent criticism.

None of this, however, may yet meet the second basic objection to history mentioned earlier in this chapter. Indeed it may well confirm the worst suspicions of those who condemn history as an industry devoted, through the manufacture of myth and propaganda, to under-pinning the basic assumptions of its own society. Accepting the basic premises of this chapter that historians 'play the same role in our society as the bards of less-developed people', a not unsympathetic observer (Philip Bagby) continues:

> They revivify and remould the past in order that it may serve as an inspiration for the present. We need not condemn them, as Aristotle did, for imitating the tragedians and the epic poets. After all, the poet is as necessary and useful as the scientist. . . . The writing of history . . . as it has been practised up to the present is only a semi-rational activity.

Having in this chapter asserted the social necessity for history, I shall hope in most of the remainder of this book to show that history none-theless is a fully 'rational' activity, competent to meet the highest standards of scientific scholarship.

History as a social activity is as old as human society. History as a scholarly discipline *and* a social activity is still quite young. It is easy, but not very rewarding, to condemn the discipline through reference to writers who make little pretence at scholarship; by quoting out of context the pronouncements of those scholars who were conscious – too conscious perhaps – that they were carrying through a revolution in historical studies it is possible to make both them and their subject sound ridiculous. It is easy, too, to make it seem that different historians or different schools of history held views about the nature of history and about the historian's tasks which flatly contradict each other. Most historiographers fall into one or other of two categories: the relativists, who present the thesis of the 'varieties of history', embodying the notion that all great historians are essentially equal, though they may find it impossible to agree upon any one interpretation of the nature of history; and the extremists, who present a definite standard of judgement (usually either that current at the time of writing or one borrowed from some other discipline, such as sociology), by which certain eminent historians are held in fact to be rather bad – thus, for instance, Ranke and his school are often said to lie at the root of all the evil which has afflicted the historical profession since the early nineteenth century. The next two chapters are designed to show the manner in which the modern practice of history as a discipline which at the same time has to meet social demands has developed. To stress the variousness of history is to turn one's face entirely in the wrong direction. Undoubtedly, as has already been stressed, the fashion and style of history changes as styles of life, politics and economic organisation change. Yet the history of historical writing canot be chopped up into neat compartments: on the one hand there is a continuity of purpose which it will be a main task of the next chapter to stress; on the other there has at all times been a vociferous opposition to whatever orthodoxy has in conventional historiography been regarded as the prevailing one of the time.

The argument will be that despite many set-backs and much asininity, historical study has on the whole advanced towards more refined techniques and more sophisticated concepts. Whatever the public stand of the ordinary bread-winners in the profession, thoughtful historians have always been aware of the difficulties and imperfections inherent in their subject. Critics may well object to the wholesale borrowings historians have made from the social sciences: but the last thing history today can be accused of is imperviousness to developments in other disciplines.

NOTES

1. Robert V. Daniels, *Studying History: How and Why* (1966) p. iii. See also H. S. Commager, *The Nature and the Study of History* (1965).
2. Richard Pares, *The Historian's Business* (1961) p. 5.
3. Robert K. Merton, *Social Theory and Social Structure* (1957) p. 16.
4. Both Sidney and Pope are quoted in C. N. L. Brooke, *The Dullness of the Past* (1957).
5. May McKisack, *History as Education* (1956) p. 10.
6. The first analogy is suggested by G. J. Renier, *History: Its Purpose and Method* (1950) p. 29; the second, privately, by Denys Hay.
7. *History in a Changing World* (1955) pp. 29–30.
8. In Mirra Komarovsky, *Common Frontiers of the Social Sciences* (1957) p. 264.
9. H. Stuart Hughes, 'The Historian and the Social Scientist' in *American Historical Review*, LXVI (1960) 46.

2 The Development of Historical Studies to the End of the Nineteenth Century

1 FROM THE BEGINNINGS TO THE ENLIGHTENMENT

THE governing influences upon our life today, and therefore upon the writing and study of history today, are the continuing scientific and technological revolutions of the seventeenth century and onwards, and the continuing national and democratic revolutions of the late eighteenth century and onwards. Historians of historiography disagree over which age should be credited with producing the first recognisably modern historian. The first era in which the influence of the scientific revolution fully permeated the arts, industry and letters was named at the time, and may be so named by us now, the Enlightenment: Voltaire, the greatest ornament of eighteenth-century intellectual life, is often identified as the first modern historian. Other commentators have preferred to lay emphasis on the great revolution in historical scholarship carried through by German historians at the beginning of the nineteenth century, while recently much has been written about the 'historical revolution' of the seventeenth century. It is useful once again to think of the two levels of meaning attaching to history (apart from its meaning as 'the past'): history as a functional social activity stretches back to the beginning of human society; it took a relatively sophisticated shape in the period of classical antiquity, lapsed somewhat after the fall of the Roman Empire into that older condition in which myth and an objective past were inextricably bound together, then, under the stimulus of Renaissance learning in the sixteenth and seventeenth centuries, history achieved a higher level of rational perception and a more advanced methodology than ever before. Many crudities remained, however, and it was the achievement of the Enlightenment to sweep these away. Voltaire and his contemporaries, therefore, might best be regarded as standing, not so much at the beginning of a new historical tradition, but at the highest point of an old one. For history in the final sense, history as a scholarly discipline, begins only with Ranke and his German compatriots at the beginning of the nineteenth century. This does not mean that we single out great historical writers of the period before the nineteenth century (and perhaps several since) and say that they are 'not historians' – though we may possibly, if we like, make distinctions between, say, 'amateur historians' and 'professional historians'. Everything really depends on which level of meaning we are attaching to the word 'historian', and we cannot blame Voltaire, Tacitus or anyone else for not having a conception of history which did not come into being till a later age. What is of interest is to note the fundamentals to which all historians of all ages have subscribed, and to assess the contributions to modern historical study which various writers have made down the ages.

The Western historical tradition in the broad sense goes back to Herodotus (*c.* 484 B.C.–*c.* 425 B.C.) and Thucydides (*c.* 455 B.C.–*c.* 400 B.C.), writing towards the end of the great classical age in Ancient Greece, Polybius (*c.* 198 B.C.–117 B.C.) writing when Greece was falling under the dominion of Rome; and to Livy (59 B.C.–A.D. 17), Tacitus (*c.* A.D. 55–120) and Plutarch (A.D. 50–120), the great historians of Imperial Rome (Plutarch was himself actually a Greek). History was then quite unabashedly a preparation for life, especially political and military life. Essentially it was a narration of memorable events designed to preserve the memory and propagate the knowledge of glorious deeds, or of events which were important to a man, a family, or a people. Political incidents, wars and revolutions, predominated – though this is not to deny that Tacitus, for instance, was a highly sophisticated observer and a superb stylist.[1] That today rather elementary general books of this sort are occasionally produced, while no tribute to the subtlety of author or readers, does testify eloquently to the elemental thrust behind historical study.

In the post-classical period the tradition was left almost exclusively in the hands of monkish chroniclers, whose annalistic accounts lack the elements of reflection or analysis which would make them history. Occasionally a chronicler would pause in his headlong flight through the years for a judgement such as this by the Anglo-Saxon Chronicler on William the Conqueror (d. 1087):

> King William, of whom we speak, was a man of great wisdom and power, and surpassed in honour and in strength all those who had gone before him. Though stern beyond measure to those who opposed his will, he was kind to those good men who loved God. . . . Such was the state of religion in his time that every man who wished to, whatever considerations there might be with regard to his rank, could follow the profession of a monk. . . . Among other things we must not forget the good order he kept in the land, so that a man of any substance could travel unmolested throughout the country with his bosom full of gold. No man dared to slay another, no matter what evil the other might have done him. If a man lay with a woman against her will, he was forthwith condemned to forfeit those members with which he disported himself. . . . He ruled over England and by his foresight it was surveyed so carefully that there was not a 'hide' of land in

England of which he did not know who held it and how much it was worth. . . . Assuredly in his time men suffered grievous oppression and manifold injuries.[2]

The Venerable Bede (d. 735) showed more of the qualities of true historical scholarship. He paid special attention to chronology; he enumerated his written sources and he made some effort to test and evaluate oral traditions. His premises and assumptions are vastly different from ours, yet at times it is possible to feel a real contact with what is continuous in human experience. Bede quotes in full the reply of Pope Gregory to the questionings of Augustine who has newly established the see of Canterbury. Gregory comes through as a man of intense humanity and warm common sense, as for instance in his reply to Augustine's anxieties regarding the variations in religious practice to be found in Britain:

> My brother, you are familiar with the usage of the Roman Church, in which you were brought up. But if you have found customs, whether in the Roman, Gallican, or any other Churches that may be more acceptable to God, I wish you to make a careful selection of them, and teach the Church of the English, which is still young in the Faith, whatever you can profitably learn from the various Churches. For things should not be loved for the sake of places, but places for the sake of good things.[3]

Though medieval historians often showed a deeper sense of historical understanding than has been credited to them by the historiographical textbooks, they often found it difficult to distinguish clearly between sacred and profane matters: events, from time to time, are expressed as judgements of God, and miracles are accepted. Such writers as Otto of Freising (*c.* 1110–58), Matthew Paris (d. *c.* 1259), Joinville (*c.* 1224–1319), Froissart (*c.* 1337–*c.* 1410), provided fairly reliable accounts of their own times, but none found it easy to shake off the all-pervasive influence of St Augustine's *City of God* (426), a work of Christian apologetics portraying the history of the world as the long unfolding of God's will. Though often themselves expert forgers, medieval chroniclers were quite uncritical in their treatment of documentary evidence. They accepted in full the sanctions of tradition, and, since they believed in divine intervention they were inhibited in their analysis of historical causation.

Renaissance writers turned again to the example of the classical historians. Their great achievements were the rational, secular approach which they brought to bear on matters formerly held to be part of the divine mystery, and their development of a form of critical scholarship. The latter, however, owed a great deal to medieval scholars who had developed the technique of the 'gloss' or explanatory note: Valla (*c.* 1407–57) had used critical techniques to expose the forged Donation of Constantine, upon which many of the claims of the medieval Church were based.

The real goad to historical study in the Renaissance was external circumstance. Geographical exploration created a demand for exact information, historical as well as geographical. The invention of printing created a new emphasis on communication – one of the basic features of historical writing. In the scientific and intellectual revolution which culminates in the work of Sir Isaac Newton (1642–1727) history, along with all other scholarly pursuits, took its share. Everywhere among the intelligent and articulate there was an awareness of, and interest in, the processes of change. Hot on the heels of the intellectual and secular revolt came the battles of the Reformation and Counter-Reformation, which provided further stimulus to historical study, as each side endeavoured to demonstrate the historical validity of its position: Luther's associate Melanchthon (1497–1560) brought to the German universities at which he taught an enthusiasm for the academic study of history, and Flacius Illyricus (1520–75) directed the publication of the 'Magdeburg Centuries', an ecclesiastical history (to 1200 or thereabouts), which though strongly biased in the Lutheran cause, did contain masses of source material.

The first great vernacular writers were Niccolò Machiavelli (1469–1527) and Francesco Guicciardini (1483–1540), though the way had already been lit by Leonardo Bruni (1374?–1444), whose *Florentine History* (1415–29) shines like a beacon in Renaissance historiography. To Machiavelli more than any other writer belongs the credit for bringing to history a genuine inductive method – arguing from the evidence rather than 'deducing' from some *a priori* theory. Apart from his famous *The Prince* (completed in 1513, published in 1532), Machiavelli, significantly enough, also published a series of *Discourses* (1516) on the classical historian Livy; his *History of Florence* was published in 1522. *The Prince* is a work of political philosophy as well as history, for there is no sense of the complete autonomy of history till the nineteenth century (and even in the twentieth century it was common for political science and history to be taught in the same university department); yet essentially *The Prince* is a realistic presentation of the nature of Italian Government, politics and diplomacy at the beginning of the sixteenth century, rather than, as often popularly thought, a guide to the worst techniques of *Realpolitik*. Guicciardini's *History of Italy* (uncompleted on his death in 1540) offers a highly skilled analysis of political motivation; its purpose, in keeping with a long tradition, was to give the reader 'wholesome instructions'.

The great Italians had no immediate disciples. In England Sir Walter Raleigh's *History of the World* (1614) is very much a mixture of medieval and modern elements. William Camden's *Britannia* (six editions, 1586–1607), however, was based on deep learning and extensive research: in his preface Camden (1551–1623) touched again on the fundamental justification for the study of history: 'If there are any who desire to be strangers in their own country, foreigners in their own cities and always children in knowledge, let them please themselves: I write not for such humours.' Camden's great essay in contemporary history, his *History of Elizabeth* (1615) was based on the great mass of records made available to him. In writing his *Survey of London* (1598), John Stow took it for granted that his historical treatment would be of intrinsic interest to his readers. The scientific method, detailed examination of evidence and vigorous enquiry into causal relationships, was best represented in the work of Sir Francis Bacon (1561–1626), for whom history – his only complete work was the *History of Henry VII* – was but one of many interests. Greatest of all English historians before the Enlightenment was Edward Hyde, Earl of Clarendon, a statesman who played a leading part in the Royalist cause during the revolutionary period in English history. Accordingly his *History of the Rebellion and Civil Wars in England begun in the year 1641* is far from being a piece of detailed scholarship, though, dealing as it does with matters of great complexity, it is a masterpiece of organisation: the nearest parallels in modern times are Winston Churchill's histories of the two World Wars.

Throughout Europe the sixteenth and seventeenth centuries were marked by the great scholarly enterprises which brought together precious collections of original documents. In part this was simply a reaction to the unhappy dispersal of valuable materials during the periods of religious strife: after the dissolution of the monasteries in sixteenth-century England, complained a contemporary with pardonable exaggeration, the new owners used the contents of their libraries for profitable sale overseas, 'to rub their boots', or to 'serve their jakes'.[4] The positive interest of Elizabeth's Privy Council can be seen in a letter of 1568 when holders of records are instructed to make them available to the deputies of Archbishop Parker, 'so as both when any need shall require, resort may be made for the testimony that may be found in them, and also by conference of them, the antiquity of the state of these countries may be restored to the knowledge of the world'.[5] (Not that there was anything specially novel in this: Edward I had done the same in regard to Scotland.) The greatest advances in historical scholarship were made in seventeenth-century France, where such men as Duchesne, Baluze, Mabillon and Montfaucon created 'the science of history and placed new tools such as palaeography, archaeology, and diplomatics in the historian's hands'.[6] The greatest work in the scholarly compilation of collected texts was carried through by the

French Benedictines at St Maur. Another great enterprise was that of certain Belgian Jesuits, followers of John Bolland (1596–1665), who initiated the *Acta Sanctorum*. The great theorist of historical study was Jean Bodin (*c.* 1530–96) who declared the subject to be both of intellectual interest and of pragmatic value for morals and politics: if studied carefully, he maintained, history did manifest certain orderly principles.

In historiography emphasis is naturally placed on the brilliant achievements of such men of genius as Voltaire and Gibbon. Yet it is important to remember that contemporaneously with these famous 'interpreters' those who laboured in the school of 'erudition' continued the great work of collecting and criticising historical records. However it was undoubtedly the dramatic successes of the great men which prepared the way for the nineteenth-century revolution in historical study: while the *érudits* advanced the cause of scholarship, the interpreters created the first great narrative histories of high literary and artistic quality, and, more critically, made the first serious attempts to analyse the development of human civilisation.

The French Enlightenment historians carried through the final destruction of the theological base of historical writing which had persisted through the Renaissance and had, in some ways, been revivified by the Reformation and Counter-Reformation, when it was most brilliantly presented in France by Jacques Bénigne Bossuet (1627–1704), Bishop of Meaux in France. Both Montesquieu (1689–1755) and Voltaire (1694–1778) wrote in a fashion directly antithetical to that of Bossuet. Montesquieu's *The Spirit of Laws* (1748) stresses the importance of physical environment and of tradition, but is lacking in any real concept of history as process through time. Save for the efficiency and elegance of the narrative there was nothing outstandingly original about Voltaire's *History of Charles XII* (1731): it was while working on *The Century of Louis XIV* (published in 1751) that he began to develop the broader cultural and social approach which characterised his *Essay on the Manners and Character of the Nations* (first complete edition published in 1756). In eloquent testimony to the principle that no new method is ever as new as its eager sponsors believe, or, if you like, to the principle that each age must rediscover old truths for itself, Voltaire now insisted that the historian must give due attention to the civilisations of India and China, that religions should be treated comparatively, with no suggestion that any automatic primacy was inherent in Judaeo-Christianity, and that economic, social and cultural matters were as much the concern of the historian as the doings of popes and kings.

The broad view of history is a characteristic of the great eighteenth-century Scottish school of historiography. That the two most celebrated figures in the Scottish eighteenth-century Enlightenment, one a philosopher, the other an economist, should both also in some sense be historians, is further demonstration of the central importance of history in human activity. David Hume (1711–76) is best known as a philosopher – though the lines delimiting history were still not firmly drawn; of great general importance was his demonstration of the absurdity of the idea that human society had originated in a 'social contract'. His *History of England* was published in six volumes between 1754 and 1762. Largely a work of interpretation rather than exhaustive original scholarship (Hume once referred to research as the 'dark industry'), the *History* had a tremendous popular success; the first volume brought the author £2000, the others a good deal more. The main text was essentially straight political narrative but Hume did include, in the form of appendices, details of wages, prices, dress and other matters conventionally referred to as social history. The rationalist element in Hume's thinking is very clear in his *Natural History of Religion* (1759). In an essay called 'Of the Study of History' Hume referred to the subject as an 'agreeable entertainment' more interesting than fiction. In history, Hume said, one observes 'the rise, progress, declensions and final extinction of the most flourishing empires; the virtues which contributed to their greatness and the vices which drew on their ruin'. Most important of all with regard to the central argument of this book, Hume declared that 'a man acquainted with history may, in some respect, be said to have lived from the beginning of the world'.

Adam Smith (1723–90) is renowned as the founder of the classical school of political economy, but his *The Wealth of Nations* (1776) is essentially historical in its approach to the study of man's economic activities. Smith, perhaps more than any of his contemporaries, was aware of the economic imperatives underpinning human society, and he had already, in the *Theory of Moral Sentiments* (1759) made the point that man can 'subsist only in society'. Although a minister of the Scottish Presbyterian Church, William Robertson (1721–93) was the complete Enlightenment historian. Dividing his *History of Scotland* (1759) into four periods, he remarked of the first that it 'is the region of pure fable and conjecture, and ought to be totally neglected, or abandoned to the industry and credulity of antiquarians'. His *The History of the Reign of the Emperor Charles V* (1769) was important both for its attempt to deal with social as well as political matters, and for the extensive scholarly apparatus: Robertson provided bare references in the text, then an appendix of 'Proofs and Illustrations' as long as the text itself. That there was nothing parochial about Robertson's approach to history was shown by his *The History of America* (1777–94) which again demonstrated his concept of history as the development of human society and civilisation.

Most interesting of all the Scottish historians was John Millar (1735–1801), Professor of Civil Law at the University of Glasgow from 1761 to his death in the second year of the nineteenth century. Millar, as his fellow Scot, Francis Jeffrey, pointed out in 1806, sought 'to trace back the history of society to its most simple and universal elements – to resolve almost all that has been ascribed to positive institution into the spontaneous and irresistible development of certain obvious principles – and to show with how little contrivance or political wisdom the most complicated and apparently artificial schemes of policy might have been erected'. In *The Origin of the Distinction of Ranks* (1771) Millar endeavours to explain changes in the power-structure of society and of groups within society: in proto-Marxist style he associated these with changes in property relations. His *An Historical View of the English Government* (1787) divided English history into three periods, each based on the predominant system of property-holding obtaining at the time: the 'feudal aristocracy' to 1066, the 'feudal monarchy' to 1603, and 'the commercial government' thereafter.[7]

Frequently careless in detail, the Scottish writers did have a broad, sociological conception of historical study. It was the greatest English historian of the eighteenth century who, in enunciating an important but partial truth, helped to set history in English upon the narrow path that it was for too long to follow in both Britain and the U.S.A.: 'Wars, and the administration of public affairs', wrote Edward Gibbon (1737–94) in the preface to his *Decline and Fall of the Roman Empire* (1776–88), 'are the principal subjects of history'. Nonetheless Gibbon's monumental work was a miracle of organisation and of sustained narrative: it brought him the fame and fortune he had sought from the moment he realised that history was the most popular of all forms of literature. Gibbon announced himself a man of the Enlightenment in his empirical treatment of the development of Christianity: 'The theologian', as he remarked in a famous sentence, 'may indulge in the pleasing task of describing Religion as she descended from Heaven arrayed in her native purity'; he, as a historian, was happy to explain the successes of early Christianity in terms of 'exclusive zeal, the immediate expectation of another world, the claim of miracles, the practice of rigid virtue, and the constitution of the primitive church'. Gibbon's view of history was a disenchanted one: he accepted, in another famous phrase, the 'melancholy truth . . . that the Christians in the course of their intestine dissensions have inflicted far greater severities on each other than they experienced from the zeal of the infidels'. Indeed he came closer to the world-view of the disillusioned twentieth century than to the nineteenth-century belief in the progress of human history: every page, Gibbon wrote, 'has been stained with civil blood . . . from the ardour of contention, the pride of victory, the despair of success, the memory of past injustice and the fear of future dangers . . . [which] . . . all contribute to inflame the mind and silence the voice of pity'.

Historians of the eighteenth century did make a stab at the cultural and sociological approach, though not always a very powerful one. There were still plenty of critics then, as now, to join in the lament (1789) of the great agricultural journalist and pioneer social researcher, Arthur Young, that

> to a mind that has the least turn after philosophical inquiry, reading modern history is generally the most tormenting employment that a man can have: one is plagued with the actions of a detestable set of men called conquerors, heroes, and great generals; and we wade through pages loaded with military details; but when you want to know the progress of agriculture, of commerce, and industry, their effect in different ages and nations on each other – the wealth that resulted – the division of that wealth – its employment – and the manners it produced – all is a blank. Voltaire set an example, but how has it been followed?

But the history of the age of Gibbon and Voltaire had three more fundamental weaknesses. First, and most important, it was remarkably innocent of any sense of human development and change; thus both Gibbon and Voltaire could exercise their magnificent wit upon the obvious fact that men in past ages had not always disported themselves in a fashion considered suitable in the eighteenth-century 'Age of Reason'. The Middle Ages in general were treated scrappily and with little respect; Gibbon was seriously in error in deprecating the achievements of the Byzantine Empire. Secondly, although important scholarly work continued side-by-side with the great interpretative works, there was little contact between the two. 'Woe to details', exclaimed Voltaire, with some reason: 'they are a sort of vermin that destroys big works.' Yet in their contempt for basic scholarship and research the eighteenth-century historians sometimes showed an unjustifiable carelessness. The charge cannot with great justice be laid upon Gibbon, who was scrupulous in his search of the available evidence; but that evidence was essentially the product of the labours of seventeenth-century scholarship. One problem, certainly, was that many important archives were simply kept closed to scholars. History at its highest must be interpretation, not fact-grubbing. But without a continued sponsorship of detailed research, conducted with the widest available collection of mechanical and conceptual aids, and, more important, a constant intercourse between interpretative history and primary research, history must quickly wither.

The third great weakness still attending upon history in the eighteenth century was that nowhere was it efficiently taught as an intellectual discipline, save in the palaces of princes and statesmen. True, the Camden chair had been established at Oxford in the Elizabethan period: but Camden professors confined themselves to Roman history. In the

1720s George I instituted Regius Chairs of Modern History at Oxford
and Cambridge, but this was essentially a political rather than an
educational move, designed to bring Whig nominees into these centres
of Toryism. The early incumbents of the chairs were completely without
distinction in historical studies. The second Oxford Professor, his
present successor, Hugh Trevor-Roper, tells us, was remembered only
for bringing 'one Handel, a foreigner, who they say was born in
Hanover' with his 'lousy crew' of 'fiddlers' to play in the Sheldonian
Theatre. From 1757 history was taught on a more serious basis at the
University of Göttingen in Germany; and in 1769 a Chair of History
and Morals was established at the Collège de France. But till history
was admitted to all the main centres of learning, it could not hope to
develop as a true intellectual discipline.

2   RANKE: HIS DISCIPLES AND HIS CRITICS

It was from the simultaneous attack on these three weaknesses that
modern history, in the final sense of the term, history as an academic
discipline, was born. After the great revolutionary upheavals at the end
of the eighteenth century it was no longer possible to believe in the
unchanging character of human nature, or in the immutable nature of
social institutions. Niebuhr (1776–1831), the great forerunner of Leopold
von Ranke in the launching of the Berlin revolution in historical studies,
explained the new interest in historical origins and historical change:
'It was a time when we were experiencing the most incredible and
exceptional events, when we were reminded of many forgotten and
decayed institutions by the sound of their downfall.' The hitherto
neglected ideas of Vico (whose *New Science* had been published in
1725) and Herder (whose short *Philosophy of History* of 1774 was
followed by a four-volume *Philosophy of History*, published between
1784 and 1791) now gained a wide currency among historians.

Giambattista Vico (1668–1744) has been described as 'a half-educated
Neapolitan literary hack', who in confused and ungrammatical style
presented a scheme of the development of human civilisation in three
stages, 'divine', 'heroic' and 'human': such a scheme was new to
European historiography, though not unusual in Chinese and Muslim
historiography. Vico's real contribution, however, was his appreciation
of the cultural differences between different ages and different nations:
in contrast to the main Enlightenment historians he was aware of the
danger of importing ideas, or judgements, into the history of earlier
ages. Johann Gottfried von Herder presented similar ideas in much
more sophisticated and coherent form: he conceived of history as an

onward march; he stressed (as Montesquieu had done) the importance of geography, and developed for the first time the concept of 'national character' which he believed greatly influenced the history of any nation. Herder coined the verb *einfühlen*, as used in his injunction to historians: 'First sympathise with the nation, go into the era, into the geography, into the entire history, *feel* yourself into it'. Herder was the first to oppose to the confident contempt of the Enlightenment historians the notion that everything, *relatively*, is right *in its own historical context*.

The desire to see the past from the inside, 'as it really was', in the celebrated (and notorious) words of Ranke, was but a part of the great outpouring of the romantic imagination, typified at this time in the novels of Sir Walter Scott, who had himself set out with the fixed purpose of portraying the manners and morals of the past ages, and whose novels had a profound direct influence on Ranke and other historians. Definitions, as we have seen, are very loose in historiography: the most exact, if rather clumsy, title for this new way of looking at history is *genetic relationism* – 'genetic' (some writers use the simpler word 'historical', but this is a trifle vague) because of the stress laid on origins and the notion of every phase developing out of a previous phase, 'relationist' (some writers say 'relativist', but this makes for confusion with the twentieth-century American school of relativists) because of the insistence that every person, every activity, every institution must be seen in *relation* to the age in which it is set. Pushed too far, genetic relationism became a stultifying influence on historical studies, but nonetheless it is a concept which lies at the heart of the activities of every modern historian. Overstatement is the venial sin of all mighty innovators, and Ranke was undoubtedly guilty of it when, in the modest and self-deprecating preface to his first book, *Histories of the Latin and Germanic Nations 1494–1514* (1824), he permitted himself the following much-quoted, and much-traduced, pontification:

> To history has been assigned the office of judging the past, of instructing the present for the benefit of future ages. To such high offices this work does not aspire: it wants only to show what actually happened (*wie es eigentlich gewesen*).[8]

Historians who for a century and a half have followed Ranke's precept to the letter have been guilty of a sorry failure of imagination which did much to bring history into disrepute. Yet the issue is crucial: the historian may judge, must, if only implicitly, instruct – but before all else it is important that he *understand*.

Just when a new emphasis was being placed on historical change, historians began to insist upon a new precision of documentation (again this is a facet of the switch from the classical general to the romantic particular). At the head of this new tradition of critical method stands

Barthold Georg Niebuhr, a native of Denmark, who from 1806 worked in the service of the Prussian Government. In 1810 he was appointed to give lectures at the newly founded University of Berlin (a product of the Prussian reform movement with which Niebuhr himself was closely associated). The lectures, published in two volumes in 1811–12 as the *History of Rome* (with a completely revised, three-volume edition in 1827–32), were a reconstruction of the historical origins of the Roman state, employing the most advanced methods of philology and textual criticism. The upshot was a complete discrediting of Livy and the various narrative accounts based on Livy. Clumsily written – Niebuhr himself believed that you couldn't have both historical accuracy and persuasive style (and too many latter-day professionals have endorsed this curious doctrine) – the *History of Rome* can nonetheless be said without exaggeration to inaugurate modern historical methodology. Ranke was explicitly following this methodology when he described the sources for his first book as 'memoirs, diaries, letters, diplomatic reports, and original narratives of eye-witnesses; other writings were used only if they were immediately derived from the above-mentioned or seemed to equal them because of some original information.' Ranke added that these sources would be identified on every page, and, in the form first used by Robertson, 'a second volume, to be published concurrently, will present the method of investigation and the critical conclusions.'⁹ The new methodology in its barest form was seen in the inauguration of the great collection of texts, the *Monumenta Germania Historia*. In France, under the direction of the historian-statesman Guizot, committees were established for the publication in hundreds of volumes of thousands of manuscripts, charts, memoirs and correspondence. Augustin Thierry (1795–1856) explained how in writing his *History of the Norman Conquest of England* (1825) he had to 'devour long folio pages, in order to extract a single sentence, or even word, among a thousand'. In 1821 the École des Chartes was founded for the purpose of providing a training in the handling of historical sources. So, by the intensive application of critical techniques, by sheer industry and pertinacious research, was a new and more refined historical methodology created. Eventually the notion of the primacy of the 'original source' could become an excuse for perpetrating the most tiresome pedantries; but in joining so impressively a dedication to the critical use of primary materials to a profound sense of historical change ('genetic relationism'), Leopold von Ranke performed an inestimable service to historical studies which justly entitles him to be regarded as the founder of the modern discipline of history.

Ranke, too, played a central part in a third important development: the establishment of the teaching of history at university level. At Berlin Ranke conducted his famous seminars which inculcated basic research techniques. Other countries lagged far behind: until the late 1860s university history teaching in France was very incoherent, there being various chairs of history in different institutions of different types, such as the Collège de France, the Faculties of Letters, and in some of the 'special schools', notably the École Normale Supérieure and the École des Chartes. Largely owing to the efforts of Frenchmen impressed by their experiences in Germany, the École Pratique des Hautes Études was established at the Sorbonne in 1868 where instruction in research techniques was provided by the historical and philological section. As a consequence there was a general improvement in the teaching of history at the Faculties of Letters. As we shall see later in this chapter, the German example spread also to Britain and the United States. Outside Germany the process was slow; but by the second half of the nineteenth century history was beginning to establish itself throughout the Western world as an autonomous academic discipline, with much of the paraphernalia which is today associated with that elevated status. In 1859 the first of the great and, some would add, infinitely tedious, historical journals, the *Historische Zeitschrift* was launched. It would, its founders declared, be above all else a 'scientific' periodical: 'Its first task, therefore, should be to represent the true method of historical research and to point out the deviations therefrom.'[10]

Too many histories of historical writing treat of Niebuhr and Ranke as being concerned purely with the more pedantic aspects of historical method, as never going beyond Ranke's precept that 'the strict presentation of facts is the supreme law of historical writing'. In fact, as any great historian must, Ranke brought to his work definite concepts as to the working of historical processes, and Niebuhr's study of ancient Rome was illumined by his own direct knowledge as a professional civil servant of practical affairs. Above all else, as we have seen, the great historians of the romantic era shared in a sense of historical development: the new history, being no longer content with mere erudition, 'endeavoured to ascertain the significance and continuity of events, to perceive and to understand the development of history'.[11] Such an aim inevitably involves, in however tenuous a form, some kind of 'philosophy of history' – in our simplest sense of a set of basic attitudes. The key figure in the development of nineteenth-century German philosophy is Georg Wilhelm Friedrich Hegel (1770–1831). Hegel and the German historians of the Ranke school were in agreement in seeing history 'as a providential process, in which every event and circumstance was justified in the light of the whole'.[12] (This, incidentally, is how some authorities would define that dread term *historicism*.) More particularly Hegel stressed the importance in human development of the political state: Ranke spoke of states as 'thoughts of God', and, partly because the newly opened archives in which he was particularly interested were necessarily the archives of princes and prelates (the poor do not leave much in the way of primary sources), he gave history a firm orientation towards 'past politics' and the relations between states ('diplomatic history').

Ranke hoped, with more modesty than he is sometimes given credit for, to present by means of scrupulous methodology an objective account of the past. Though he was aware that other competent historians could yet hold a subjective point of view – he referred to his American contemporary, George Bancroft (1800–91), as a great 'democratic' historian – he seems to have been unaware of the strength of his own prejudices. Ranke was in fact an extreme conservative, supporting the repressive Press law passed in the German Confederation after the 1830 upheavals, and he rejoiced in the events of 1870–1 'as the victory of Conservative Europe over the revolution'. However, if Ranke came close to lending his scholarly reputation to propaganda on behalf of the Prussian power state, that cannot diminish his stature as the great innovating historian. And whatever might happen later in the name of his innovations, he was himself in no sense a narrow specialist: his final work, indeed, was a *Universal History*, completed after his death by his students. Already Ranke had written: 'Universal history comprehends the past life of mankind, not in its particular relations and trends, but in its fullness and totality.' Although absolutely dedicated to the necessity for specialised research, Ranke was aware of 'the danger of losing sight of the universal, of the type of knowledge everyone desires':

> For history is not simply an academic subject: the knowledge of the history of mankind should be a common property of humanity and should above all benefit our nation, without which our work could not have been accomplished.[13]

Here Ranke the overt adherent of the social necessity theory of history and Ranke the nationalist are presented in subtle blend. In the work of Ranke's young compatriot, Heinrich von Treitschke (1834–96), however, nationalism trenched on chauvinism: the German state was glorified, and so was war.

It must be remembered that while the methodological revolution of Niebuhr and Ranke had a powerful and salutary influence throughout the world of historical studies, that world by no means succumbed to the overlordship of Ranke: in fact many prominent historians strongly denounced the less attractive features of Rankean scholarship, or at least resisted the idea that the central theme in historical development was the rise of the state. Such leading German historians of the nineteenth century as Dühring, Droysen, Lorenz and Lamprecht were all critics of Ranke: John Gustav Droysen (1808–84), Professor of History at Berlin from 1859 to 1884, was responsible for the famous remark that the objectivity of Ranke was 'the objectivity of a eunuch'. Most famous

counterpoise to the totality of Rankean orthodoxy was the work of
Jacob Burckhardt (1818–97), Professor of History at Basel from 1845.
Burckhardt, descendant of a patrician Swiss family, studied under
Ranke at Berlin and from him derived his basic understanding of
historical method; but Burckhardt reacted against what he believed to
be Ranke's suppression of the poetry in history, and he later showed his
hostility to the Rankean tradition by refusing to become Ranke's
successor in the Berlin chair in 1872. Burckhardt established his reputation with *The Era of Constantine the Great* (1853), *The Civilisation of
the Renaissance in Italy* (1860), and the *History of the Renaissance in
Italy* (1867). Often weak in detail, these works played an impressive
part in furthering the concept, in whose interest Voltaire had laboured,
of history as the history of culture and civilisation in all its manifold
aspects; and they remain an essential starting-point for any study of the
period. Burckhardt, incidentally, was even more conservative in general
political outlook than Ranke: where Ranke could retain a proud
nineteenth-century optimism over human development, Burckhardt was
deeply pessimistic.

Burckhardt's approach to history owed much to the French contemporaries of Ranke, Augustin Thierry and Jules Michelet (1798–1874).
Thierry said that the essential object of his *History of the Norman
Conquest of England* (1825) was to 'envisage the destiny of peoples and
not of certain famous men, to present the adventures of social life and
not those of the individual': attacking 'writers without learning who
have not known how to observe', and 'writers without imagination
who have not known how to paint', he expressed the hope, which many
historians in the mid-twentieth-century crisis in historical studies have
heartily echoed, that he might produce 'art at the same time as
science'. Thierry was a romantic, and his work suffered excessively
from the faults of romanticism: over-dramatisation and luxuriance in
emotionalism. Michelet, also a romantic and a political partisan, nonetheless played an important role in the three key advances by which
history became a modern academic discipline. First, he did much for
the teaching of history in France, publishing two useful little textbooks,
the *Précis of Modern History* (1827) and *An Introduction to Universal
History* (1831), as well as lecturing at the École Normale, the Sorbonne
and the Collège de France (where he received the history chair in 1838).
Secondly, Michelet was at one with the school of historical writing
which saw the need to see history from the inside, to 'resurrect' the
past as Michelet himself put it; it was indeed Michelet who brought the
neglected work of Vico to the attention of other scholars. Finally
Michelet shared the passion of his contemporaries for primary source
materials: in 1831 he was appointed Chief of the Historical Section of
the National Archives. Michelet is seen at his best in the first six

volumes of his seventeen-volume *History of France* (1833–67) – the later
volumes are spoiled by his growing anti-clericalism – and in his *History
of the French Revolution* (1846–53). Often marked by romantic exaggeration, this work is characterised by that sympathy with an era and
its people which is the first requirement in a modern historian. Beyond
that Michelet showed that, in this age of historical revolution, history
should be concerned not just with politics and diplomacy, but with all
facets of human societies.

All the writers of this era, then, had their weaknesses and their blind
spots; while Ranke set his close followers off on a too narrow study of
diplomacy and politics, those historians who aimed rather at the study
of human civilisation were still often guilty of imprecision and romantic
overstatement. The first half of the nineteenth century brought to birth
modern historical study: but many further refinements and new
syntheses were still to come.

3 POSITIVISM AND MARXISM

We have noted the influence on the new nineteenth-century school of
historians of the great political upheavals of the late eighteenth century
and of the romantic revival which followed. Nineteenth-century intellectuals were also influenced, to a far greater degree than any of their
predecessors, by the triumphs of modern science. And so, once again, we
come to yet another of these problems of definition which constantly
afflict any discussion of the nature and methods of history. When men
talk of history as being 'scientific' they can mean one or other of two
things: they can mean that it is exact and painstaking in the collection
and sifting of evidence – it was in this sense that Ranke, as quoted in
the previous section, used the word. But a natural science is more usually
characterised by the manner in which it establishes general laws to
which the phenomena of the particular science conform: in the nineteenth century there were various attempts to establish a 'scientific'
history of this type, partly indeed as a reaction against those followers
of Ranke who repeated by rote that history could not answer questions,
could only show 'how things really were'. Later I shall consider the
real nature of science as understood in the mid-twentieth century,
taking up the point I touched on at the beginning of this book, that the
historian and the scientist in many ways share the same activity, the
attack upon that which is not yet known. Meantime, without accepting
that in practice they justified the claims made on their behalf, we shall
look at the extremely important attempts made in the nineteenth century
to present history as a kind of natural science with certain general laws.

Whether or not Auguste Comte (1798–1857) was a 'historian' is an unproductive question (was Machiavelli? Adam Smith?): he certainly had a profound effect on the development of historical studies. When the demarcation lines are drawn, Comte is cut off as the founder of the modern discipline of sociology; but for over a century now there has been a constant interaction, sometimes violent, usually fruitful, between history and sociology (a topic which, again, I shall take up in detail later). Comte's objective was to introduce into the study of society the same scientific observation of the laws which prevail in the natural, or as he called them, 'positive', sciences. Comte impinged, as all social scientists must, on the study of history through his acceptance that history provided the raw material for the understanding of society (and he was the man most responsible for securing the establishment of a Chair of History in the Collège de France in 1831). Comte, in effect, was seeking the laws underlying the development of history, laws which would, he believed, enable man to predict the future course of events. Comte's two major works, *Course of Positivist Philosophy* (1830–42) and *System of Positivist Politics* (1851–4), are ponderous, convoluted, ill-written studies which certainly did not justify the claims he made for his 'positivism'; nonetheless they are of outstanding importance as an unequivocal statement that human society is amenable to scientific study. From positivism sprang modern sociology, which does not in practice offer one overarching system of general laws, but seeks such laws in specific spheres of human activity.

Much wider claims were made for the theory of history which originated with Karl Marx. Marx was born in 1818, son of a lawyer in the German Rhineland, but he lived much of his writing life in England, where he died in 1883. He never presented a full and rounded account of his theory, known alternatively as the Marxist, or the 'materialist' interpretation of history. The fullest early statement of this interpretation is to be found in the *German Ideology*, written in collaboration with Friedrich Engels and completed in 1846, though only a part was published during Marx's lifetime; no complete edition appeared till 1932. There is a lively sketch in the rousing *Communist Manifesto* (1848), in which Engels again collaborated, and a brief summary in the preface (first published posthumously in 1897) which Marx wrote for his *A Contribution to the Critique of Political Economy* (first published in 1859). His major work, *Capital* (1867–94), which like Adam Smith's *Wealth of Nations* is historical in approach, concentrates on the development of the capitalist economy, which Marx saw as the dynamic factor in modern history. Other writings by Marx, and by his close associate Friedrich Engels, add various glosses; to this have been added the explanations and extrapolations of admirers and disciples, both scholarly and polemical. If much tedious rubbish has been written

by Marxist historians (leaving aside the propagandist official histories
of allegedly 'Marxist' countries), it must also be said that some of the
most stimulating of all historical work being written today is that of
scholars who are happy and proud to describe themselves as 'Marxists'.
The distinction is between Marxism as a crude, and sometimes untenable, system applied by rote in the same unimaginative way that many
disciples of Ranke applied the master's teachings, and Marxism as a
stimulating and liberating approach to the manifold problems of
history. Modern Marxists in the latter school would probably not now
accept in full Lenin's claim on behalf of the materialist conception of
history that it had discovered 'the objective law behind the system of
social relations' and had 'made it possible for us to examine, with the
precision of a natural science, the social conditions influencing the life
of the masses, and the changes taking place in these conditions'. Much
attention in recent years has been given to the random insights into
historical processes appearing in various of Marx's works aside from
the basic premises of the materialist interpretation. To talk of a Marxist
school of history (apart from the hacks and the propagandists) is probably to exaggerate Marx's importance as a historian; but it is almost
impossible to deny his influence in some manner or another on almost
everything of importance relating to history published since the late
nineteenth century. Since the materialist conception of history has this
importance, I shall here briefly indicate its main points.

First of all a distinction is made between the basic economic
structure of any society, constituted by the 'conditions of production,
taken as a whole', and the 'superstructure' of laws, institutions and ideas.
History has unfolded through a series of stages, Asiatic, antique, feudal
and modern bourgeois, each determined by the prevailing conditions of
production. The motor for this development from era to era is provided by the 'class struggle', classes themselves being determined by
the relationships of particular groups to the conditions of production:
the bourgeoisie, for example, own the means of capitalist production.
The first section of the *Communist Manifesto* actually begins with the
challenging statement: 'The history of all hitherto existing society is the
history of class struggles.'[14] When a stage is reached where the material
productive forces of society come into conflict with the existing relations of production, there begins, says Marx, 'an epoch of social
revolution'.

Few now accept, completely uncritically, everything that Marx
wrote (supposing that everything he wrote was self-consistent). No one
accepts everything Comte wrote (supposing it all to be comprehensible).
Grand theories of historical development are not usually approved of
by modern historians; in general they lack that quality of understanding
the past from the inside which is at the base of all true historical

study. If it is rash to state that no acceptable universal history of this sort will ever be written, it can be stated with confidence that no such history has yet been written. But this does not mean that the historian should not employ general concepts such as those of Marx, or of Toynbee, or of his own, as hypotheses against which to test the empirically observed facts, as tools of analysis, or as possible organising principles. Comte and Marx, the positivists and the Marxists provided a valuable corrective to the too literal interpretation of the Rankean teachings which seemed to lay too great a stress on the mere accumulation of facts and too little on their essential interconnections.

It is not necessary to accept in full the programme adopted by Thomas Henry Buckle (1821–62), the self-taught English historian who sought to follow the positivists in their search for the general laws of human development; but one can still appreciate the deep insights contained in his *History of Civilization in England* (the two volumes published in 1856 and 1861 in fact covered European as well as English history). Not least in importance is his salutary comment that among historians

> a strange idea prevails, that their business is merely to relate events, which they may occasionally enliven by such moral and political reflections as seem likely to be useful. According to this scheme, any author who from indolence of thought, or from natural incapacity, is unfit to deal with the highest branches of knowledge, has only to pass some years in reading a certain number of books, and then he is qualified to be an historian; he is able to write the history of a great people, and his work becomes an authority on the subject which it professes to treat.

'The establishment of this narrow standard,' said Buckle, and all historians should heed him, 'has led to results very prejudicial to the progress of our knowledge.'[15]

4 ANGLO-SAXON ATTITUDES

The Berlin revolution in historical studies was slow to affect history in Britain and America. Indeed in Britain the main thrust of Ranke's immediate contemporaries was to re-emphasise history as a literary art rather than as a science in either of the two senses mentioned in the previous section. Foremost among these was Thomas Babington Macaulay (1800–59), whose approach to history, in some measure at least, is illumined by the much-quoted sentence he penned in 1841: 'I shall not be satisfied unless I produce something which shall for a few days supersede the last fashionable novel on the tables of the young ladies.' His *History of England* (four volumes, 1848–55, the fifth volume being incomplete at his death) enjoyed an unrivalled success in both Britain and America: according to Westfall Thompson, sales in the U.S.A. exceeded those of any book ever printed, save the Bible and some school texts; in the U.K. 140,000 copies had been sold by 1875. In common with the Enlightenment historians, with whom he should really be ranked, Macaulay took the view that 'facts are but the dross of history'. He was enough a man of the romantic revival to state that 'the perfect historian is he in whose work the character and spirit of an age is exhibited in miniature'; but his work was marked by 'the constant avowed or unavowed comparison . . . with the present' which S. R. Gardiner, a later English disciple of Ranke, declared 'is altogether destructive of historical knowledge'. Macaulay did some service to history as a discipline in providing so magnificent a demonstration of the literary effect to be achieved through the exercise of the highest powers of selection and organisation. Historians must be directed by precepts other than those which guided Macaulay; but since history is essentially social in function, since history among so many other things is also communication, no harm, and indeed much good, is done if they strive also for the literary grace in which Macaulay excelled. By the standards of historical scholarship established since the early nineteenth century, Macaulay sometimes falls short as a historian. In his search after effect he sometimes cheated, his rendering of the past was less 'truthful' than, given the resources available to him, it could have been. One notorious example of this is the passage in the first volume of the *History* describing the speech in which William III bade farewell to the States of Holland before setting out for Britain. Macaulay writes:

> In all that grave senate there was none who could refrain from shedding tears. But the iron stoicism of William never gave way; and he stood among his weeping friends calm and austere, as if he had been about to leave them only for a short visit to his hunting-grounds at Loo.

Macaulay had no reliable source for this fanciful description. In fact it is a direct plagiarism (conscious or unconscious) from the *Odes* of Horace, the description of Regulus making his farewell to the Senate.[16]

Macaulay's other great failing is of interest in connection with the point about history being a 'dialogue between present and past'. In a limited party sense Macaulay was a 'Whig historian': to his historical work he brought the bias of a practising Whig politician and his writings, in an obvious way, are an example of history as propaganda. More significant is Macaulay's contribution to what has become famous and notorious as the 'Whig interpretation of history', conceived in the broader, non-party sense as a product of the intellectual and material developments of the time and the reaction of liberal upper-class intellectuals to these developments. Macaulay was actually born in the first year of the nineteenth century; with the ruling class of his time he could confidently state (in the first chapter of his *History*): 'The history of our country during the last hundred and sixty years is eminently the history of physical, of moral and of intellectual improvement.' The first Whig historian (in both narrow and broad senses) was Henry Hallam (1777–1859), whose *Constitutional History of England from the Accession of Henry VII to the Death of George II* was published in 1827, and the tradition was continued throughout the nineteenth century by historians who would have repudiated the overt party bias which attached to Macaulay. All shared with Hallam a spoken or unspoken assumption that the central theme in English history was the development of liberal institutions: thus in the study of remote ages they greatly exaggerated the importance of 'parliaments' or of bodies, real or imagined, that they thought were parliaments; and they tended to interpret all political struggles in terms of the parliamentary situation in Britain in the nineteenth century, in terms that is, of Whig reformers fighting the good fight against Tory defenders of the *status quo*.

Thomas Carlyle (1795–1881) stands at an even greater remove from the accepted canons of historical scholarship than does Macaulay. His works are literature, prophecy even: in that they are full of lessons and morals for his times, in that they were very widely read, they demonstrate clearly the social affiliations of historical writing. They had a considerable effect on the attitudes of the wider public towards the problems of history, and upon the teaching of history at the lower levels. On the whole the influence was an unfortunate one, for Carlyle, who often seemed to regard 'history' as synonymous with 'biography', greatly exaggerated the importance of 'great men', which in turn served to foster at lower educational levels the most naïve forms of historical analysis. At the same time it should be noted that Carlyle's *Letters and Speeches of Oliver Cromwell* made an important contribution to historical interpretation: for two centuries the Puritan dictator had been described as one of the most evil villains of English history; thanks to Carlyle he now began to take his place as one of the 'great men' of English history.

The attitudes of the great English historical writers of the early nineteenth century were amply reflected in the absence of any efficient provision for the systematic teaching of history at the university level. History in Britain, much later than history in Germany and France, remained a branch of literature, or a study to be pursued purely for its more obvious utility to soldiers, statesmen and lawyers. Only against strong resistance was history established as an autonomous academic discipline, and even then the literary and the utilitarian traditions proved very enduring. In fact the first big changes in the ancient Universities of Oxford and Cambridge came about as a by-product of the utilitarian concept of history, for the men who wished to reform the slumbering condition of the universities were strong believers in history as a 'useful' subject for study. Thus in 1850 when history was first given status as a subject suitable for academic study at Oxford, it was as part of a combined school of Law and History. In attacking even this project, a contemporary broadsheet raised a number of questions which, in the continuing debate over the nature of history, have not always been satisfactorily answered:

> Is the subject suitable for Education? Is it an exercise of the mind? Is it not better left till Education is completed? Is it not sufficiently attractive to ensure a voluntary attention to it? Is it a convenient subject for Examination? Where is the standard author like Thucydides, etc.? If there is not a standard author, how are the comparative merits of the candidates to be judged?[17]

'Will it not', queried the anonymous author, putting a point over which somebody, some of the time, has worried ever since, 'supersede those subjects where a severer discipline is required?'

There had been a Regius Professor of History since the early eighteenth century: from the deliberations of the Royal Commission on Oxford University there followed a Professorship of International Law and Diplomacy and the Chichele Professorship of Modern History ('Modern' as distinct from 'Ancient'). Yet in the new history school standards remained far from rigorous: history's purpose, the Regius Professor openly boasted, was 'the better education of the gentry'.[18] Instruction took the very rudimentary form of commentary on a textbook: examination papers were provided with a small space into which the student could insert his answers. Only with the appointment in 1866 of William Stubbs (1825–1901) to the Regius Chair, was the basis laid for the serious study of history at Oxford. Much later than in the leading European countries the British Government had initiated a redirection of energies towards the publication of basic source materials in British history; Stubbs had for many years been working on editions of the twelfth-century chroniclers for the *Rolls Series*, begun in 1857. Stubbs had produced nearly twenty volumes of texts, all magnificent works of critical scholarship, when in 1870 he produced his volume of *Select Charters* which long remained a basic source book in constitutional history classes. Between 1874 and 1878 he published his *Constitutional History of England*, based as no other work of an English historian had been on meticulous scholarship and exhaustive study of all available sources. For all that, Stubbs could not, any more than Ranke, escape the prejudices and received attitudes of his times. As Sir Ernest Barker once remarked, 'he wrote his *Constitutional History of England* in spectacles – the spectacles of Victorian Liberalism, which are all the more curious on his nose when one remembers that he was a natural Tory' – the Whig interpretation of history, we have noted, was no narrow party matter. Stubbs began with high hopes of teaching history based 'not upon Hallam and Palgrave and Kemble and Froude and Macaulay, but on the abundant collected and arranged materials now in course of publication'. While Ranke had stressed diplomatic history, Stubbs, child of an era when British parliamentary institutions still stood forth in men's eyes as one of humanity's great inventions, saw in constitutional history the sturdy discipline upon which to base his teaching.

Stubbs retired from his chair in 1884 (to become Bishop of Chester and, later, Oxford), a disappointed man. Despite the founding of the Historical Manuscripts Commission in 1870, publication of source materials in Britain was lagging far behind the achievements in this respect of Germany. And although in the long term Stubbs had as profound an effect on historical scholarship and teaching in Britain as Ranke had in Germany, resistance at Oxford to any complete adoption of German methods was too strong for Stubbs to overcome. 'Research! Research! A mere excuse for idleness; it has never achieved, and never will achieve, any results of the slightest value!' Such was the conviction of Benjamin Jowett, Master of Balliol, and promoter of the famous Oxford tutorial system. There was, of course, good sense in the continued insistence at Oxford on the utilitarian aspect of historical studies, on history as a basic ingredient in a liberal education. The Oxford system, with what a recent Professor has termed its 'peculiar mixture of intellectual excitement and practical usefulness', served a valuable social function (if only to a somewhat select element in society): but history as a subject, and therefore history as social memory, quickly becomes sterile if battle is not constantly engaged at the frontiers of research, criticism and methodology.

Stubbs's successor in the Regius Chair, Edward Augustus Freeman (1823–92), expressed many of the basic features of the Oxford attitude in his brief but memorable aphorism: 'History is past politics, and politics is present history.' To John Richard Green (1837–83) is often given the credit for mounting the challenge to the assumptions behind the first part of this aphorism. In his *Short History of the English People* (1874) Green deliberately turned away from what in a fine phrase he called 'drum and trumpet history': 'I have devoted more space', he declared, 'to Chaucer than to Cressy, to Caxton than to the petty strife of Yorkist and Lancastrian, to the Poor Law of Elizabeth than to her victory at Cadiz, to the Methodist revival than to the escape of the Young Pretender.' In view of the reputation history has gained in some circles for being over-concerned with politics and great men, it is important to note that there have always been historians of impeccable scholarship (as was Green) to raise the flag on behalf of social history. It may be, though, that Green contributed to the idea of social history as an inferior kind of history because the records available to him were still of the type upon which a political or constitutional narrative could most easily and reliably be constructed. He was in fact very much in the Whig tradition, entertaining quaint notions about the essentially democratic character of the English 'people': in his history the men of the Middle Ages speak with the accents of Victorian reformers.

The best rejoinder to the implications of the second part of Freeman's aphorism was that of Samuel Rawson Gardiner (1829–1902), an Oxford historian in the style of Ranke and Stubbs, who was for a time Professor of History at King's College, London. Gardiner declared: 'He who studies the society of the past will be of the greater service to the society of the present in proportion as he leaves it out of account.' Here we are back to the central point in the social necessity theory of history: Gardiner is recognising the necessary service to present society of history, but stresses that the quality of the history, that is to say the value of that service, will be higher the more the historian disabuses his mind of the preoccupations and values of present society. The 'past-minded' historian renders the truer service to the present than does the 'present-minded' historian. Gardiner's sixteen-volume *History of England from 1603–1660*, based on the highest canons of scientific scholarship, is still an essential starting-point for all students of seventeenth-century English history.

At Cambridge historical study began to glimmer into life after the appointment (in 1869) of Sir John Seeley (1834–95) to the Regius Chair in immediate succession to Charles Kingsley, who as a novelist and Christian socialist has some claims to historical eminence, though none to eminence as a historian. The real founder of the Cambridge school of history was Lord Acton (1834–1902), of whom more in the next section. Seeley was an active politician, and one of the group of intellectuals who played a part in the development of the ideals of British imperialism at the end of the century: his most important book, *The Expansion of England* (1883), one of the earliest ventures into the realm of imperial history, is remembered for the classic remark about the British Empire being acquired (in the seventeenth and eighteenth centuries) 'in a fit of absence of mind'.

It was Oxford which gave the lead to historical studies in other British universities. When a Chair of History was created at the new Owen's College, Manchester, it was given (on the advice of Hallam) to a recent graduate from the new Oxford School of History and Jurisprudence, Richard Copley Christie. However, so far was history from full autonomy that Christie's successor held the chairs of both History and English. In 1890 Thomas Frederick Tout (1855–1929), a pupil of Stubbs, became Professor: Tout built Manchester into one of the great history schools in the United Kingdom. The Scottish historians of the eighteenth century, unlike their English counterparts, had been university teachers, but in the intervening years historical studies had sunk low in the Scottish universities: in the 1880s R. L. Stevenson, the novelist, was seriously considered for the History Chair at Edinburgh. At the beginning of the new century the Edinburgh history school, followed by those of the other Scottish universities, was remodelled on the Oxford pattern, that is, the hard core was provided by constitutional history, involving some study of documents; the softer outer flesh was a combination of history as a literary, and history as a useful 'liberal' subject.

As has been the case in certain other spheres, the United States of America proved more receptive to the best European historical ideas than did Britain, though for much of the nineteenth century the literary approach to history, informed by noble liberal sentiments, predominated. George Bancroft (1800–91) was as much a nationalist as a democrat: his ten-volume *History of the United States from the Discovery of America* (1834–87) established the legend of the glories of the American Revolution carried through entirely by disinterested patriots on behalf of the liberties of mankind. But American literary historians were not parochial: while John Motley (1814–77) turned to the study of the Dutch Republic, William H. Prescott (1796–1859) wrote his impressive and colourful pioneering studies of the Spanish expansion in South America. As American historical study on a formal basis was developed in the last quarter of the nineteenth century the influence of Ranke was undoubtedly very strong, though it would be wrong to suggest that American scholarship succumbed entirely to the great German and his less great apostles. At the other extreme positivism, at least in the somewhat reduced and common-sense form of a desire for synthesis and a search for patterns and tendencies, was accorded more respect by some American professionals than was the case in Britain. Among leading scholars in both countries, however, there was to be found in abundant degree a stress on the usefulness of history. The Rankean seminar method was imported into America in the 1870s by Herbert Baxter Adams of Johns Hopkins University; and Ranke himself was made first and only honorary member of the American Historical Association (A.H.A.) on its foundation in 1884. Justin Winsor, President in 1887, was a strong Rankean, and the German 'scientific' approach was developed by Henry Adams (1838–1918), who inaugurated graduate studies in history at Harvard. First President of the A.H.A. was Andrew D. White, who as Professor of History at the University of Michigan had endeavoured to establish contact with European standards. But on the whole White, an influential educator (he became President of

Cornell University), stressed the utility of history and was rather impatient of detailed research. He did do something to combat the view, sponsored by Bancroft, and fostered by the disciples of Ranke, that the main concern of history was politics. Alfred T. Mahan (1840–1914), like White, was interested in the 'lessons' afforded by history, rather than in deep primary research: he was thus led to his important and creative idea of the vital importance in warfare of control of the sea (expressed in two books, *The Influence of Sea Power on History, 1660–1783* and *The Influence of Sea Power on the French Revolution and Empire, 1793–1812*). On the whole it can be said that American historical study only began its phenomenal expansion in the twentieth century.

5 THE END OF THE CENTURY

Although the influential works of Niebuhr and Ranke and the teaching seminar of the latter dated back to the first quarter of the nineteenth century, the remainder of the century had passed before history as an academic discipline had properly established itself in Western Europe and North America. This does not mean that any monolithic party line had been established among professionals: critics from the outside, transfixed by some of Ranke's more extreme pronouncements and justifiably bored by the pedantries of some of his followers, often ignore the continuing debate among historians themselves. Undoubtedly one sign that history was developing an autonomous methodology of its own was the appearance of a number of manuals of historical technique; yet as C. V. Langlois and Charles Seignobos (1854–1942), authors of the best of these manuals, *Introduction to the Study of History* (Paris and London, 1898), remarked, hostility to such books from within the profession was strong. Langlois and Seignobos quoted one critic's opinion that 'generally speaking, treatises of this kind are of necessity both obscure and useless: obscure, because there is nothing more vague than their object; useless because it is possible to be an historian without troubling oneself about the principles of historical methodology which they claim to exhibit'.

Langlois and Seignobos, in fact, adopted a somewhat forbidding tone, declaring that of all branches of study, history most requires a consciousness of method:

> The reason is, that in history instinctive methods are, as we cannot too often repeat, irrational methods; some preparation is therefore required to counteract the first impulse. Besides, the rational methods of obtaining historical knowledge differ so widely from the methods of all other sciences, that some perception of their distinctive features is necessary

to avoid the temptation of applying to history the methods of those sciences which have already been systematised.

Furthermore, say Langlois and Seignobos, the greater part of those who embark upon historical study have no idea of why they are doing what they are doing: probably they have been good at the subject at high school or they fancy 'that history is a comparatively easy subject'. The two French historians would not even allow 'the same kind of romantic attraction which, we are told, determined the vocation of Augustin Thierry' as a legitimate reason for taking up the subject.

The great change, they argued, had taken place around 1850, when history ceased, both for the historians and the public, to be a branch of literature. Previously, and the comment is particularly apposite in regard to the work of Macaulay, historians republished their works from time to time without feeling any necessity to make any changes in them:

> Now every scientific work needs to be continually recast, revised, brought up to date. Scientific workers do not claim to give their work an immutable form, they do not expect to be read by posterity or to achieve personal immortality; it is enough for them if the results of their researches, corrected, it may be, and possibly transformed by subsequent researches, should be incorporated in the fund of knowledge which forms the scientific heritage of mankind. No one reads Newton or Lavoisier; it is enough for their glory that their labours should have contributed to the production of works by which their own have been superseded, and which will be, sooner or later, superseded in their turn.

Only works of art, Langlois and Seignobos declared, 'enjoy perpetual youth'.

It should be noted that Langlois and Seignobos were opposed to the study of the trivial, to the mere accumulation of obscure facts. Nonetheless as the heralds of the new dawn, whose crepuscular light was the light of Leopold von Ranke, they undoubtedly adopted an extreme posture: they spoke of certain 'idle questions' which were not worthy of consideration – 'whether history is a science or an art; what are the duties of history; what is the use of history'. Yet with the principle upon which they made their stand there need be no quarrel: 'The aim of history is not to please, nor to give practical maxims of conduct, nor to arouse the emotions, but knowledge pure and simple.' Apart from man's general attack on the unknown, there is, I have argued, a special social need for the type of knowledge with which the historian is concerned: if, of course, the pursuit of this knowledge produces practical lessons, if the manner of its communication gives pleasure, that undoubtedly is all to the good.

As a form of literary art, history had failed in its social function in that the 'memory' of the past that it presented was less 'truthful' than it could have been: in stressing the need for history to be scientific, in the sense of employing painstaking empirical methods of research, the followers of Ranke performed an invaluable service. Most famous of all turn-of-the-century pronouncements was that of J. B. Bury in his inaugural address (1902) as successor to Lord Acton in the Regius Chair at Cambridge:

> If, year by year, history is to become a more and more powerful force for stripping the bandages of error from the eyes of men, for shaping public opinion and advancing the cause of intellectual and political liberty, she will best prepare her disciples for the performance of that task, not by considering the immediate utility of next week or next year or next century, not by accommodating her ideal or limiting her range, but by remembering always that, though she may supply material for literary art or philosophical speculation, she is herself simply a science, no less and no more.[19]

The last phrase has been much quoted, not always in a manner favourable to Bury or to the state of historical studies at the turn of the century. In general historians of the twentieth century have been less certain (and Bury too, in common with all men of intelligence, changed his views, as we shall see in the next chapter) that the painstaking accumulation by empirical means of 'fact' would ultimately produce a scientifically accurate representation of the past. Yet, whatever reservations they may have about the universal validity of their findings, all reputable historians of today still have as the core of their activities the 'scientific' study of evidence as understood by Ranke, Langlois and Seignobos and Bury. Concepts of science have changed since the turn of the century when the absolutes of Newtonian physics still held sway: certainties have given way to probabilities, the absolute to the relative. In fact the whole concept of the nature of human understanding and knowledge has become more complex and more subtle. When Bury said 'history is a science, no less and no more', science to him meant something concrete and ultimately knowable. Science has changed, and so has history: they have indeed changed in parallel, and it remains true that the historian and the scientist are engaged in the same kind of activity, the attack on the unknown.

Bury was a man of wide culture and a writer of great literary grace. He believed that history had developed in scope since the time of the great master, Ranke:

> The exclusive idea of political history, *Staatengeschichte*, to which Ranke held so firmly has been gradually yielding to a more comprehensive definition which embraces as its material all records, whatever

their nature may be, of the material and spiritual development, of the culture and the works, of man in society, from the stone age on-wards.[20]

This had come about, Bury believed, because of the rise of nationalism with its emphasis on peoples rather than states; but, he argued, it owed most to the application of 'the historical method' to all the manifestations of human activity – social institutions, law, trade, the industrial and the fine arts, religion, philosophy, folklore, literature. And certainly in the very home of *Staatengeschichte* (though Bury did not refer to this) a great battle had been raging for a quarter of a century between the 'economic' historians and the Rankeans. Wilhelm Roscher (1817–94), who has been credited, somewhat meaninglessly, with the 'invention' of economic history, was both a pupil of Ranke's and some-thing of a positivist in his search for general historical laws. Gustav Schmoller (1838–1917) and Karl Wilhelm Nitzsch (1818–80) both wrote economic history of a more specific and limited character. The Rankean counter-charge was laid in resounding style by Dietrich Schäfer, now re-membered only for the phrase 'History is not a feeding trough'. It fell to Karl Lamprecht (1838–1917), who in 1886 had published a blameless three-volume, statistic-ridden study of economic life in the middle Rhine and Mosel valley, to lead the anti-Rankean cause. He proposed a *New Direction*, a sociological history with general laws (nothing, I shall have to say again and again, is really new in historiography), and in 1909 he founded the Royal Saxon Institute for Cultural and Universal History. In Britain there was no intellectual battle, and indeed there was only one real piece of solid economic history, though a massive one at that: between 1866 and 1902 there appeared seven volumes of *A History of Agriculture and Prices in England* by J. E. Thorold Rogers (1823–90). On the fringes Arnold Toynbee the elder had begun the debate on what was then as much a current social and political, as historical, topic, *The Industrial Revolution in England* (1884). More of that later.

History then, said Bury, was concerned with 'the constant inter-action and reciprocity among all the various manifestations of human brain power and human emotion'. It is important to note this broad conception of the nature of history, for historians have long been attacked for having a too narrow view of the past. The trouble, of course, is that although in inaugural addresses leading historians might preach the ideal of total history, in practice most of Bury's contemporaries did relapse into a concentration on political and constitutional history. There was a theoretical justification for this: only in political and constitutional history were there source materials suitable for scientific study; and however desirable the study of folklore or the conditions of the poor, the evidence was too fragmentary to make anything but charlatanism possible (though Thorold Rogers had shown what could be done). There remains today a fundamental divide between historians who believe that one should first decide what questions require answers, then wring answers out of whatever material is available, however unsatisfactory, and historians who prefer to be guided by the available material and to ask only those questions to which the material provides well-substantiated answers.

The most impressive memorial to the 'scientific' concept of history to which Bury subscribed, is the *Cambridge Modern History*, launched by Bury's predecessor in the Regius Chair at Cambridge, Lord Acton (1834–1902). Aiming to 'meet the scientific demand for completeness and certainty' the *Cambridge Modern History* was to be, as are most important advances in natural science, the work of many hands. 'Contributors will understand', Lord Acton wrote,

> that our Waterloo must be one that satisfies French and English, German and Dutch alike; that nobody can tell, without examining the list of authors, where the Bishop of Oxford laid down the pen, and whether Fairbairn or Gasquet, Liebermann or Harrison took it up.[21]

Although there would be extensive bibliographies, there were to be no footnotes. As historians have lost confidence in the objective history which the *Cambridge Modern* was supposed to provide, footnotes have crept back in: they are not, as readers and publishers often think, the last words in complacent pedantry; they imply in fact an admission of fallibility on the part of the historian, who is indicating his premises to the reader so that the reader may, if he wishes, work out different conclusions of his own. Increasing use of sociological techniques in our own day has provided greater opportunity for joint enterprise in historical research of a style long known in the natural and social sciences. Completely new versions of the Cambridge *Histories* are issued from time to time: characterised by brilliant individual chapters, they serve as invaluable works of reference, but they do not, and cannot, satisfy the demand for a re-creation of the rich texture of the past. Such joint enterprises bear witness to the great flowering of historical endeavour achieved by the end of the nineteenth century; but they are predicated upon an incomplete understanding of the nature of history.

NOTES

1. See Ronald Syme, *Tacitus* (1958).
2. *The Anglo-Saxon Chronicle*, ed. G. N. Garmonsway (1953) pp. 219–220.
3. Bede, *A History of the English Church and People*, ed. Leo Sherley-Price (1955) pp. 72–3.

4. Quoted by F. Smith Fussner, *The Historical Revolution* (1962) p. 23.

5. Ibid.

6. J. H. Brumfitt, *Voltaire: Historian* (1958) p. 2.

7. For Millar, see S. W. F. Holloway, 'Sociology and History' in *History*, XLVIII (1963) 157–61.

8. Quoted in Fritz Stern (ed.), *The Varieties of History* (1956) p. 57.

9. Ibid.

10. Quoted in Stern, p. 171.

11. J. Westfall Thompson, *History of Historical Writing* (1942) II 149.

12. Emery Neff, *The Poetry of History* (1947) p. 173.

13. Quoted in Stern, pp. 61, 62.

14. There is an excellent paperback edition of *The Communist Manifesto* (1967), with an introduction by A. J. P. Taylor.

15. Quoted in Stern, p. 124.

16. See C. G. Crump, *History and Historical Research* (1928) pp. 151–2.

17. Quoted in R. W. Southern, *The Shape and Substance of Academic History* (1961) p. 9.

18. My colleague Mr C. T. Harvie points out that by this remark Professor Goldwin Smith meant that he was offering the landed classes their last chance to educate themselves for government.

19. Quoted in Stern, p. 223.

20. Ibid., p. 221.

21. Quoted in Stern, p. 249.

3 The Development of Historical Studies: the Twentieth Century

1 LITERARY HISTORY

THE nineteenth-century revolution in historical scholarship provided the basis for the modern study of history; but as with most revolutions, this one produced many sectarians as well as a few men of vision. History in the twentieth century, while firmly rooted in the canons of scholarship established by the end of the nineteenth century, has been characterised by a series of reactions against the narrow forms into which history, under the influence of the more unimaginative followers of Ranke, was being forced. None of the new trends was quite as new as their enthusiastic exponents liked to believe: nineteenth-century historians had already explored the whole range from positivism to eruditism. And, as always, many were more ambitious in their announced intentions than they proved to be in their actual historical practices. But all the important new trends were in some degree products of an intellectual environment conditioned by the upheavals of modern total war and by the uncertainties fostered by Freudian psychology and the Theory of Relativity.

However, the first reply to the view of history enunciated so clearly by Bury in his inaugural address came in the form of an appeal to the older literary tradition which the disciples of Ranke had supplanted. In the December 1903 edition of the *Independent Review* George Macaulay Trevelyan (1876–1962), grand-nephew of Macaulay, published the celebrated essay 'Clio, a Muse', which was republished in 1913 in slightly less polemical form. History, Trevelyan argued, could perform neither of the functions properly expected of a physical science which he defined as 'direct utility in practical fields'; and, 'in more intellectual fields the deduction of laws of cause and effect'. The only fashion in which Trevelyan would allow that history could be scientific was in 'the collection of facts, the weighing of evidence as to what events happened'. Trevelyan then continued:

> In dealing even with an affair of which the facts are so comparatively well known as those of the French Revolution, it is impossible accurately to examine the psychology of twenty-five million different persons, of whom – except a few hundreds or thousands – the lives and motives are buried in the black night of the utterly forgotten. No one,

therefore, can ever give a completely or wholly true account of the French Revolution. But several imperfect readings of history are better than none at all; and he will give the best interpretation who, having discovered and weighed all the important evidence obtainable, has the largest grasp of intellect, the warmest human sympathy, the highest imaginative powers.[1]

Carlyle, Trevelyan claimed, had fulfilled these last two conditions in his *French Revolution*, so that his 'psychology of the mob' and his 'portraits of individual characters'

> are in the most important sense more true than the cold analysis of the same events and the conventional summings up of the same persons by scientific historians who, with more knowledge of facts, have less understanding of Man.

Trevelyan believed that he was rescuing history from the trammels of the Rankeans: critics of history have been even-handed in denouncing the pedantries of the Rankeans, and the presumption of Trevelyan and the literary historians in propagating the idea of the ineffable psychological insight possessed by the historian. The development of modern psychology, which was scarcely out of the womb when Trevelyan penned his reply to Bury, has rendered a substantial part of his argument invalid. 'You cannot', said Trevelyan, 'dissect a mind; and if you could, you could not argue thence about other minds. You can know nothing scientifically of the twenty million minds of a nation.' Therefore, Trevelyan concluded,

> in the most important part of its business, history is not a scientific deduction, but an imaginative guess at the most likely generalisations.

There is a pleasing honesty about this, though Trevelyan was unwise to state so categorically the limits of what is scientifically knowable. History today still employs 'imaginative guesses' – so indeed do all intellectual pursuits – but no historian today could discuss the French Revolution, or any similar topic without acquainting himself with the discoveries of the sciences of individual and social psychology.

Concluding then that history had no 'scientific value' (by this somewhat dubious phrase Trevelyan meant that history yielded neither useful inventions, nor causal laws of human behaviour in the mass), Trevelyan declared, as many in the opposition camp – Langlois and Seignobos are examples mentioned above – had long agreed, that history's purpose is educative. The justification for the pursuit of historical studies which Trevelyan now developed is the one which, among teachers of history, has most successfully held the field ever since, although, as I argued in the opening chapter, it is not really more than a corollary of the basic proposition of the social necessity of history. History, said

Trevelyan, provides a basic training in citizenship. The value, for
example, of Lecky's Irish history is not that Lecky proves Irish Home
Rule to be 'right or wrong, but he trains the mind of Unionists and
Home Rulers to think sensibly about that and other problems'. History
should not only remove prejudice, it should provide the ideals which
inspire the life of the ordinary citizen. A knowledge of history enhances
the understanding of literature, and doubles the pleasures of travel.

Returning again to the question of whether history is an art or a
science, Trevelyan concluded, rather as Thierry had done before him,
and as contemporaries like Stuart Hughes have agreed since, in this
fashion: 'Let us call it both or call it neither. For it has an element of
both.' Trevelyan distinguished between three distinct functions of
history: the *scientific* (collecting and weighing evidence as to facts),
the *imaginative* or *speculative* (selection and classification, interpretation
and generalisation) and the *literary*. This last function, whose importance
Trevelyan deliberately stressed, he defined as 'the exposition of the
results of science and imagination in a form that will attract and
educate our fellow-countrymen'. The remainder of 'Clio a Muse' took
the form of a lament that since the 'scientists' had taken over, the
intelligent layman had ceased to read history:

> The *Cambridge Modern History* is indeed bought by the yard to
> decorate bookshelves, but it is regarded like the *Encyclopaedia Britan-
> nica* as a work of reference; its mere presence in the library is enough.

Together with the man whose legacy he so vigorously combated,
Leopold von Ranke, Trevelyan is one of the great sitting targets in the
contemporary controversy over the nature of history. His clarion call
found an echo in the hearts of those with an amateur interest in history
rather than in those of professionals, whether in historical or other
disciplines. Theodore Roosevelt was one of the 'amateurs' who expressed his views in a letter to Trevelyan's father, George Otto
Trevelyan:

> I am sorry to say that I think the Burys are doing much damage to the
> cause of historic writing. . . . We have a preposterous organisation
> called I think the American Historical Association. . . . They represent
> what is in itself the excellent revolt against superficiality and lack of
> research, but they have grown into the opposite and equally noxious
> belief that research is all, that accumulation of facts is everything, and
> the ideal history of the future will consist not even of the work of one
> huge pedant but of a multitude of small pedants. They are honestly
> unconscious that all they are doing is to gather bricks and stones, and
> that whether their work will or will not amount to anything really
> worthy depends upon whether or not some great master builder here-
> after arrives who will be able to go over their material, to reject the

immense majority of it, and out of what is left to fashion some edifice of majesty and beauty instinct with the truth that both charms and teaches. A thousand Burys, and two thousand of the corresponding Germans whom he reverentially admires, would not in the aggregate begin to add to the wisdom of mankind what another Macaulay, should one arise, would add. The great historian must of course have scientific spirit which gives the power of research, which enables one to marshal and weigh the facts; but unless his finished work is litera- ture of a very high type small will be his claim to greatness.[2]

The trouble with this controversy as it unfolded historically at the be- ginning of the present century is that in fact Bury was almost as fine a prose stylist as Trevelyan, though unlike Trevelyan he made no song and dance about the difficulties of writing coherent historical narrative. Furthermore it may well be true that in the 1970s as many readers are repelled as are attracted by the high-flown phraseology which accounted for Trevelyan's great popularity in the early part of the century. None- theless, however overstated and unfair, Trevelyan's main points were important: there is, in human societies, both an educational necessity and a poetic craving for history; to fulfil his social function, the historian must *communicate*. Trevelyan was himself an 'amateur' in that after holding a fellowship for a short time at Trinity College, Cambridge, he severed all formal connection with teaching institutions till his appoint- ment as Regius Professor at Cambridge in 1927. But he was also very much a part of the 'industry' of history – a captain of industry one could say – in that his historical writings suited perfectly the prejudices and beliefs of the upper and middle classes in twentieth-century Britain. Like Macaulay and like Stubbs, Trevelyan was in fact a Whig historian, glorifying English common sense, English toleration, and English liberal institutions. Apart from a special concentration on British history in the early eighteenth century – his *England in the Reign of Queen Anne* is an outstanding achievement by any standard – Trevelyan's other important area of specialisation was the Italy of the Risorgimento. The series, initiated with *Garibaldi's Defence of the Roman Republic*, published in 1907, was completed just at the time Mussolini came to power. Trevelyan's triumphant affirmation of the virtues of nationalism was not one which later historians found per- suasive.

His greatest disservice to historical studies lay in his giving currency to a concept of social history which he himself described as 'history with the politics left out' and which critics have rightly termed 'polite chat about the past'. Much of the widespread feeling that 'social history' is somehow an intellectually inferior version of the real thing can be laid to the account of his travesty of an *English Social History*, written during the First World War when patriotic sentiment was at its height.

Fat-headed, jingoistic (in a nicely Whig way) pronouncements abound. The hard grit of statistical evidence is ignored, the precision of sociological inquiry nowhere to be found. Life in the past is idealised, never pinned down with any kind of psychological or quantitative objectivity.

However it would be unfair to condemn Trevelyan for ignoring methodologies which were only coming into being towards the end of his very long working life. Similarly, too much should not be made of his Whig bias: he was himself clear that it was idle for the historian to attempt to be dispassionate. It is open to the reader, participating in that second dialogue which I mentioned in the first chapter, to reject the overpraise of English virtues and yet to profit from Trevelyan's very deep involvement with the past. Trevelyan ignored the nastiness of life in former ages, but he brought to his subject the most important quality required by any worker in any task: love.

The re-emphasis on the poetic quality in history, on its educational value, and on its validity as a literary form profoundly influenced historical studies in Great Britain, not so much, perhaps, because of Trevelyan's powerful advocacy as because there was a strong predisposition in this direction anyway among many working teachers. At the undergraduate level this often meant that a gentlemanly sensibility and an elegant style became the prime qualifications for entry into, and success in, a course of study in history. Sometimes the same qualifications served for the writing and teaching professional. In North America and on the Continent of Europe there was much greater willingness to take a firm grasp of the problems facing historical study in the aftermath of the nineteenth-century revolution. But everywhere in the lesser institutions of learning there was a sufficiency either of dull pedants or of literary charlatans to provide a damning brief for history's critics.

2 New Approaches: Economic

One obvious reaction to, or, more accurately in many cases, development from the *Staatengeschichte* of the nineteenth century was the proliferation in the twentieth century of various sub-histories directing attention to aspects of human activity which had been largely ignored by historians concerned with 'past politics'. In a direct line from the positivists, Marx and such writers as Roscher and Schmoller lay the special interest in and emphasis on economic history which, at the beginning of the twentieth century, certain historians in all the Western countries began to cultivate assiduously. Latest and most important of the Germans was Werner Sombart (1863–1941), author of many important works, including *War and Capitalism* (1913) which laid emphasis on the part played by war in stimulating eighteenth-century industrialisation.

The other main line of specialisation also in essence originated from Germany, where Friedrich Meinecke (1862–1954) sought in a kind of 'intellectual history' to fuse the teachings of the two great masters who had formerly seemed to stand at opposite poles in historical study: Ranke, who had glorified the might of the political state, and Burckhardt, who contemplated (somewhat pessimistically) the development of human civilisation and its creative artefacts. Clearly the stronger pull was that of Ranke, and Meinecke's essential interest proved to be the history of *political* ideas. After taking his Berlin doctorate in 1886, Meinecke worked for fourteen years in the Prussian state archives. His first book (two volumes, 1895 and 1899) was a biography of General Hermann von Boyen, an activist in the early nineteenth-century Prussian reform movement. In 1906 and 1907 there followed two further studies of Prussian liberalism; and in 1908 he published a book on the origins of the German nation state. His most famous work was *The Doctrine of Raison d'État and its Place in Modern History* (Munich and Berlin, 1924).

The nineteenth-century revolution, then, produced 'diplomatic' history, and 'constitutional' history; the continuation of, and reaction against this revolution, produced 'economic' history and 'intellectual' history. There was really no 'social' history: social history was either seen as a further refinement of economic history, or else as the impressionistic 'polite chat about the past' of such writers as Trevelyan. Effectively all history (the study of man and society in the past) is really social history, so that the term is really tautological; but it has the virtue of tautology – extra emphasis. To speak of social history is a means of emphatically denying an exclusive interest in diplomatic or constitutional or, for that matter, economic or intellectual history. Today many of the sub-histories have become areas of arid specialisation, distinguished more by bitter demarcation disputes than by creative research. Economic history, necessarily, has recently developed refined techniques of its own, though for many years it existed in many places as a sort of non-discipline, history with the difficult bits left out.

For the moment we are concerned with great pioneers, who though they may have concentrated on one aspect of history rather than another, sought to illuminate, not to fragment: their lesser disciples, as always, were the bores and sinners who created the worthy tedium of the separate sub-histories. Any rigid categorisation, accordingly, would do an injustice to the breadth of outlook of most of the historians considered here; certain historians in the United States, for instance, almost simultaneously stressed both economic and intellectual factors; Henri Pirenne, though he set out as it were from the direction of economic institutions, was in every sense a *complete* historian. My grouping, therefore, is as follows: in the remainder of this section I shall consider those historians who can, in a more or less broad way, be termed 'economic' historians (if for no other reason than that this was the term adopted by their self-avowed disciples); in the next section I shall look at those magnificent ventures in the United States and in France whereby the attempt was made to create a 'New History' or a 'Total History'[3] bringing in economic, intellectual, and all other relevant factors.

Henri Pirenne, Belgium's greatest historian, was born in 1862. After a long and thorough training in what had become the established European manner, in which he developed a deep and abiding interest in 'scientific' historical methodology in the Rankean sense, he taught throughout his life at the University of Ghent save for the untoward interruption while he was the defiant prisoner of the Germans during the First World War. He died in 1935. Doubtless the best explanation of Pirenne's great contributions to historiography would be to say that he was a born historian equipped with the best training his time could offer. However his career does illustrate some aspects of the inevitable 'dialogue' between the historian's environment and his approach to the past. Pirenne belonged to a country which had had an independent political existence only since the 1830s; it is not therefore surprising that he should have turned so readily to a study of economic and cultural forces in early Belgian, and, by extension, European history (since there were no *Belgian* political institutions). Secondly, Belgium at the end of the nineteenth century was an urban society: and in the length of their continuous history, the towns of Belgium rivalled those of Italy. Finally, men of the later nineteenth century were very conscious of the fact that urbanisation was one of the major features which distinguished their culture from that of earlier ages: hence, among historians, there was a lively controversy over the origins of medieval towns.

From 1893 onwards Pirenne began publishing articles, based mainly on Belgian evidence, giving his thesis on the origins of Medieval towns, which, briefly, he associated with a revival of trade in the eleventh and twelfth centuries: the final statement appeared in *Medieval Cities: their origins and the revival of trade* (Princeton, N.J., 1925). Meantime Pirenne became involved in the bigger controversy of how and why the classical ages gave way to what, since the Renaissance, had been dubbed 'the Middle Ages'. Pirenne's famous thesis on this issue probably emerged first in his lectures at Ghent in 1910, though it appeared in print only in 1922 and 1923, and then in the form of two learned articles in the professional journals. A brief statement followed in the opening pages of *Medieval Cities*; the full statement was published posthumously in *Mohammed and Charlemagne* (1937). Through a study of economic rather than political institutions, Pirenne reached the conclusion that a Roman civilisation, based on the Mediterranean, survived the barbarian invasions, and did not collapse till the Muslim expansion of the seventh century. Medieval civilisation began only with the Carolingians: 'Without Mohammed, Charlemagne would have been inconceivable.'

Pirenne's other achievements, his seven-volume *History of Belgium* (1899–1932) and his works of popularisation, such as his *Economic and Social History of Europe*, still stand unchallenged, though his two major theses have both been subject to damaging attack by subsequent researchers. Pirenne's own stated position, to which one can only add a loud 'hear, hear', was that

> Every effort at synthesis, however premature it may seem, cannot fail to react usefully on investigations, provided one offers it in all frankness for what it is.

The Pirenne theses, indeed, served as a most useful goad and stimulus to further valuable attempts to conquer that which is not yet known. More important than this, Pirenne and those fellow-workers who shared his outlook, if not his genius, permanently broadened the channels of medieval history, which, despite the best efforts of some of the 'constitutional' historians, did more and more become a true 'social history'. In this respect, indeed, medieval history outstripped modern history, as a glance at that great enterprise of the 1930s, *The Oxford History of England*, will confirm: the medieval volumes are 'social history', the modern ones very largely political and institutional.

On account of his war experiences, Pirenne became a national hero: although in essence a medievalist, he was deeply interested in the problems of contemporary Belgian history; and of course he was a committed participant in two important academic controversies. Yet he kept himself within the accepted tradition of historical professionalism when at the beginning of the final volume of the *History of Belgium* he declared: 'My sole end has been to seek to understand and to explain.'

If the origins of modern professional history lie in nineteenth-century Germany, the greatest advances, unfortunately all too readily ignored in other countries, have been made by a select few in twentieth-century France. The dynamic couple Lucien Febvre and Marc Bloch we shall discuss in the next section; here we consider the austere George Lefebvre (1874–1959), who from the severe disciplines of Langlois and Seignobos evolved a quantitative and finally a quasi-psychological approach to history. Echoing the great masters ('No documents, no history'), he said 'Without scholarship there can be no history.' Later he added what was to become the password for a whole generation: 'Il faut compter.' It is perhaps due to the good health of the French historical establishment that Lefebvre ranks, not as an 'economic' historian, but as a 'historian of the French Revolution'; or perhaps it is due after all to the parochialism which has been a less desirable feature of French historical study. After a long, careful, impoverished and somewhat obscure apprenticeship, Lefebvre published his first book (two volumes, of course) in 1924, *Les Paysans du Nord pendant la Révolution française*, which established his primary interest and his primary virtue: studies in depth of the French peasantry during the Revolution, a meticulous attempt to establish the concrete realities of the social structure. Lefebvre accepted the existence of the class struggle; his Marxism was of the liberating creative sort. In 1932 there followed *Questions Agraires au temps de la Terreur*, the work which took him into the realms of social psychology. Lefebvre believed that in the future historians must make use of the discoveries of the social psychologists, the sociologists and the social anthropologists. For himself, however, he preferred to stick to the traditional materials of the historian, his documents.

Lefebvre was leftist and working-class in his political associations, and doubtless this helped to guide the direction of his researches, though, as he believed, it would not affect his conclusions. A growing interest among the intellectual classes in the working-class movement and in socialism generally was undoubtedly a motive in spreading an interest in economic history. Particularly was this true in Great Britain. Arnold Toynbee the elder was an upper-class pioneer of the university settlement movement who is generally given the credit for popularising, if not inventing, the concept of an Industrial Revolution: his major theme was the harsh effects industrialisation had had on the lower classes. A similar interest lay at the heart of the pioneering studies by J. L. and Barbara Hammond: *The Village Labourer* (1911), *The Town Labourer* (1917) and *The Skilled Labourer* (1919). The primary concern of the two great Fabian intellectuals Sidney (1859–1947) and Beatrice (1858–1943) Webb was to establish the social facts upon which to predicate social reform: they were thus led into producing a number of historical works, which for many years remained as standard authorities: *History of Trade Unionism* (1894) and *English Local Government* (nine volumes, 1906–29). R. H. Tawney (1880–1962), an Oxford graduate who later became a teacher at the London School of Economics, was also directly involved with the working-class movement through his activities in adult education and in the Labour Party. His first book, *The Agrarian Problem in the Sixteenth Century* (1912), was concerned with the decline of the English peasantry – the former 'yeomen of England' – in face of what he saw as the unscrupulous 'rise of the gentry'. Following a path which has proved to be not unusual among historians, Tawney began to reach from economic history into the realm of intellectual and sociological history. Much influenced by two famous articles on 'The Protestant Ethic and the Rise of Capitalism' published in 1904 and 1905 by the great German sociologist Max Weber, Tawney in 1926 published his own best-known work: *Religion and the Rise of Capitalism*. As is the way with great seminal works, Weber's thesis had been somewhat simplistic in establishing a direct link between Protestantism and capitalism. Tawney's work was at once much more specific and much more subtle, merely suggesting some of the associations between Protestant ethics and capitalist enterprise, and giving full weight to the exceptions and anomalies. It was also superbly written: a silent testament to history as communication, without all the attendant huffing and puffing of a Trevelyan.

The giant among twentieth-century economic historians, certainly in Britain, perhaps in the whole English-speaking world, is J. H. Clapham (1873–1946). Although Clapham had taken his First at Cambridge shortly before Acton took over as Regius Professor, the great man nonetheless influenced his first ventures in historical research – conventional studies of the politics of the French Revolution and of the origins of the war of 1792. However, Clapham also came in contact with the economist Alfred Marshall, who in 1897 sent the following important and revealing letter to Acton:

> I feel that the absence of any tolerable account of the economic development of England in the last century and a half is a disgrace to the land, and a grievous hindrance to the right understanding of the economic problems of our time. London and Cambridge are the only places where the work is likely to be done well; but till recently the man for the work had not appeared. But now I think the man is in sight. Clapham has more analytic faculty than any thorough historian whom I have ever taught; his future work is I think still uncertain; a little force would I think turn him this way or that. If you could turn him towards XVIII or XIX century economic history economists would ever be grateful to you. . . .[4]

In these days, when economics was still essentially political economy, a change in direction was not difficult. In 1902 Clapham accepted appointment as Professor of Economics at the college which was shortly to become the University of Leeds. While based in this centre of the textile trade, Clapham seized the opportunity to make full acquaintance with the world of business: in 1907 he published his first book, *The Woollen and Worsted Industries*. There followed at once his return to King's, Cambridge, as assistant tutor in History *and* Economics; he celebrated with a not very exciting book which cleared off his former interest in the politics of the French Revolution. It was not until after the First World War that Clapham revealed his talent for sustained economic narrative in areas formerly illumined only by the occasional monograph: *The Economic Development of France and Germany, 1815-1914* was published in 1921. Clapham now devoted himself to his major life's work, *An Economic History of Modern Britain*, published in three massive volumes between 1926 and 1938.

In the original preface to the first volume Clapham offered three justifications for his labours. First, that the story had never previously been handled on this scale. This was true: the standard economic history then (and, at a less exacting level of scholarship, since) was *The Economic History of England* which Ephraim Lipson (1888-1960) had started publishing in 1915: his three relatively slender volumes covered the whole gamut of English history, in vividly written but not entirely rigorous fashion. Clapham's second justification was that he intended to challenge certain widely accepted 'legends':

> Until very recently, historians' accounts of the dominant element of the nineteenth century, the great and rapid growth of population, were nearly all semi-legendary; sometimes they still are. Statisticians had always known the approximate truth; but historians had often followed a familiar literary tradition.

Actually Clapham's explanation of population increase as due to a falling death rate would not now be accepted by many historians employing the most sophisticated statistical techniques, so that there is a slightly hollow ring about Clapham's complacent reference to 'historians who neglect quantities'. In his preface Clapham cited also 'the legend that everything was getting worse for the working man, down to some unspecified date between the drafting of the People's Charter and the Great Exhibition'. This 'legend' – which had appeared most forcefully in the work of the Hammonds – he attributed to the way in which 'the work of statisticians on wages and prices' had been 'constantly ignored by social historians'. Against the psychological intuitions and emotional sympathies of the Hammonds, Clapham placed the quantities of the economist and the characteristic modern faith in the virtues of economic growth. The great 'standard of living controversy' had begun: by no means all of the shrewdest arguments supported the Clapham position, which indeed seemed somewhat lacking in elementary human perception and understanding. 'Thirdly', claimed Clapham in his preface,

> it is possible, all along the line, to make the story more nearly quantitative than it has yet been made. Dropped here and there in the sources – in the blue books above all – lie all kinds of exact information, not only about wages and prices, but about the sizes of businesses and farms and steam-engines and social groups. . . . Much approximation must be tolerated, and some guessing; but if the dimensions of things are not always clear, at least an attempt has been made to offer dimensions, in place of blurred masses of unspecified size.

The information was often less exact than Clapham thought: more because of temperament than because of the technical point that he worked exclusively in printed sources, Clapham was probably further from the real stuff of history than Lefebvre. But together they enunciated the thesis which was to dominate economic sub-history, and later was increasingly to influence general history: one must count.

By the late 1920s the intellectual autonomy of economic history had been accepted in Britain. In 1926 Lipson played the leading part in founding the Economic History Society, with its learned journal *The Economic History Review*. In 1928 Clapham was appointed to the first Chair of Economic History in the University of Cambridge; subsequently departments of economic history were founded in the various British universities. (There were already many lectureships – before the first world war George Unwin had taught Economic History at both Edinburgh and Manchester. The first Chair of Economic History in North America was established in 1893, with the first incumbent the Englishman W. J. Ashley.)

3   INTELLECTUAL HISTORY AND TOTAL HISTORY

In European history there has been no more prolonged or more fertile debate than that over the 'Pirenne thesis'; a similar role in American history has been fulfilled by the 'Turner thesis' on the significance of the American frontier. The eminence of Frederick Jackson Turner (1861–1932) in American history is obvious; where to place him in the development of historical studies is rather more difficult to determine. His essay on 'The Significance of the Frontier in American History' was read to a meeting of the American Historical Association in 1893. In one form or another the thesis (not completely unique to Turner, but he was the one who expressed it most vividly) has affected American historical thinking ever since, soon provoking a violent reaction. Turner was a great teacher and a great influence; but he did not himself publish a great deal. In 1906 he published *The Rise of the New West*, covering American history in the years 1820–30. The continuation, *The United States 1830–1850*, never completed, was published after his death in a version edited by his students. The most important of only thirty or so articles were grouped in two volumes, *The Frontier in American History* (1920) and *The Significance of Sections in American History* (1932). It has been argued that he never gave any valid demonstration of his thesis, but simply reiterated it over and over again.

The thesis, as Turner put it to the American Historical Association, was that

Behind institutions, behind constitutional forms and modifications, lie the vital forces that call these organs into life and shape them to meet changing conditions. The peculiarity of American institutions is the fact that they have been compelled to adapt themselves to the changes of an expanding people – to the changes involved in crossing a continent, in winning a wilderness, and in developing at each area of this progress out of the primitive economic and political conditions of the frontier into the complexity of city life.

The frontier to the Americans, said Turner, was what the Mediterranean had been to the Greeks, and, an adherent of the Pirenne thesis might add, to Roman civilisation. The second Turner thesis concerned the significance, once the frontier had disappeared, of a geographically determined 'sectionalism' in the American nation: the 'physical map' of America, he argued, 'may be regarded as a map of potential nations and empires'. Turner was attacked, particularly in regard to 'the significance of sections' for ignoring economic imperatives, the growth of capitalism, the nature of class antagonism; for ignoring technology and the true inspiration behind cultural and artistic endeavour; above all Turner was attacked for fostering isolationism and nationalism, and denying the European roots of American civilisation. To read only Turner's critics is to receive a picture of a nineteenth-century obscurantist who cast a blight on twentieth-century studies. In fact, in his isolationism at least, Turner was very much of the America of the inter-war years, an emphatic example of that dialogue between present and past to which we have so often referred.

The most astonishing weakness in the frontier thesis was Turner's failure to make any comparative study of the experience of other nations and other frontiers. Nonetheless Turner's pupil, Professor Avery Craven, has argued first, that prior to Turner's bold revisions the 'germ' theory of the European origins of American institutions remained unquestioned; and second, that there had been a general neglect of economic, social and geographical factors. 'Against such attitudes', Professor Craven writes, 'Turner revolted':

> A Wisconsin background enabled him to take a more penetrating view. He could enter by the back door. Because he had been part of a rapidly changing order, he saw American history as a huge stage on which men, in close contact with raw nature, were ever engaged in the evolution of society from simple beginnings to complex ends. Historians had answered 'what' long enough; it was time to inquire as to 'how' things came about. America, as it then existed, was the product of the interaction of 'economic, political and social forces in contact with peculiar geographic factors'. Such an understanding would give a new American history.[5]

The 'new history', in fact, was the label consciously adopted by James

Harvey Robinson (1863–1936). The general tenor of the attack on the 'old history' was perhaps not altogether new: that it was pedantic, lacking relevance, neglectful of vast territories of the human experience. To take each criticism in turn. The 'new history' aimed to avoid the mere recital of facts; the question must be asked:

> Is the fact or occurrence one which will aid the reader to grasp the meaning of any great period of human development or the true nature of any momentous institution?

It was deliberately 'present-minded' in that it sought to use history to explain the present. It would give special attention to economic forces, as to intellectual and any other relevant forces; in so doing it would make use of the discoveries of the social scientists. The programme has been repeated often since; the virtue, we are coming to realise, lies not in the programme, but in the manner in which and the extent to which it is carried out. Already a sufficient number of people, both inside and outside the profession, have told the historian what, ideally, he ought to do. Only those who have faced up to the practical problems, particularly in terms of sheer hard labour, of what they recommend deserve to be listened to.

Robinson himself was not much given to scholarly research and the best practical example of the new history is the work produced in collaboration with Charles A. Beard, *The Development of Modern Europe* (1907–8). Beard (1874–1948) was an outstandingly gifted scholar. In the early years of the century he shared in the fascination with the economic aspects of history which, as we have seen, was so evident in Europe. His *An Economic Interpretation of the Constitution* (1913) has much of the hard-edged quality one finds in Clapham: essentially he saw the framers of the American constitution as realistic appraisers of man's economic instincts, rather than as liberal-minded idealists. At the time Beard probably believed that he was offering *the* key to the American constitution, though later he was to contend that he had only offered *one* key among many, that, as his title had stated, this was merely *an* interpretation. The book at any rate was a stimulating one, and a valuable corrective both to the predominantly political orientation of American historiography at that time and to the myth-making of Bancroft. Two years later there followed an even more penetrating study, the *Economic Origins of Jeffersonian Democracy* (1915).

Another American who participated in the general interest in economic history was Edward P. Cheyney, who as early as 1901 published his *Introduction to the Industrial and Social History of England*. While in general economic history in America was to become even more professionalised and specialised than it did elsewhere, Cheyney belonged to that style of economic historians who have followed their positivist ancestors in seeking general historical laws. Cheyney in fact formulated six such laws, which were, however, more obviously informed by generous liberal sentiment than by scientific marshalling of evidence. The six laws were: first, The Law of Continuity, which states that 'all events, conditions, institutions, personalities come from immediately preceding events, conditions, institutions, personalities' and, further, that 'the immediate, sudden appearance of something, its creation by an individual or a group at some one moment of time, is unknown in history'. Essentially this is simply a restatement of the fundamental genetic view held by all historians since the time of Ranke; but since the Second World War not all historians would accept it as completely axiomatic. Second, The Law of Impermanence, which states that institutions must adapt or perish. Third, The Law of Interdependence: by this Cheyney held that no nation could make permanent gains at the expense of another, and he cited the case of the French occupation of the Ruhr (1923) which had not greatly benefited France. This one sounds suspiciously like liberal propaganda, as do the fourth, fifth and sixth laws, the Law of Democracy (proven only by demonstration of the 'failure' of all other systems), the Law of Necessity for Free Consent (coercion, being 'against human nature', would necessarily produce resistance) and the Law of Moral Progress: in support of the last Cheyney advanced the highly dubious proposition that 'the people, always more moral than their rulers, would not at any time within the last four centuries have supported their governments in wars merely of plunder, aggression or revenge.'

Beard wrote a lot of history; Robinson wrote a lot about what he thought historians ought to write; Carl Becker (1873–1945) wrote more than was then customary about what he thought historians actually were writing. We shall consider Becker's views on history in general in the next section; at this stage the important point is to consider Becker's part in developing another of the 'sub-histories' which led away from the purely constitutional and political approach: intellectual history. As with Meinecke, Becker's abiding interest was in political ideas. From the German intellectual historians he took over the notion that each age can be characterised by a specific mode of thinking, 'a climate of opinion'. This was a simple but fruitful notion; unfortunately it has become one of the stock platitudes of history, the cover for reams of sloppy thinking. In 1920 Becker published one of the first 'intellectual' histories of his own country: *The United States: an Experiment in Democracy*. Becker's primary research interest, however, was the development of rational and liberal ideas at the time of the Enlightenment, and his most famous single work, *The Heavenly City of the Eighteenth Century Philosophers* (1932), is devoted to this theme.

It may seem strange that historical studies in the early years of the twentieth century should simultaneously try to face in two different directions: in the direction of economics and in the direction of ideas. Some would argue that these are opposite directions; that the very heart of human activity is dominated by an oscillation between two opposites, the *idea* and the *economic imperative*. However, this turning in different directions was all part of the same internal revolution within historical studies: the bad old men of the dying generation had ignored both economic and intellectual factors, so the brave young men of the present must explore one or other or both. The turning to economic history, which had its origins deep in the nineteenth century, obviously makes sense in the context of a developing technological civilisation. The fashion for intellectual history was essentially a more temporary one, associated with the tide of philosophical doubt which swept the Western world in the aftermath of the First World War, washing away much of the older faith in the existence of solid historical 'facts'. 'Everything is relative' and 'It's all in the mind, anyway' were the cant phrases which affected and reflected thinking at all levels of intellectual activity.

The most important second-generation product of the new history movement was Arthur M. Schlesinger Sr (1888–1965).[6] As a graduate student at Columbia, Schlesinger was formally under the supervision of the Rankean traditionalist Herbert L. Osgood, from whom he derived an enduring respect for the canons of good scholarship. But the men who most influenced the thrust of his work were Robinson and Beard. His dissertation, finally published in 1918 under the title *The Colonial Merchants and the American Revolution, 1763–1776*, gave him, he has written, 'an opportunity to examine the interrelation of economics and politics, something which Beard had so deeply interested me in'. The result, he believed, combined 'the research methods of Osgood with the insights of Beard'. While teaching at the State University of Iowa, Schlesinger in 1922 instituted a course on the 'Social and Cultural History of the United States', the first of its kind. This led naturally to his sponsorship of a multi-volume, co-operative *History of American Life* (first four volumes 1927). A triumphant exposition of Schlesinger's dictum that the Great Man is 'merely the mechanism through which the Great Many have spoken', the series nonetheless had some unfortunate overtones of Trevelyan's 'history with the politics left out', and, despite the scrupulous scholarship and (above all) editorship, presented finally a certain spineless quality. Still, the bid to give 'ordinary life' a genuine place at the heart of academic study was an important and valuable one.

All of the leading American historians in the first quarter of this century were concerned to broaden the base of history, to enrich man's understanding of the richness of his past. But again by what might be termed the Iron Law of Historiographical Tedium the insights of men like Beard and Becker hardened into grimly partitioned sub-histories: congeries of 'economic' historians and of 'intellectual' historians, clasping firmly to their one means of identity, pursued topics of research even narrower and less intellectually stimulating than those pursued by nineteenth-century political historians.

In America much was written and there was much heart-searching, but the really concrete advances in developing a genuinely new and wider approach to history took place in France. The guiding influence was that of Henri Berr (1863–1954), who sought through the journal he founded in 1900, the *Revue de Synthèse historique*, and through his projected one-hundred-volume *l'Évolution de L'Humanité*, to bring together in one great synthesis all the activities of man in society, calling to his aid the methods and insights of sociology and the other social sciences. But the two men who more than any others demonstrated how the perennial but vague aspirations after a history more truly representative of the richness of man's life in society could be turned into reality were Lucien Febvre (1878–1956) and Marc Bloch (1886–1944).

Lucien Febvre, born into a cultivated middle-class family, received a thorough historical training in keeping with the best traditions of late nineteenth-century scholarship. At the same time he found himself greatly attracted by the ideas and objectives of Henri Berr, whom he affectionately described as the 'Trojan horse in the territory of traditional scholarship'. A stress on the importance of geography had been part of French historical scholarship since the time of Michelet, and Febvre's first book was in fact predominantly geographical: *The Regions of France: Franche-Comté* (Paris, 1905). His long apprenticeship was completed with the publication in 1911 of his dissertation *Philippe II and the Franche-Comté*. Based on deep researches among extensive archival materials, the book was strong in knowledge both of geography and of economics. Already profoundly dissatisfied with the simple monocausal explanations of earlier political historians, Febvre was concerned to demonstrate what he called 'the multiple action of profound causes'. This work was followed immediately by a *History of Franche-Comté*, then, after an interval spent in the French Army during the First World War, Febvre swung to something much more general, a volume on *The Earth and Human Evolution* for Henri Berr's multi-volume series: among the large number of points which Febvre made which have now become platitudes was the rebuttal of the idea that rivers make 'natural frontiers' – in fact they serve to link human groups together in common activities. From a special interest in geography, Febvre, in a manner typical of many twentieth-century intellectuals, moved to an interest in group psychology. The new interest was revealed first in a study of *Martin Luther*, published in 1928; but his most impressive venture into what he himself called 'historical psychology' was his study of religious unbelief in the sixteenth century, *Le problème de l'incroyance au XVI siècle* published just after the Second World War (1947).

Marc Bloch also came from a comfortable family: since his father was a Professor of Ancient History at the Sorbonne it has been said of him that he was 'by birthright a member of the intellectual élite of the Third Republic'. Significantly he graduated in both history and geography, and his earliest publication, paralleling that of Febvre, was a geographical study of *L'Île de France*. His historical apprenticeship was served in searching the archives of northern France for materials for a study of medieval society in the Île de France. At the end of the First World War (through which he served with distinction) he was appointed to a chair at Strasbourg, to which university Febvre had already been summoned. With Febvre, Bloch shared an interest both in geography and in collective psychology. Beyond that he sought to borrow from sociology an exactness of method and a precision of language which, as he lamented, was too often lacking in traditional historians, and he studied archaeology, agronomy, cartography, folk-lore and linguistics – the last subject with particular reference to place names and the genealogy of language. Bloch was an early believer in both the *comparative* and the *regressive* method. Comparative study (his interest in which, he said, had been derived from Henri Pirenne), involving comparisons within a single country or between different countries, is of immense value, since in highlighting both similarities and differences it can be a source of new syntheses, new questions and, sometimes, convincing answers. The regressive method involves using evidence drawn from a later age of matters – customs, traditions, place names, field patterns – which may well have endured from an earlier age, in order to illuminate that earlier age. In a manner which in some ways echoes the early approach of Frederick Jackson Turner, and more obviously that of the great French master Michelet, Bloch himself tramped around the French countryside talking to the men who in the twentieth century still tilled the soil in a manner not too far different from that of their medieval predecessors.

Bloch's interest in collective psychology, in, above all, the manner in which the irrational imposes patterns on human behaviour, was seen most strongly in his book on *Les Rois Thaumaturges* (1924): in this Bloch showed that although the belief that both French and English kings were endowed with healing powers grew up almost by accident, that belief became a fundamental part of the concept of royalty and an important element in maintaining its strength. But Bloch's main contributions to historical study were his investigations into the nature of feudal society. *Rois et Serfs: un chapitre d'histoire capétienne* (1920) is a

rather brief work, but it shows clearly the manner in which Bloch
viewed feudal society from the standpoint of the peasants rather than
that of the lords and kings. *The Basic Characteristics of French Rural
History* (1931) turned firmly away from the historian's traditional preoccupation with legal and administrative institutions: Bloch endeavoured
to show that the forms of French agricultural life depended less on such
matters than upon the persistence of the forms of tenure and organisation established in the early Middle Ages. Through his refusal to
examine only institutions and communities for which traditional primary materials existed, Bloch helped to rescue from oblivion the medieval village community, hitherto largely ignored by medieval historians
who preferred to follow where the documents took them, that is to the
seignorial manor and its legal apparatus. Bloch struck bold and powerful blows on behalf of the kind of history which questions first, then
seeks around for any scrap of evidence of any kind which may provide
answers: too many historians shoot first and ask questions later. *Feudal
Society* (1940), though a sketch rather than a fully rounded work, drew
upon the many types of source and the many methodologies with which
he had familiarised himself.

   The great vehicle for the broader history desired by Bloch and Febvre
was the famous journal which they jointly launched in January 1929,
Annales d'Histoire Économique et Sociale, widely known thereafter,
despite slight changes in the details of the title, as *Annales*. The first
editorial committee of *Annales* consisted of Albert Demangeon, Professor
of Human Geography at the Sorbonne, G. Espinas, Archivist of the
French Foreign Ministry, Maurice Halbwachs, Professor of Sociology at
the University of Strasbourg, Henri Hauser, Professor of Economic
History at the Sorbonne, A. Piganiol, Professor of Roman History at
Strasbourg, Charles Rist, Professor of Political Economy at the Faculty of
Law, Paris, André Siegfried, Professor at the School of Political Science,
Paris, the Deputy Governor of the Bank of France and Henri Pirenne.
In their introductory address to their readers, Bloch and Febvre referred
to the gulf which had developed in historical and social studies:

> While historians apply their good old hallowed methods to the docu-
> ments of the past, more and more people are devoting their activity to
> the study of contemporary societies and economies. . . . Among the
> historians themselves, as among the students of contemporary problems,
> there are plenty of other lines of demarcation: ancient historians,
> medievalists and modernists; students dedicated to the description of
> societies termed 'civilised' . . . or, on the contrary, drawn to those
> which for lack of better terms, can be called 'primitive' or exotic.
> Nothing would be better, we absolutely agree than for each person,
> concentrating on a legitimate specialisation, laboriously cultivating his
> own back yard, nonetheless to force himself to follow his neighbour's

work. But the walls are so high that, very often, they hide the view. . . . It is against these deep schisms that we intend to raise our standards. Not by means of articles on method or theoretical dissertations, but by example and accomplishment. Brought together here, scholars in different disciplines and different specialities, all motivated by the same spirit of exact objectivity, will present the results of their researches in subjects which they have chosen and in which they are expert. . . . Our enterprise is an act of faith in the exemplary virtue of honest labour, backed by solid and conscientious research.[7]

The great enterprise and 'act of faith' of Febvre and Bloch has endured in a manner which surpasses the labours of the various American pioneers of 'new' history, important though their work also was. Today *Annales* is probably the most respected and most prestigious of all historical journals, though it is likely that a large number of those who speak highly of it do not actually peruse its pages, let alone attempt to contribute to it. *Annales* was ambitious in scope, catholic in attitude in a way in which the old historical *Reviews*, and indeed the new *Economic History Review*, were not: but the final explanation of its success lies in the way in which breadth of approach was combined with a rigorous insistence on the highest standards of scholarship, 'exact impartiality' and 'the exemplary virtue of honest labour, backed by solid and conscientious research'.

What *Annales* stated really was that there could be no short cut to a more interesting, a more 'total' (Febvre's word),[8] a more 'human' (Bloch's word) history. If the older school of political and constitutional history was unsatisfactory, it was not necessarily because it was laborious and painstaking, but often because it was lacking in these qualities, was too prone to easy remedies and oversimplified conclusions. The lay reader, then, will find *Annales* a rather forbidding journal: like any other learned journal, it does not try to fulfil the necessary historical role of communication with the wider audience, society as a whole. But the example of *Annales*, as well as the direct teaching of Bloch and Febvre, gave rise to a whole school of better historical writing. Febvre was the more rounded historian; much of Bloch's writing has a provisional character about it, and he is not always easy to read. Both made some of their most stimulating contributions to our deeper knowledge of the nature of history in the pages of *Annales*, often in the form of short reviews. However, Bloch left behind after his death the unfinished manuscript published in English as *The Historian's Craft*. In this work there are obvious and understandable imperfections, but overall it succeeds marvellously in being a very human testimony to a personal faith in history, and a manifesto on behalf of the most advanced school of historical writing of the inter-war years. Bloch begins with the question: 'What is the use of history?' First he dwells on the poetry of history, on its 'unquestionable fascination'. However, to entertain is not enough: the use of history is that it aids understanding; 'to act reasonably, it is first necessary to understand'. Recognising the human and social need for history, Bloch remarks that 'we become indignant if . . . it seems incapable of giving us guidance'. History, of course, is 'but a fragment of the universal march towards knowledge', and it is only 'a science [Bloch uses the word in the Continental sense, as discussed in our next chapter] in infancy . . . it is still very young as a rational attempt at analysis'. Bloch is proud of the soul-searchings, the hesitancies of his craft, but he hopes to see ever-increasing numbers of historians 'arrive at that broadened and deepened history which some of us – more every day – have begun to conceive' – that is, the history of the *Annales* school.

After this introduction, Bloch attempts a definition of 'history': history is 'the science of men in time'; the critical element is the human one. Dismissing the debate over history as art or science, Bloch nonetheless makes a fine personal statement on behalf of the aesthetic and humane quality of history:

> Between the expression of physical and of human realities there is as much difference as between the task of a drill operator and that of a lutemaker: both work down to the last millimetre, but the driller uses precision tools, while the lutemaker is guided primarily by his sensitivity to sound and touch. It would be unwise either for the driller to adopt the empirical methods of the lutemaker or for the lutemaker to imitate the driller.

In a section entitled 'Understanding the Present by the Past', Bloch elaborates one of his simplest but most impelling ideas, and one which is incidentally a perfect ancillary justification for the study of history: 'Man spends his time devising techniques of which he afterwards remains a more or less willing prisoner.' Although admitting the great technological transformation which has set the present apart from even the immediate past, Bloch singles out the 'understanding of the Protestant or the Catholic Reformation' as most important 'for a proper grasp of the world today'. In the section 'Understanding the Past by the Present', Bloch defends his famous regressive technique of historical research, then comes to the heart of his own humane affirmation: the 'faculty of understanding the living is, in very truth, the master quality of the historian'.

With the chapter on 'Historical Observation' Bloch moves into the realm of the historian's methods. Here he admits that not all historians in the past have made the best use of the wide variety of source materials open to them. He looks forward to the time when historians will be better equipped with linguistic and social science techniques, and hopes to see much more in the way of co-operative research. The manifesto-writer is very apparent in his plea that 'history as it can be' should not be made 'the scapegoat for the sins which belong to bad history alone'. Chapter Three, on 'Historical Criticism', deals with the problems of forgery, reliability of records and the like. Bloch makes a strong claim on behalf both of the difficulties of the historian's tasks and of his success in overcoming them, and, as one would expect from the editor of a scholarly journal, he looks for the highest standards in the use of references and other scholarly apparatus. In the next chapter Bloch goes on to affirm his abiding interest in group psychology as a basic study in history. His faith is in a total, integrated history, but since the individual cannot grasp history in its wholeness, he believes that each historian must be content with analysing one particular aspect of society. Bloch's treatment of the historian's use of words like 'serfs', 'bourgeoisie', 'Middle Ages' is so important that we must leave it for separate discussion in a later chapter (see below, pp. 167ff.). The book concludes with an unfinished fragment on historical causation, where there is a clear echo from Lucien Febvre: 'History seeks for causal wave-trains and is not afraid, since life shows them to be so, to find them multiple.'

Marc Bloch was a hero of the French Resistance, and after cruel tortures he was shot by the Germans in 1944. Nothing could bring out more forcefully his simultaneous commitment to present and to past. His commitment to the present provided the driving force of his historical inquiries: his importance in the development of historical studies lies in the way he linked this commitment to a demonstration (in collaboration with Lucien Febvre) of what a 'broadened, deepened' history could mean in practice, linked in turn to an insistence upon the most rigorous scholarly standards.

4   PHILOSOPHIES

Richard Pares noted the reluctance of historians to philosophise about their subject. One very good reason for this is that historians change their minds, not, I would argue (if they are good historians) about the essential core of their activities, but over the other issues which have been a perennial source of debate. J. B. Bury, for instance, is permanently interred in the textbooks as the apostle of 'scientific' history. Unhappily great men do not always die immediately after making their most quotable remarks. And for a generation after the famous 'a science, no less and no more' address, Bury continued to publish various asides on the nature of history. Even in that address he had remarked that the great interpretative works of the past, while retaining permanent value as 'memorials to their age', would be of diminishing value as history. In some of the later essays Bury came very close to the full position of what was called 'relativism', the view that even the most 'scientific' history will be superseded as new ages adopt different interests and viewpoints. He was saying in fact that really there could be no 'scientific' history, only 'relative' history, history whose 'truthfulness' could only be assessed relative to the age in which it was written. Here, of course, we are back with our old friend, the dialogue between present and past.

Common-sense British historians, such as the later Bury, or the Elizabethan expert J. B. Black, referred to this dialogue in passing: Black, for instance, in his study of the Enlightenment historians, *The Art of History* (1928), remarked that 'direct observation of historical events is out of the question: they must always be seen indirectly, reflected so to speak, in the mirror of the present'.   However, a number of American historians felt that the excesses of the 'scientific' historians, the intensive pursuit of hard facts, had got so out of hand that a clear theory of 'historical relativism' must be raised as a counter-agent. In stressing that history must be written with the needs of the present in mind, J. H. Robinson and the 'new' historians, of course, were adopting a kind of relativist position. The most mature early statement of historical relativism, however, appears in an essay published by Carl Becker in 1910.[9] Approvingly quoting Voltaire's aphorism about history being simply 'a pack of tricks we play on the dead', Becker proceeded with great wit to demolish the pretensions of that mighty labour of many hands, the *Cambridge Modern History*. He remarked that despite the historian's 'chiefest ambition' to make 'a permanent contribution to knowledge', histories in fact were constantly falling out of date. In the nineteenth century, an age of political revolution, there had been growing agreement that 'history is past politics'; 'in an age when industrial problems are pressing for solution the "economic interpretation" of history is the thing'. The advent of 'the social state', Becker said with considerable foresight, given that he was writing four years before the First World War, 'will doubtless give us some new formula'. Historical synthesis, Becker then concluded, could be true in only one sense, 'true relatively to the needs of the age which fashioned it'. It was in the inter-war years, however, when Einstein's theories had entered the popular imagination, and when scepticism and disillusionment with old absolutes was at a height, that the most thoroughgoing relativist statements were made. Charles A. Beard (though he subsequently repudiated the ultimate absurdities in which the relativists indulged) dismissed the aspirations of the scientific historians as a 'Noble Dream' in which 'facts' like 'the Sleeping Beauty of the fairy tale' awaited the 'advent of her bespectacled, seminar-trained deliverer'.[10]

Becker spoke of 'everyman' being 'his own historian'. Professor Conyers Read announced the growing recognition of 'the relativity of all history'.

Today one suspects that these historians of the inter-war years were simply participating in a universal fashion for 'relativity', giving a somewhat grandiose title to a rather simple idea. In the development of historical studies, however, they did play a valuable role in forcing a reassessment of assumptions which underlay the post-Rankean school of historical study. In general, however, working historians continued to operate with a vague mixture of Rankean 'scientific' history lightened by a few dabs of relativism. This mixture has been much under attack from the sociologically orientated historians of recent years. In David M. Potter's mild overstatement:

> After living for a long period under the dominion of scientific history, historians at last threw off this creed and embraced historical relativism. As they did so, they passed from the belief that they could attain truth without troubling themselves about theory to the belief that they could not attain truth even if they invoked theory.[11]

Historical relativists then were a rather humble school of historians, humble about the aims and possibilities of their discipline. Modesty, even false modesty, was certainly not the failing of the two most famous historical philosophers of the twentieth century, Benedetto Croce (1866–1952) and R. G. Collingwood (1889–1943). Croce served as Minister of Education in the Italian Government of 1920–1. He was a distinguished opponent of fascism and he wrote a fair amount of 'orthodox' history. But he also produced a number of philosophical essays on the nature of history, which are not themselves very easy to follow; where they are easy to follow they do not always seem to be very coherent or self-consistent. In that polarity between the ideal and the economic (or material) which has already been mentioned as a fundamental in the study of social development (above, p. 71), Croce was firmly and unreservedly attracted to the ideal. He insisted that there was a fundamental distinction between historical and scientific knowledge, and seemed to see the former as essentially a kind of intellectual intuition. Finally, since the past itself has no existence (an argument many philosophers have used to challenge the validity of history as a discipline at all), history has reality only in the mind of the historian: 'all history', then, in one of Croce's famous phrases, 'is contemporary history' – that is, it has existence only in the minds of contemporaries. If this has any meaning at all, it simply seems to be a conflation of the relativist and present-minded attitudes. Croce, however, was also convinced that historical thinking was superior to all other kinds of thinking: the relativity of history was not a confession of weakness but an assertion of intellectual and imaginative power. As a historian of Italy Croce was perceptive and liberal-minded; as a philosopher of history he left a confusing legacy, which, in the arrogant claims it made on behalf of the subject, perhaps restored some self-confidence to puzzled researchers in the age of relativity, but which did not contribute much to the development of historical studies.

Croce's ideas were refined and expounded in lucid and poetic style by R. G. Collingwood, who, it is important to note, was primarily a philosopher rather than a historian, though he was also a practising archaeologist and historian of Roman Britain and he held an Oxford lectureship in history along with his Chair of Philosophy. Based on lectures given in 1935 and 1936, *The Idea of History* was put together and published after Collingwood's death in 1944. Beautifully written and poetic in its sensibility, it is for me a puzzling and unsatisfactory book, and I shall not attempt here the impertinence of a summary. Nevertheless, in the course of a very full life Collingwood expressed with his own peculiar talent many of the ideas which lie at the heart of the twentieth-century reaction to the nineteenth-century revolution in historical studies. In 1930 he published for the Historical Association (of Great Britain) a pamphlet on the *Philosophy of History*. Though clearly much inferior to *The Idea of History*, this pamphlet does make an easy point of entry into some aspects of Collingwood's thought. After a somewhat elaborate argument justifying the concept of historical relativism, Collingwood then attempted to refute the criticism that the historian is essentially selective in his approach to evidence. History, being the creation of the historian (that is, it is not synonymous with 'the past'), only begins when the historian asks a question. 'History' is the answering of this question: 'the historian does not select, because no past facts are "there" before him, to select from, until he has put them there by sheer historical thinking.' This was a neat twist: critics in the past had so often said that history was all in the mind of the historian: Collingwood was proud of it. Collingwood ended his pamphlet with a fine exposition of the Crocean notion that all history is contemporary history. All history, he said, brings its narrative down to the present day, 'not necessarily as history, but as the history of history'. (By this remark Collingwood seems to mean that the book standing on the shelf is not history, it only becomes history when taken down and read by the contemporary seeker after historical knowledge: rephrased less dogmatically, this recalls the point that *included in* history – though not the fundamental *essence* of history, as Collingwood seems to argue – is the dialogue between historian and reader.) Thus, Collingwood continues in familiar fashion, 'every age must write history afresh':

> Everyone brings his own mind to the study of history, and approaches it from the point of view which is characteristic of himself and his

generation; naturally, therefore, one age, one man, sees in a particular historical event things which another does not, and vice versa. The attempt to eliminate this 'subjective element' from history is always insincere – it means keeping your own point of view while asking other people to give up theirs – and always unsuccessful. If it succeeded, history itself would vanish.

But history does not thereby become something arbitrary and capricious, as the layman would be only too justified in suspecting. Collingwood is excellent in his efforts to meet the doubts of the layman: 'if my thoughts about Julius Caesar differ from Mommsen's . . . must not one of us', he asks, 'be wrong?' The answer is 'no' because, he says, 'the object differs':

> My historical thought is about my own past, not about Mommsen's past. Mommsen and I share in a great many things, and in many respects we share a common past; but in so far as we are different people and representatives of different cultures and different generations we have behind us different pasts, and everything in his past has to undergo a slight alteration before it can enter into mine. . . .
>
> Finally, since the past in itself is nothing, the knowledge of the past in itself is not, and cannot be, the historian's goal. His goal, as the goal of a thinking being, is knowledge of the present; to that everything must return, round that everything must revolve. But, as historian, he is concerned with one special aspect of the present – how it came to be what it is. In this sense, the past is an aspect or function of the present; and that is how it must always appear to the historian who reflects intelligently on his own work, or, in other words, attempts a philosophy of history.

With Croce, Collingwood played an important part in restoring to the twentieth-century historian a confidence that what he was doing was not quite as daft as it sometimes seemed. Everyone interested in history should know something of Collingwood's ideas. But it must be stressed again that he does not stand in the mainstream of the development of historical studies: full of deep insights, he is no sure guide to what historians actually do or how they think.

The most interesting account of Collingwood's thinking occurs in his *Autobiography*, written unhappily when he was already seriously ill. Collingwood reckoned that until the end of the nineteenth century history had been very much a 'scissors-and-paste' matter, and the historian's main business was to know his 'authorities' (there is a much fuller discussion of 'scissors-and-paste' in *The Idea of History*):

> to his authorities' statements he was tied by the leg, however long the rope and however flowery the turf over which it allowed him to circle. If his interest led him towards a subject on which there were no

authorities, it led him into a desert where nothing was except the sands of ignorance and the mirage of imagination.

This statement was accurate perhaps for the current state of history in the ancient English universities rather than for historical studies as a whole: however, what Collingwood now went on to say about the effects on his conception of history of his experiences on his father's archaeological digs echoed the broadening of historical thinking everywhere. He learned that

> scissors and paste were not the only foundation of historical method. All you wanted, I could see, was a sufficiently extensive and sufficiently scientific development of such work, and it would teach you, not indeed everything, but a great deal, about subjects whose very existence must remain permanently unknown to historians who believed in authorities. I could see, too, that the same methods might be used to correct the authorities themselves, when they had been mistaken or untruthful. In either case, the idea of an historian depending on what the authorities tell him was exploded.

In all this Collingwood was at one with Bloch, Febvre and the *Annales* school. However, immediately after this common-sense appraisal came the rather silly argument taken from Croce which not only insisted that historical thinking was different from scientific thinking, but that somehow historical thinking was supreme because there is always a 'historical element' in scientific method. On examination this appears to mean no more than that when a scientist frames a theory he uses 'certain historical knowledge in his possession as to what experiments had been tried and what their results had been'.

With Croce, Collingwood believed that 'all history is the history of thought' and in this, of course, he was in key with the new emphasis on intellectual history developing in the twenties and thirties. To demonstrate his point Collingwood drew a distinction between history and such 'pseudo-histories' as geology, palaeontology and astronomy:

> History and pseudo-history alike consisted of narratives; but in history these were narratives of purposive activity, and the evidence for them consisted of relics they had left behind (books or potsherds, the principle was the same) which became evidence precisely to the extent to which the historian conceived them in terms of purpose, that is, understood what they were for; in pseudo-history there is no conception of purpose, there are only relics of various kinds, differing among themselves in such ways that they have to be interpreted as relics of different pasts which can be arranged on a time-scale.

This in itself is an illuminating commentary on one part of the historian's method. But Collingwood's contention was that there 'is nothing else except thought that can be the object of historical knowledge':

Political history is the history of political thought: not 'political theory', but the thought which occupies the mind of a man engaged in political work. . . . Military history, again, is not a description of weary marches in heat or cold, or the thrills and chills of battle or the long agony of wounded men. It is a description of plans and counter-plans: of thinking about strategy and thinking about tactics, and in the last resort of what the men in the ranks thought about the battle.

The reader may well share my conviction that this last passage is absolute rubbish, well illustrating what can happen when a highly refined mind pushes a pet theory too far (in fairness, Collingwood's illness must also be recalled). All that needs to be said is that history can very well be 'a description of weary marches . . . the long agony of wounded men'. Why on earth not?[12]

Collingwood surmised in 1939 that we might well be standing on the 'threshold of an age in which history would be as important for the world as natural science had been between 1600 and 1900'.[13] At least he was convinced of the importance of history, and in his writings he expressed the dignity of the subject; for these services all historians must be grateful. But the odd mystical outbursts simply provided material for history's enemies: those who, rightly, derided a history which turned out to depend solely on the historian's intuition. Perhaps in wrapping up in fine words what many historians were doing anyway, Collingwood prepared the ground for the violent reaction against the glorification of intuition which came after the Second World War.

Collingwood's interests and thoughts were not those of a conventional historian; professional historians, however, have generally been much more respectful towards Collingwood than they have towards a contemporary whose approach to history followed a rather different tangent: Arnold Toynbee (born 1889). Once upon a time Toynbee would have been called a philosopher of history: the material of his philosophising is the past itself (Collingwood, on the other hand, was concerned with history as the historian's activity). Toynbee would like us simply to call him a historian: but the word which best encompasses the immense scope and lofty aims of his work is 'metahistory'.[14]

The writing of metahistory in many ways belongs to the tradition pioneered by the positivists in the nineteenth century. Toynbee's precursor in the twentieth century was Oswald Spengler (1880–1936), whose *Decline of the West* (1918) was a comparative study of the rise and fall of whole civilisations which claimed to have the key to historical development in an analogy with a living organism, which is born, matures, ages and dies. When Toynbee became preoccupied with the problem of the genesis of civilisations (the civilisation, he has often said, is the smallest unit which the historian should consider), he sought guidance first from Spengler: but he found Spengler's rigid,

Germanic *a priori* system of little value; he himself would try 'English empiricism' instead.

Toynbee has described how he became preoccupied with the comparative study of civilisations:

> The general war of 1914 overtook me expounding Thucydides to Balliol undergraduates reading for *Literae Humaniores*, and then suddenly my understanding was illumined. The experience that we were having in our world now had been experienced by Thucydides in his world already.

There is nothing reprehensible or necessarily 'unscholarly' about such flashes of illumination, which most working historians (and, for that matter, many working scientists) have experienced from time to time. Toynbee has never, indeed, concealed the intuitive nature of his historical vision, having described vividly his feeling of having the tide of history flowing in his veins. Toynbee's own specialised expertise lay in the world of Greek history and literature: from 1919 to 1924 he held the Chair of Byzantine and Modern Greek Language, Literature and History at London University. For thirty years thereafter he was Director of Studies at the Royal Institute of International Affairs in London and throughout the inter-war years he was responsible for the year-by-year *Survey of International Affairs* published by the Institute: these annual surveys are standard works, both for the information they contain and as models of the writing of contemporary history.

After a number of false starts, Toynbee made his first jottings for the famous *A Study of History* (vols I-III, 1934; vols IV-VI, 1939; VII-X, 1954) while on a train between Alexandria and Nish:

> This time I had not deliberately set myself to make the plan. I had spent the day looking out of the railway carriage window, and the plan that I had jotted down at the end of the day had seemed to come of itself.

From the Californian philosopher F. J. Tegart (himself influenced by Turgot) Toynbee got the idea that the best entry into a comparative study of history was to decipher the local differences in the cultures of living societies, and to work back into the past from there. At this stage Toynbee was not familiar with Jungian psychology, though many of his later generalisations about social behaviour were in keeping with the basic tenets of that school. But from the encounter between God and Mephistopheles in Goethe's *Faust* he took a central idea: 'an encounter between two personalities in the form of challenge and response: have we not here the flint and steel by whose mutual impact the creative spark is kindled?'

The second world war bulldozed a gap in the sequence of publication between the first six volumes and the last four; in the meantime

Toynbee's own opinions changed slightly, and the final volumes are marked by a kind of messianic revivalism which was absent in the early volumes, and which undermined Toynbee's constantly reiterated claim that his methods were exclusively empirical and inductive.

Toynbee has identified twenty-one civilisations, which, he claims, have passed through similar stages of growth, breakdown (including a 'time of troubles') and eventual dissolution, the final phase in each case being characterised by the formation of a 'universal state'. Certain 'laws' are advanced to account for certain critical developments, for example, the famous challenge and response mentioned above:

> Briefly stated, the regular pattern of social disintegration is a schism of the disintegrating society into a recalcitrant proletariat and a less and less effective dominant minority. The process of disintegration does not proceed evenly, it jolts along in alternating spasms of rout, rally, and rout. In the last rally but one, the dominant minority succeeds in temporarily arresting the society's lethal self-laceration by imposing on it the peace of a universal state. Within the framework of the dominant minority's universal state the proletariat creates a universal church, and after the next rout, in which the disintegrating civilisation finally dissolves, the universal church may live on to become the chrysalis from which a new civilisation eventually emerges.

The first six volumes of the book are pervaded by the deep pessimism of a man who knows that his own civilisation is in decay: but the revivalist Toynbee shines through in the four published after the Second World War:

> . . . if a vehicle is to move forward on a course which its driver has set, it must be borne along on wheels that turn monotonously round and round. When civilisations rise and fall and, in falling, give rise to others, some purposeful enterprise, higher than theirs, may all the time be making headway, and, in a divine plan, the learning that comes through the suffering caused by the failures of civilisations may be the sovereign means of progress.

Whatever one may feel about this as objective history, Toynbee's own pronouncements about his objectives in writing *A Study of History* do make good sense, and fit well into many of the preoccupations we have detected among historians reacting against the nineteenth-century legacy. Remarking that *A Study of History* had been written side by side with the *Survey of International Affairs*, Toynbee argued that he could not have done either piece of work if he had not been doing the other at the same time. There is here a distinct element of that 'present-mindedness' we have seen in other twentieth-century historians:

> A survey of current affairs on a world-wide scale can be made only against a background of world-history; and a study of world-history

would have no life in it if it left out the history of the writer's own lifetime, for one's contemporaries are the only people whom one can ever catch alive. An historian in our generation must study Gandhi and Lenin and Ataturk and F. D. Roosevelt if he is to have any hope of bringing Hammuraki and Ikhnataon and Amos and the Buddha back to life for himself and for his readers.

Secondly, Toynbee has stressed the way in which his comparative study of twenty-one civilisations has broken with the tradition of Western-orientated history, increasingly outmoded as formerly 'underdeveloped' parts of the world rise to power, and as archaeological discoveries bring further ancient civilisations to light. Toynbee, thirdly, has referred to the division between history and the social sciences:

> In the study of human affairs the first thing now to be done is to explore how far we can carry, in this field, the scientific method of investigating 'laws', regularities, uniformities, recurrences.

While claiming to recognise the value of specialised studies (though he has also poured much scorn on some of the activities of professional historians), Toynbee sees his own work as a counterpoise to excessive specialisation. He has aimed, he says, at giving a synoptic view of the new knowledge which has recently come to light on different civilisations. Finally Toynbee, in an astonishing echo of some remarks of Langlois and Seignobos, who would have deplored his entire approach to history, gives himself a definite social purpose:

> The historian can help his fellow men of different civilisations to become more familiar with one another, and, in consequence, less afraid of one another and less hostile to one another, by helping them to understand and appreciate one another's histories and to see in these local and partial stories a common achievement and common possession of the whole human family.

Toynbee has been acclaimed by the reading public and denigrated by professional historians. In general there is professional agreement that whatever Toynbee has written in *A Study of History*, it is not history. Basically the arguments are that far from arguing inductively as he claims, he has first established an *a priori* system, then made the facts fit. Many of the 'facts' indeed are not in accord with the latest researches in the fields into which he so boldly treads. Among the present generation of younger historians there has been a slight reaction in favour, if not of Toynbee, of some of the things he was trying to do. What has been missing in the wholesale denunciations of Toynbee is a recognition of that second dialogue at the heart of history, the dialogue between historian and reader. We do not have to swallow whole the entire mystic apparatus of the Toynbee system; but we can perhaps agree that, as in such deceptively simple notions as challenge and response, Toynbee has in fact made a very genuine contribution towards our understanding of the past. Toynbee is perhaps a great poet, and a not-so-great historian; but in the mansion of history there are many chambers. It is as helpful to say that Toynbee is 'not a historian' as it is to say that Carlyle is not a historian: no less and no more.

5 THE STRAIGHT-LINE PROFESSIONALS

While Beard, Bloch, Tawney and the others laboured to broaden the base of historical studies, the vast majority of practising historians continued to operate within the boundaries which had been defined at the end of the previous century by such authorities as Langlois and Seignobos, continued to deal exclusively with constitutional and political matters, continued to put the patient accumulation of facts above sweeping interpretation, the study of documents above the use of tools borrowed from other disciplines. At the highest level of historical activity categorisation of this sort must not be taken too far: the man who insists most strongly on the primacy of written documents is often the man who is most aware of how much, and how little, other sources and other methods will yield in the particular inquiries with which he is preoccupied. In this section we shall be concerned with some of the greatest names in twentieth-century studies, men who showed that it is not necessary to talk loudly about 'new' history or about healing schisms between art and science to make a substantial contribution to man's better understanding of the past. They are in many cases men of the broadest intellectual outlook and awareness of subjects beyond their own discipline. In the United States in the nineteen-thirties there was indeed a somewhat wordy battle between relativist and 'new' historians on the one side, and the 'straight-line' professionals on the other: but in the main the battalions of those attacking that in the past which is not yet known advanced in fair amity, too slowly no doubt, but from time to time firing off the new weapons forged by a Lefebvre or a Schlesinger. The achievement of the 'new' historians of all descriptions was to open up to scholarly study areas of the past which had formerly been either neglected or subject only for windy speculation. The achievement of the 'professionals' was, through a developing ability to empty study of the past of the grosser preoccupations of the present, to rid well-worn traditional topics of much of the mythology which surrounded them.

Professional methods, derived from the nineteenth century, but informed by a twentieth-century scepticism, and, in many cases, illumined by a true appreciation of the totality of human society, yielded vital work in the study of medieval English institutions. By the strict rule of chronology I should have mentioned the name of F. W. Maitland (1850–1906) in the previous chapter. But although all his masterpieces were published in the last decade of the nineteenth century, he above all represents the vital bridge between the centuries. Practically no one reads Stubbs today, and few read Tout, yet Maitland's work is constantly on call. This may well be the most convincing demonstration, if tables of greatness are called for, that he was, as H. E. Bell believed, 'the greatest English historian'.[15]

Maitland played a worthy part in the great campaign waged by Stubbs to make available the basic texts of medieval English history. He produced many volumes for the Selden Society and his first noteworthy publication was his edition of *Bracton's Note Book* (1895). Bracton was a thirteenth-century lawyer, and Maitland's starting interest was the law (traditionally history and law were closely associated in British universities), but it was informed by a deep perception of social and economic necessities: as Trevelyan remarked, Maitland used medieval law 'as the tool to prise open the mind of medieval man'. His *History of English Law to 1272*, written in conjunction with Frederick Pollock, first published in 1895, is still a standard work. Maitland moved away from the stuffier Ranke–Seignobos school in insisting on the importance of asking questions. One key to the continuing regard in which Maitland is held is the manner in which so often one pregnant sentence of his has provided the stimulus for a later scholarly monograph. In a manner which anticipated the 'regressive' techniques of the *Annales* school, Maitland recommended working 'backwards from the known to the unknown, from the certain to the uncertain'. This was precisely the counsel he followed in his epoch-making venture into the social and legal history of early England, *Domesday Book and Beyond* (1897). Maitland was a true professional, meticulous in his use of sources, preoccupied above all with the problems of *analysis*, and, though a brilliant stylist, not at all interested in the writing of historical *narrative*. Two of his many aphorisms set the tone of professional history for the first half of the twentieth century. History, he said, in a restatement of the historicist position, is a 'seamless web'; and 'the only generalisation is that there are no generalisations.'

Impossible (and not very desirable) to catalogue here all the fascinating work accomplished in medieval studies at the beginning of this century in the wake of Maitland and his two distinguished contemporaries Sir Paul Vinogradoff (1854–1925), the Russian émigré scholar, and James Tait (1866–1944) of the celebrated Manchester school. However, mention must be made of the way in which the study of place-names was introduced into the professional investigation of English medieval history. In Britain one agency of scholarly reform in an otherwise backward country has been provided by the newer universities.

Immediately before the 1914–18 war the recently established University College at Reading had as a Research Fellow, Frank Stenton (1880–1967), whose early work was in the field of place-names. After publishing a number of monographs relating to various English counties, Stenton proceeded to the more conventional editing of various manuscript source collections; he was also an authority on the various artefacts left by early times, particularly coins. From his secure base in a deep familiarity with the primary sources, conventional and unconventional, Stenton became a leading authority on early medieval England and author of the second volume in the Oxford series, *Anglo-Saxon England* (1953).

One central problem which the professionals attacked with vigour was that of the origins of the English Parliament, pride of the Whig historians. While 'new' historians and relativists sought to stress the importance of the present in the study of the past, the professionals were able to show how deep misconceptions about the medieval 'parliament' had grown up because of the present-minded character of Stubbs and his like. Some of the most important work in this area was done by American scholars, traditionally attracted either to medieval institutions as the forebears of American concepts of law, or to the late-colonial origins' of American independence (where much important myth-destruction was accomplished, see below, p. 94). Quoting with approval Tout's dictum, 'We investigate the past not to deduce practical political lessons, but to find out what really happened', the Harvard historian C. H. McIlwain explained in his 1936 presidential address to the American Historical Association how professional revisions of standard myths come about:

> They have usually come piecemeal because someone has been steeping himself in the thought and motives of some past epoch by extensive and careful reading of the records or writings of the time, and one day wakes up to find – usually to his utter amazement – that this thought or these motives and institutions are not at all the ones he has been reading about all these years in the standard modern books. Then he gets to work.

McIlwain described his own personal feeling of shock when he 'suddenly realised that men like Lambarde or Fitzherbert in Elizabeth's time, when they spoke of a parliament, were thinking of something in many ways very different from what I had learned'. That McIlwain was personally a man of strong political commitment was apparent from his reflection on the manner in which the over-extension of checks and balances in American constitutional theory tends to violate liberty, 'making government innocuous only by making it ineffective, and by splitting it up [rendering it] irresponsible'. In the end he did believe in the social

function of history, though the basic task of the historian was to
understand the past on its own terms:

> As historians, our real task is with history, not with its application;
> but when troubles come upon us, the question will always emerge – it
> will not down – whether it belongs to the historian, even if not strictly
> *as* historian, to find in all these facts and developments, assuming
> them to be accurate, any lessons of value that may be practically useful.
> I sincerely believe that it does. . . .[16]

The distinction between the historian *as* historian, concerned with
accuracy in understanding the past, and, as it were, the applied historian,
drawing out present uses of history, is a valuable one to which we shall
return.

Among British historians there is agreement that the great man of the
twentieth century is L. B. Namier (1888–1960), who probably ranks as
second only to Maitland among the greatest of British straight-line professionals. Mr A. J. P. Taylor has likened the publication of *The Structure of Politics at the Accession of George III* (two volumes, 1929) to the
publication of Darwin's *The Origin of Species*. Professor John Hale has
suggested that in historiography the present age can fairly be termed 'The
Age of Namier'.[17] Lewis Namier was a Polish Jew[18] who read history
at Balliol in the years before the First World War. He originally planned
to research into the British Empire at the time of the American Revolution. An American historian gently guided him away from the over-
crowded American end to the British. Soon after he started on this
assignment Namier became aware of how little was really known of the
nature of English politics in the later eighteenth century: under the all-
pervading influence of the Whig school it had been too readily accepted
that eighteenth-century political assumptions were the same as those of
the nineteenth century: the works of contemporary polemicists, like
Edmund Burke, were taken at their face value. What was really intended by Namier as a preliminary clearing-up operation before he proceeded to his original project grew into the greatest single contribution
made by a twentieth-century scholar to British historical study, and,
arguably, one of the most important single contributions to the development of historical methodology. The manner by which Namier became
involved in his great life's work is a not uncommon one among true
professional historians: treating problems as they come up and getting
to the bottom of each problem before passing on to the next, rather than
approaching history with some great problem ready formulated, or with
some *a priori* conceptual scheme. As he worked into the subject, Namier
knew what questions to ask and when to ask them: a supremely important gift.[19]

The fashionable Whig view of eighteenth-century political history postulated that the Glorious Revolution of 1688 had created a constitutional monarchy, to which the Hanoverian accession in 1714 added cabinet government. In 1760, however, the misguided George III had attempted through a vast central machinery of corruption, and in face of the heroic resistance of the Whigs, to put the clock back and restore a personal monarchy. The essential basis of the Namier method was the carrying out of meticulous studies of individual personages which could then be welded together into a composite portrayal of the age: instead of generalisations (that is, guesses) about what 'people', parties or groups did or thought, Namier got down to the individual unit and worked up from there. In *The Structure of Politics at the Accession of George III* he studied the separate members of parliament and the motives for their being there, showing how small was the part played by the lofty political ideals which the Whig historians loved to bandy about. Above all Namier brought out the extent of local political influence, and showed how insignificant in fact was the reputed power of corruption held by the central government. Namier's credo was essentially that of the Rankean professional: 'One has to steep oneself in the political life of a period before one can safely speak, or be sure of understanding, its language.' His materials were traditional: in fact he was the first researcher in the field to work through the five hundred volumes of the Newcastle papers in the British Museum.

England in the Age of the American Revolution (1930) was only the first volume of a projected multi-volume series under this general title. However, it contained enough meat in itself to complete the Namierite revolution. Namier had already shown the limits to eighteenth-century corruption; now, seeing the system not in terms of latter-day moralising but as men saw it at the time, he justified such corruption as did exist as necessary to the smooth running of government. More than this he demonstrated how unreal it was to see eighteenth-century Whigs and Tories as analogous to nineteenth-century Conservatives and Liberals. At the national level much of the meaning had gone out of the terms 'Whig' and 'Tory' though at the local level it was still possible to distinguish between a Whig and a Tory 'mentality'. National politics were the politics of faction and connection rather than of party in any nineteenth-century sense. Finally Namier showed that the powers of George I and II were much greater than the Whig historians had allowed for: correspondingly there was a good deal less in the contemporary and later accusations that George III was in some way 'unconstitutional' in his actions. Ministers under the first two Georges, as Richard Pares, the most brilliant of the Namierites put it, were the King's servants: but they were servants who had had 'the run of the place'.[20]

Apart from his eighteenth-century interest, Namier wrote on the diplomatic origins of the Second World War (permitting his work here to be marked by some of the passion which he strove to exclude from the eighteenth-century books) and the 1848 revolutions. But it is the books discussed here, along with the massive *History of Parliament* (on which many pairs of hands were set to work), which exemplify the Namierite approach. These are works of analysis, in which the narrative element, of which Macaulay was such a great master, is completely swamped. From outside the profession one of the great criticisms of twentieth-century professional history was to be centred on this very loss of narrative impetus. Namier, further, was a 'Tory' historian in that he appraised the individual, selfish motivations of human beings, eschewing the abstract ideals of the political philosophers. Here, consciously or unconsciously, he was implicated in the Freudian revolution, which had done so much to destroy the old high-flown theorising about human motivation. In a later work, to be discussed in the next chapter, Namier consciously adopted the concepts of modern psychology. There is another point about Namier which we shall also take up then: in a rudimentary way, his work was at bottom quantitative; instead of talking of 'the' Whigs and 'the' Tories, he was asking 'how many' Whigs, 'how many' Tories. In this he was in parallel with Sir John Clapham; but Namier was the greater historian, for he went on asking questions while Clapham was too often content simply to print the answers he found in his Blue Books.

Namierite methods were further applied to the eighteenth century by Richard Pares and a still younger generation of disciples; to the reign of Anne and the early Hanoverians by J. H. Plumb; to the sixteenth century by J. E. Neale, who in the process finally destroyed the mythology of a fully developed parliament in the Middle Ages; and to the nineteenth century by Norman Gash.

One other main brand of traditional history was much developed in the present century: diplomatic history. In most of the main Western universities where the study of history had been formalised, history was held to end some time in the nineteenth century, or even earlier, and there was no study of contemporary history. However, the preoccupation in the inter-war years with the origins of the First World War gave a tremendous stimulus to the study of recent diplomatic history. Before the war Bernadotte Schmitt was being highly adventurous when he prepared a doctoral dissertation on Franco-German relations in the period after 1870. An American, Schmitt took the Honours History School at Oxford, where the tuition in 1906 (as indeed now) consisted in the writing and discussing of a weekly essay on such topics (they haven't changed much either) as 'Was Magna Charta a Feudal Document?', 'Was the Foreign Policy of Queen Elizabeth Vacillating?' and 'Did the Stamp Act cause the Loss of America?' Schmitt reckoned that the essay-writing discipline served him well when it came to presenting the results of his own historical researches. He also remarked that the examinations for his Oxford B.A. were harder than those subsequently taken for his doctorate at the University of Wisconsin.[21]

In the years after the First World War the various nations published volume upon volume of their diplomatic correspondence, providing a plentiful supply of source material for this particular historical specialisation. In many British universities the curious tradition developed that it was all right to study diplomatic history for the recent period, though the ancient embargo still rested upon the study of recent domestic history. Although diplomatic history was soon to gain the reputation of being the most arid and sterile of all the sub-histories, with a particularly piddling expertise of its own, much of the diplomatic history of this time was very definitely present-orientated. The works of G. P. Gooch and S. B. Fay were very much part of the Western liberal climate which sought to exonerate Germany from the extreme charges of war-guilt which had been laid upon her at the time of Versailles. (Schmitt, it may be said, consistently followed a line much less favourable to Germany, and, it may be said also, more in keeping with the documentary evidence; his general line was also taken by Pierre Renouvin, the famous French diplomatic historian, and, after the Second World War, by the equally distinguished Italian scholar Luigi Albertini.) The attempt to create a League of Nations stimulated an interest in earlier forms of international organisation: Sir Charles Webster produced a study of *The Foreign Policy of Castlereagh* (1925) which did something to rehabilitate that much-hated foreign minister as, at any rate, a man of European vision. Webster, in a further study of *The Foreign Policy of Palmerston* (1930), and H. W. V. Temperley, in one of Canning,[22] both showed an almost Namierite interest in the mechanics of the Foreign Office (as distinct from the broad principles upon which foreign policy, as was once thought, was conducted). A whole generation was conditioned to feel that if history was not constitutional charters, then it must be diplomatic correspondence: a piece of historical popularisation published as late as 1964 actually began with a dismissal of 'that tortuous train of Reinsurance treaties, Dual and Triple Alliances, Moroccan crises and Balkan imbroglios which historians have painstakingly followed in their search for origins'.[23] The author was somewhat out-of-date in her historiographical knowledge but the comment would certainly have been good for a quarter of a century earlier.

In the main the diplomatic historians seem to have had a more definite sense of their social utility than would be true of the other professionals: a thorough knowledge of the origins of the previous war should be helpful in averting the next one. I propose to conclude this section with a glance at one or two other historians whose professional standing remains very high because of their ability to go very far (as far as is conceivable, in fact) towards seeing the past on its own terms rather than on those of the present. F. M. Powicke (1879–1963) wrote apparently forbidding studies of thirteenth-century England: but the reader who struggled through them really could breathe the air of the thirteenth century. Herbert Butterfield, who had first identified the *Whig Interpretation of History* (1931) and had added a pioneering study of *The Origins of Modern Science* to his front-line work in eighteenth-century radical politics, became a leading theorist on behalf of the professional doctrine that the historian must 'empty himself' of all judgements. A third British historian, though often mistrusted by his professional colleagues because of the slightness of his volumes and the delicacy of his literary touch, was actually responsible for the classic statement of the professional case: explaining how he approached the study of Victorian England, G. M. Young (1882–1959) said that he 'read and read till he heard the voices of time speaking to him'. For our present generation this view still smacks too strongly of the historian's intuition: how does he know he has not got the voices wrong? should he not be counting heads, rather than listening to voices?

Among American professionals in the 1930s, one of the most outstanding was Samuel Eliot Morison (b. 1887), a determined upholder of the Rankean principle of genetic relationism (see above, p. 35). His studies of seventeenth-century American Puritanism both stressed the elements of continuity in American intellectual life and, by setting it firmly in the context of its own time, refurbished the image of Puritanism which had been somewhat tarnished by the interpretations of the new historians. Another sturdy professional, R. L. Schuyler, had, in a number of scholarly monographs, played an important part in destroying the myths which, since Bancroft, had encrusted American accounts of the American Revolution. In Schuyler's own words:

It is only within the last generation that the Revolution has come to be studied in a more scientific spirit, with the desire to find out what happened, rather than to justify. The revolt from England, we now know, was no spontaneous uprising of a whole people in behalf of human rights. It was, on the contrary, the work of an aggressive minority, capable in leadership and strong in organisation, who managed to carry with them a more numerous body of less active persons. A large minority of the colonists, probably about one-third detested the Revolution, remained loyal to King and Empire, and suffered loss of property and every species of indignity at the hands of their exasperated and often envious neighbours. No account of the Revolution which does not represent it as a civil war, involving confiscation of property and social upheaval, is even measurably true to facts. The nationalistic school of American history disregarded what did not suit their patriotic purposes. They slighted the arguments of the Loyalists, ignored the British official side of the case, and exalted the Revolutionary cause. In short, they gave a warped and biased interpretation of the Revolution.[24]

Schuyler's language, it may be noted, is almost as emotive as that of any 'patriotic' historian, for in fact Schuyler was strongly Tory in political outlook. Although determined in the hunt of those he described as 'present-minded' in their historical writing, he was not much more successful than Ranke in keeping his prejudices out of his writing. This does not necessarily reflect on Schuyler's scholarship, though it means, as always, that it is useful to the reader, in keeping open his end of the dialogue, to know about Schuyler's Conservatism. Nor does it mean that all 'professionals' as described in this section are Conservatives, though it may be that those who are conservative in other spheres cling most firmly to established scholarly practices.

For our last example of the professional scholarly mind in operation we turn in fact to a distinguished British educationist, and, for a time, liberal statesman and framer of the well-intentioned Education Act of 1918. H. A. L. Fisher (1865–1940) was a contributor to Acton's *Cambridge Modern History* on the French Revolution, author of two volumes on the *Medieval Empire* (1898), three on Napoleon, and editor of the collected papers of both Maitland and Vinogradoff. Apart from his work on Napoleon, he is now mainly remembered for his three-volume *History of Europe* (1935) from neolithic man to Hitler, a miracle of compression. In the preface to this work he reiterated in elaborate form Maitland's dictum on generalisation, to which professionals still adhered:

> One intellectual excitement has . . . been denied me. Men wiser and more learned than I have discerned in history a plot, a rhythm, a predetermined pattern. These harmonies are concealed from me. I can see only one emergency following upon another as wave follows upon wave, only one great fact with respect to which, since it is unique, there can be no generalisations, only one safe rule for the historian: that he should recognise in the development of human destinies the play of the contingent and the unforeseen.

By the outbreak of the Second World War the solid line of historical endeavour running back to early nineteenth-century Berlin had not been broken. Of the new approaches the most fruitful were also the ones which were, in the traditional sense, the most scholarly: Arthur Schlesinger was a pupil of Osgood as well as of Beard; *Annales*, above all, was a learned journal. Many of the new approaches anyway had broken down into rather sterile sub-histories: economic history, intellectual history, history of science.

Notes

1. Quoted by Stern, p. 231.
2. Letter of 25 January 1904, quoted by Howard K. Beale in *Pacific History Review*, xxii (1953) 228.
3. The usual translation of the French *histoire intégrale*.
4. Quoted by G. N. Clark, *Sir John Harold Clapham* (1946) p. 6.
5. Turner and Craven are quoted in G. R. Taylor (ed.), *The Turner Thesis* (1956).
6. See A. M. Schlesinger Sr, *In Retrospect: The History of a Historian* (1963).
7. *Annales d'Histoire Économique et Sociale*, i i (Jan 1929): my translation.
8. In French the word is *intégrale*.
9. 'Detachment and the Writing of History', reprinted in *Detachment and the Writing of History*, ed. P. L. Snyder (1958).
10. Quoted in Stern, pp. 315–28.
11. 'Explicit Data and Implicit Assumptions in Historical Study' in Louis Gottschalk (ed.), *Generalization in the Writing of History* (1963) p. 179.
12. Colleagues whose wisdom I respect have tried to explain to me why not. But I still don't understand.
13. R. G. Collingwood, *An Autobiography* (1939) pp. 87–8.
14. For what follows, see M. F. Ashley Montagu (ed.), *Toynbee and History* (1956).
15. H. E. Bell, *Maitland* (1965). For a useful selection of Maitland's writings with a valuable introduction, see R. L. Schuyler (ed.), *Frederick William Maitland, Historian* (1960).
16. The address is printed in the *American Historical Review*, xlii (1937).
17. John Hale, *The Evolution of British Historiography* (1967) p. 79.
18. He was born near the town of Lukow which was then in the Austro-Hungarian Empire.
19. There is a useful study of Namier by Catherine S. Sim, in Herman Ausubel *et al.* (eds.), *Some Modern Historians of Britain* (1952).
20. Richard Pares, *George III and the Politicians* (paperback ed., 1968) p. 64.
21. Bernadotte Schmitt, *The Fashion and Future of History* (1960) pp. 4ff.
22. H. W. V. Temperley, *The Foreign Policy of Canning* (1925).
23. Barbara Tuchman, *The Proud Tower* (1966) p. xiv.
24. R. L. Schuyler, 'Some Historical Idols' in *Political Science Quarterly*, xlvii (1932) 5–6.

4 History, Science and Social Science

WE have seen that when Bury described history as a science he meant one thing, while the positivists and their followers, who also wanted history to be scientific, meant something rather different. Curiously the professionals of the twentieth century, those nearest in spirit to Bury, have usually been most forceful in denying that their discipline has anything to do with science. In the 1940s in Britain a star performer on the popular radio programme *The Brains Trust* was the philosopher C. E. M. Joad, who gained some fame for handling questions like 'Is history a science?' with the phrase 'It depends what you mean by a science.' The fame, perhaps, was somewhat cheaply earned. Words do not have just as many meanings as we care to give them, but important ones do usually have several shades of meaning. It would be legitimate in this particular argument to say 'It depends which particular meaning of science you have in mind.' If we are to achieve anything useful in carrying through the debate we must accept that as a matter of observed fact most institutions of learning group together physics, chemistry, biology and other 'sciences' in one faculty, school, building, or what have you, and history, philosophy, literature, classical and modern languages in another faculty or building. This is to leave totally alone the difficult subjects such as economics, sociology and political science, which are often put with history and languages, but never with physics and biology. Are these divisions there purely for administrative, or perhaps architectural, convenience?

Let us first look at the question of history and the 'natural' sciences – that is physics, biology, etc., but not economics and sociology. I have already suggested in the first chapter of this book that the historian does share with the natural scientist in a joint enterprise, the attack upon that which is not yet known. The very real, common-sense, yet perhaps minor, differences between history and the natural sciences are all too apparent to the ordinary man: scientists work in laboratories, historians in libraries; scientists produce short papers, usually in collaboration with several other scientists, historians produce long papers, and sometimes books: they seldom have collaborators. At universities professional historians spend a substantial proportion of their time in undergraduate teaching, professional scientists spend most of their time on their researches with or without their graduate students.

These differences are plain. They go a long way towards suggesting the rational explanation for the placing of natural scientists in one building with one type of facilities and historians in another with other facilities. But there is no great point in exaggerating the differences between the activities of the historian and those of the natural scientist. The big books about the 'autonomy' of history, about how the historian's thought processes are totally different from those of the scientist, are usually written by the more arrogant type of historian who in some way sees science as a lesser intellectual activity.

The great value of the 'Is history a science?' debate is the manner in which it helps clarify the nature of history and to delimit what history can, and cannot, do. To the ordinary common-sense mortal, and it is to such a person that this book is, in the first instance, addressed, the most striking difference between history and natural science is the degree to which proof can be established of the various contentions made by the scientist and by the historian respectively. I say 'degree', though the more self-regarding historians would probably join with history's severest critics in saying there is little or no similarity between the scientist's methods and the historian's 'intuition', between the scientist's empirical expertise and the historian's creative flights. Yet neither 'intuition' nor 'creation' need represent a fundamental divide between history and science. The gifted scientist will usually develop a 'feel' for his subject which may not be greatly different from the intuition of which some historians boast. The scientist of course will attempt empirically to demonstrate the validity of any hunch he may have; his 'feel' will take him in the direction of trying one kind of experiment rather than another, not towards stating untested assumptions. But again this is not terribly different from the way the professional historian (as distinct from the inspired charlatan) sets to work; intuition may suggest certain causal connections but the historian will do his best from the material at his disposal to establish at least the probability of such a causal relationship; better still he may be stimulated to seek for entirely new source materials (rather as a scientist might devise an entirely new type of experiment). On the matter of 'creativity', it is surely not to be contested that Einstein's theory of relativity is one of the great monuments to man's creative thinking. Of course most practising scientists are engaged on much more basic tasks; but then a large number of historians are engaged on pretty mundane work as well.

Rather cunningly, a few sentences ago, I introduced the word 'probability'. The historian can only show from his sources that it was likely, or at most probable, that something happened in the way he says it did. But natural science today also deals in probabilities rather than in the certainties of palmy nineteenth-century days. Many of those who so vehemently deny that history can have any resemblance to a natural science reveal appalling ignorance of the direction natural sciences are currently taking. The changing direction was apparent in the work of the great nineteenth-century physicist Clerk Maxwell, who wrote: 'If . . . cultivators of science . . . are led to the study of singularities and instabilities, rather than the continuities of things, the promotion of natural knowledge may tend to remove that prejudice in favour of determinism which seems to arise from assuming that the physical science of the future is a mere magnified image of the past.' With the 'Relativity Revolution', the Newtonian absolutes were dethroned. The discovery of 'quanta' contradicted the conception of the continuity of the infinitesimal calculus. The theory of mutations pointed to change coming through leaps, not by gradual process. Today, scientists can, from time to time, be heard calling for a revision of scientific laws: in October 1968 Professor Fred Hoyle challenged the Royal Astronomical Society with the need for a radical change of the laws of physics; only thus, he said, would it be possible to account for the 'funny things which are going on' in the universe.[1] Let us therefore agree that, save on the most banal level, there are no absolutes in the natural sciences. So when the historian fails to establish conclusive proofs for his version of past events he may not necessarily be exposing himself as thoroughly unscientific.

However, there *is* a difference, and we all know there is a difference. The physical scientist can repeat his experiments; the historian cannot call for a repeat performance of the past. The scientist, it may be argued further, can preserve an objectivity towards the phenomena he is studying, whereas the historian, as we have seen, can never be completely objective. On the whole this distinction too must be allowed to stand, though again as one of degree rather than as an absolute. After all, as has often been pointed out, the man who assembles the apparatus for a particular experiment effectively becomes a part of the experiment: even in physical science the human, subjective element can never be entirely excluded.

The other central problems in the 'Is history a science?' debate are these: the ultimate (often remote) objective in scientific exploration is the formulation of a scientific law, but there are no general laws in history (attempts in this direction having commended themselves neither to historians nor to non-historians); scientific knowledge provides the power of prediction; the historian cannot predict. The latter point is in some ways a bit of a red herring: the historian's concern, by definition, is with the past; he may well, as a result of his expertise, make some intelligent predictions about the present and future, but that is not strictly his business. E. H. Carr has given an example of the kind of prediction the historian might indulge in:

> People do not expect the historian to predict that revolution will break out in Ruritania next month. The kind of conclusion which they will seek to draw, partly from specific knowledge of Ruritanian affairs and partly from a study of history, is that conditions in Ruritania are such that a revolution is likely to occur in the near future if somebody touches it off, or unless somebody on the government side does something to stop it; and this conclusion might be accompanied by estimates, based partly on the analogy of other revolutions, of the attitude which different sectors of the population may be expected to adopt. The prediction, if such it can be called, can be realised only through the occurrence of unique events, which cannot themselves be predicted; but this does not mean that inferences drawn from history about the future are worthless, or that they do not possess a conditional validity which serves both as a guide to action and a key to our understanding of how things happen.[2]

An overwhelming majority of historians in fact will probably have no knowledge whatever of Ruritania and little knowledge of revolutions. Non-historians do have a right to expect intelligent and informed comment on current events from their historical friends; statesmen, civil servants, television commentators may reasonably be presumed to react more intelligently to current crises if they have a historical training. But this is really to move away from the kind of 'prediction' continuously practised by the professional historian in the normal line of business, a type of 'prediction' which in a small way is analogous to the prediction of the physical scientist. This comes about when the historian, using the evidence he has painfully accumulated, together with the feel for the way things happen in certain circumstances which he has developed over the years, makes an inference about something for which he does not in fact have full and sufficient evidence. He is 'predicting' what will be seen to have happened once the full evidence is forthcoming. This in the end is certainly not the *same* as the scientist's prediction (indeed the special word *retrodiction*[3] has been coined for it): again we come up against difference at least of degree.

Much time, most fruitfully, has been spent over the issue of general laws. It has now become something of a platitude that whatever the 'straight-line professionals' from Maitland to Fisher might say, whenever the historian speaks of a 'war', of a 'revolution', of 'feudalism', of 'representative government', he is using a generalisation. In each of these cases he is suggesting that there are certain general features which characterise a 'war', 'feudalism', etc. However, the use of such generalisations still leaves us a long way from the formulation of general laws. Given all the qualifications that must now be made about the nature of scientific laws, that they are working hypotheses, expressions of tendencies and probabilities, not iron-hard certainties, it still does seem that in the physical sciences there are laws which differ in scale from any generalisation which the historian might feel competent to make. Again the distinction is not an absolute one; after all, the formulation of scientific laws only exercises the physical scientist operating at the highest level: most scientists are just as immersed in detail as are most historians.

There is one further point which is sometimes thrown into the argument, notably, as we saw, by Trevelyan. This is the one about science having use, while history, of course, is 'useless'. In fact the whole tenor of this book, arguing for the social necessity theory of history, has been to show how, and in what sense, history has use. What is meant, of course, by the Trevelyans and their humble sympathisers is immediate tangible use: television sets, pasteurised beer, nuclear bombs. The natural scientist working as a scientist (and not as an industrial chemist or a scientific adviser to some government or corporation) would however deny that his researches are directed towards such utilitarian products. The scientist seeks knowledge of the phenomena of the physical universe as the historian seeks knowledge of the human past. If the scientist is anything more than a crusty misanthropist he will believe that somewhere sometime his discoveries in 'pure' science will have practical application; that belief is not fundamentally different from that of historians adhering to one or other of the justifications for history already presented in the first chapter of this book. Many scientists do of course operate in the world of applied science: they fulfil a role analogous to that of the historically trained who operate as journalists of the better sort, or as politicians – that is to say, the 'applied historians'.

All this would suggest that while there is no fundamental distinction between the main aims and methods of the historian and of the physical scientist, nonetheless there are good reasons for the common-sense assumption that differences do exist. The final point which highlights this sense of difference springs from the manner in which, in one form or another, history becomes implicated in the making of value judgements. Most historians would accept Professor Knowles's neat statement: 'The historian is not a judge, still less a hanging judge.' But they also rejoice at the delicate come-uppance which the late Professor Alfred Cobban administered to Professor Michael Oakeshott's plea for complete moral neutrality (in papers read to the second and fourth Irish Conferences of Historians):

> It is admittedly difficult, says Professor Oakeshott, to avoid 'the description of conduct in, generally speaking, moral terms'. This I take to mean that, for example, we cannot help describing the September massacres as massacres. The important thing is to avoid any suggestion

that massacres are a bad thing, because this would be a moral judgement and therefore non-historical.

The historian cannot help but make moral judgements, if only by
implication or by virtue of his selection of the facts: these judgements
are of a type not encountered in the natural sciences.

Finally, to recall a point already made, and one which I must develop later in this chapter, if the historian's activities truly are necessary
to society, he must *communicate* the fruits of his labours to that society.
There falls upon the historian a duty to write serviceable prose which
does not fall on the scientist, whose labours may best be summed up
in a few pages of equations.

The arguments of this section, I hope, are intelligible to the British
and American reader; they are probably rather less so to the French,
German or other Continental reader. For science on the continent of
Europe, as generally used, has a less exclusive meaning than that implied
in my arguments. Science on the Continent usually means (and of course
Anglo-Saxons are at liberty to prefer this usage if they like) an
organised body of knowledge. It is with this in view that Professor
Bernadotte Schmitt once wrote:

> Evidently much depends on what you mean by science. A recent
> English writer has remarked that science does not cease to be science
> because it sometimes fails to formulate its laws or adhere to the gift of
> prophecy. Thus meteorology cannot be denied the quality of a science
> because the laws according to which sunshine and storm succeed one
> another are as yet undiscovered. . . . Science, in the mind of this
> writer, can be defined as 'systematised, organised, formulated know-
> ledge', and history, the original meaning of which is investigation, is
> therefore a science if it is pursued with the sole purpose of ascertaining
> the truth, if all relevant facts are diligently searched for, if presupposi-
> tions and prejudices are eliminated, if the constants and the variables
> are noted and plotted with the same care that is the rule in the natural
> sciences. But do we really care whether the chemists and the mathe-
> maticians accord our study the title and dignity of a science? We
> believe that the critical methods which we use in the acquisition of
> historical information are every whit as scientific as those of the
> laboratory or the field expedition. For my part, I am willing to let the
> matter rest there.[3a]

Professor E. H. Carr has been rather more definite:

> The word science already covers so many different branches of know-
> ledge, employing so many different methods and techniques, that the
> onus seems to rest on those who seek to exclude history rather than on
> those who seek to include it. . . . I am myself not convinced that the
> chasm which separates the historian from the geologist is any deeper
> or more unbridgeable than the chasm which separates the geologist
> from the physicist.[4]

The most apposite words of all are those of Professor E. E. Evans-Pritchard, the anthropologist: 'When will people get it into their heads that the conscientious historian . . . is no less systematic, exacting and critical in his research than a chemist or biologist, that it is not in method that social science differs from physical science but in the nature of the phenomena they study.'[5] Here surely is the crucial point: the historian is concerned with a different kind of material, human experience in the past, from that with which the natural scientist is concerned. From this difference, all other differences spring. Perhaps I should have said this right at the beginning of the chapter: but look at the ground we have traversed since page 97.

2 HISTORY AND SOCIAL SCIENCE

Even so we have not really penetrated to the storm-centre of debate. In recognising the differences between natural science and history, E. H. Carr, with scarcely a second thought, places history with the social sciences, as does Evans-Pritchard. It may not matter, as Bernadotte Schmitt suggested, whether the chemist or physicist wishes to admit the historian to the natural scientist's club; what does matter is that some of the most devastating criticisms of history are mounted by scholars who would describe themselves as social scientists, and who would quite definitely not admit history to the social scientist's club. It can be noted also that the historians of the 'professional' cast are often to the fore in denouncing social science or, more particularly, sociology, as a non-discipline. And, in many universities, there are, in addition to the Faculty of Science which contains physics, chemistry, biology and so on, both a Faculty of Arts (including history) *and* a Faculty of Social Science. Thus although we may accept, as was suggested in the previous section, that the scholars grouped in natural science, social science and arts are all engaged in the same kind of activity which may, in a loose way, be described as 'scientific', and that the further subdivisions are merely a matter of common sense and convenience, we have still to decide whether there is any real basis for the allocation of history either to arts or to social sciences. If we examine the statements of those who automatically align history with the social sciences, we will see that there is often an element of wishful thinking, a reaching for the history-that-might-be rather than the history-that-is. The concluding exhortation in E. H. Carr's argument, indeed, is that 'we must make our history more scientific'. Certainly there need not be the same obvious differences between history on the one hand and, say, economics and sociology on the other that there are between history and the natural sciences. Yet it is significant that the very debate does exist. The objections which many social scientists level against history as currently produced by historians, and which are used to demonstrate the unscientific nature of history, cannot be conjured away by wishing history to become something which it is not.

It is probably best to look at the matter, firstly as a question of historical development, then as a question of convenience. History, we have seen, has existed in some form or other for many many centuries; history as a scholarly discipline is relatively new, yet, it has been argued in this book, there is no complete break between unscholarly and scholarly history. The social sciences do not have this long tradition as a basic semi-rational human activity: thus there are sound historical reasons for the separation between them and history. It is true that after decades of talking about this, historians are now genuinely moving in the direction of making their subject more like a social science. And historical reasons could not alone prevent us from accepting that wherever history stood in the past, it should now stand with the social sciences. But certain points of contemporary convenience immediately become relevant. History does have legitimate associations with literature and languages. If history moves in with the social sciences, should all humanities move with it? If it is convenient and necessary to draw a line somewhere, should that line not follow accepted current practice?

Let us summarise the main schools of thought on this point. First the professionals on both sides of the line are arrayed in shining armour against each other: the historians call a plague upon the social sciences for their pretentiousness, the social scientists upon the historians for their vagueness. E. H. Carr, Marc Bloch and the *Annales* school, and possibly most Continental historians, are clear that history is a social science. Some in this school have gone so far as to argue that history is the central social science, off which all the others must feed. History, H. C. Darby has suggested, is basic to social science rather in the way that mathematics is basic to natural science.[6] There is much force in this particular argument, yet in the end it does not really seem to be saying other than that history is the study which links together all facets of human experience: by that account history is also basic to literature and philosophy. If the members of this school are not, as suggested above, victims of wishful thinking, they often seem to be ignorant of what exactly the social scientists are about these days. The reader might best be advised to pick up a standard work of history, and a standard work of sociology, or of economic theory: that there is a difference somewhere will be readily apparent. Most of the statements which align history most solidly with the social sciences (as presently constituted) are declarations of intent only: and often they are declarations by those least qualified to make them. In a famous article in the *Times Literary Supplement*, Keith Thomas, member of the editorial board of *Past and Present* (Britain's worthy imitator of *Annales* – see below, chapter 6), threw down the gage: after attacking history for its lack of intellectual and analytical rigour, he looked forward to the co-operative research, based on statistical methods, of the 'age of the historical factory'.[7] It was Geoffrey Elton, now, as Professor of Constitutional History at Cambridge, a leading British professional, who neatly pointed out that to the best of his knowledge, 'Mr Thomas . . ., the author of some excellent articles, has never worked even within sight of these "factories".'[8] And Professor W. O. Aydelotte of Iowa State University, who by use of statistical methods has immensely deepened our knowledge of the post-Reform Bill House of Commons, has been foremost in indicating the limits to the uses which historians can make of statistics.[9]

There is, therefore, a third school, deeply interested in the contributions to man's knowledge of man to be derived from the social sciences, but which, in the words of Professor Richard Hofstadter, sees the 'historian as having contacts with the social sciences rather than as being a social scientist'.[10] Others in this school have reverted to a notion put forward from time to time by distinguished historians in the past, that history is 'both art and science'. Others again have resolved the issue – to their own satisfaction at least – with the reflection that history, being neither truly art nor science, is *sui generis*.

It would be tedious to rehearse the traditional arguments, which are largely those discussed in the section on history and natural science. It can reasonably be stated that history and sociology or economics stand closer to each other, being concerned with man and his activities in society, than sociology or economics stand to those sciences which are concerned with natural phenomena. The basic difference we postulated between history and natural science (that of the *material* studied) can therefore be eliminated. But since the social sciences model themselves on the natural sciences in a way in which history so far, wittingly, has not done, four secondary distinctions are worth further examination. These concern *experimental data, generalisation, value judgements* and *communication*. Social scientists do, in greater or lesser degree, conduct 'experiments', in the form, principally, of opinion samples, or studies of behaviour patterns and responses to controlled stimuli of small groups. Historians, of course, make extensive use of social surveys, census returns and so on conducted in the past by 'pure' or 'applied' social scientists; and they may, as we shall see, derive a great deal of benefit from participating in controlled surveys conducted in their own time. Nonetheless it remains true that the historian, as historian, does not conduct controlled experiments; his evidence is always that little bit more impressionistic than is that of the man working on the frontiers of the social sciences.

Some of the misconceptions surrounding the use and non-use of generalisation we have already discussed. Yet when all qualifications have been made, it remains true that the social scientist far more regularly uses models and theoretical constructs than does the historian, and that these constructs are nearly always of a more abstract character than the historian would be prepared to accept. The familiar platitude probably overstates the case but it nonetheless contains a vital kernel of truth: the historian must always accommodate the unique and the contingent, the social scientist is essentially orientated towards the universal, towards the recurrent pattern. Value judgements, inevitably, will intrude further into the work of the social scientist than into that of the natural scientist; but through his use of empirical data and abstract models the social scientist will avoid the constant entanglement with them which besets the historian. Finally, the social scientist does not have that direct involvement with a wide audience which is one of the special characteristics of the historian. The great historians are at least readable; some of the greatest social scientists are practically unreadable. And, seemingly, proud of it.

The fact is there is no easy answer to all the issues raised here: to discuss them is extremely valuable; to answer them is only really necessary when it comes to university organisation and administration. Professor Fritz Stern has referred to the 'Solomon's judgement' which took place when the University of Chicago set up separate divisions of the social sciences and the humanities and some historians went to one division, some to the other.[11] In British universities there not infrequently exists a split between economic history and, sometimes, social history, which are grouped with the social sciences, and general history, which remains with the arts. In theory a deplorable division in that it suggests a perpetuation of the sub-world of the sub-histories, this often works well in that almost inevitably there is a co-operation between different historians which transcends faculty barriers.

In harmony with one of my main themes in this book, which is the *development* (rather than the *variety*, or the *conflict*) of history, I believe that historians are less confused and self-contradictory about all this than the reader may well be after ploughing through this exposition. Consider again the notion of all scholarly activities as the attack upon that which is not yet known. The forces are spread widely across the extensive plain of man's present knowledge. At one end are the mathematicians, then the mathematical physicists, then the physicists, the chemists and the biologists; somewhere towards the middle come the geologists. At the other end are the painters, the musicians, the poets, concerned also (whether avowedly or not) with broadening man's perception of himself and of his environment. But the plain is really a continuum for it may well be, as is suggested by those who talk of the beauty of mathematics, that the one extreme touches closely upon the other. But let us proceed on-wards from the geologists: soon we come to the social scientists, then to history, then to languages, literature and philosophy. Any model of this sort must seem contrived and arbitrary: where for instance do we put psychology? – long regarded as a social science, but now becoming more and more biological in content. And indeed we have such subjects as social biology, and social medicine. So indeed there is a continuum. But the present divisions, provided they are taken as divisions within a deeper unity, serve a useful purpose, and have a certain common-sense validity. It follows, however, that each discipline, as traditionally con-ceived, must at all times be ready to make useful borrowings from other disciplines. Of no subject is this more true than history: it is to history's vital contact with the social sciences that we now turn.

3 HISTORY AND GEOGRAPHY

Between history and geography, now universally regarded as a genuine social science, there are venerable ties. Diplomatic history and military history of the standard type obviously require some rudimentary geo-graphical knowledge. Domestic history, too, clearly requires to be set within the appropriate geographical context. In the preface to his *Histoire de France* (1833) Michelet stated that history in essence was founded upon geography; he himself spent a great deal of time wandering through France collecting first-hand impressions of the changing country-side. The preface to the 1869 edition contained the more positive assertion that:

> Without a geographical basis, the people, the makers of history, seem to be walking on air, as in those Chinese pictures where the ground is wanting. The soil, too, must not be looked upon only as the scene of action. Its influence appears in a hundred ways, such as food, climate, etc.

This concern with the geographical context of history was later very noticeable in the work of Lucien Febvre and Marc Bloch, and indeed was something of a characteristic of French historical study in general. Bloch, who himself observed the precepts of Michelet, has noted that:

> In certain of its fundamental features, our rural landscape, as has been previously mentioned, dates from a very remote epoch. However, in order to interpret the rare documents which permit us to fathom its misty beginnings, in order to ask the right questions, even in order to know what we were talking about, it was necessary to fulfil a primary condition: that of observing and analysing our present landscape. For

it alone furnished those comprehensive vistas without which it was impossible to begin.

In his study of *Tudor Cornwall* (1941) A. L. Rowse has remarked upon the fascination of attempting 'to decipher an earlier, vanished age beneath the forms of the present and successive layers that time has imposed':

> So it is that beneath the towns and villages, their roads and fields of today, we may construct under our eyes out of the evidences that remain, a picture of a former age.

The geographical context in fact is something of a common-sense matter, well in keeping with the old amateur tradition in history, requiring no professional expertise to unveil its significance: indeed professional expertise in the twentieth century often tended to obscure what had formerly been obvious: the dependence of history upon geography. The common-sense, amateur apprehension of this can best be seen in Macaulay's famous third chapter setting the scene for the commencement of his history. J. R. Green, in his *The Making of England*, called landscape 'the fullest and most certain of all documents'. Maitland, the great professional, had a vivid understanding of the importance of geography to historical investigation. Many general histories since then, though often more, it would seem, as a matter of rote rather than as a matter of conviction, have included an introductory geographical chapter, usually with some such title as 'The Face of the Country'.

This use of geography has often been impressionistic and uninformed. Though history's close relationship with geography has been recognised more universally and over a far longer period than any other possible relationship between history and a social science, it is only recently that historians have turned to the geography of the geographers in place of their own undisciplined observation. One of the many strengths of Febvre and Bloch and the *Annales* school was that they did not just invent their geography but sought the co-operation of professional geographers. In his *A Geographical Introduction to History* (1925) Febvre declared that the study of the relationship of past societies to environment must rest upon 'a sound study of physical geography'. It is scarcely to be expected that historians, unless preoccupied with a specific environmental problem, will find the time to master the scientific (in the sense of natural science) intricacies of physical geography, but there can be no doubt as to the value for any historian of a knowledge of the classificatory categories employed by the geographer.

The climate of the British Isles is notorious: at times, as with the heat-waves of 1911 (associated with strikes and violence) and 1959 (associated with Conservative electoral victory) or with the hard winter of 1946–7, or the east coast floods of 1953, it may have impinged directly upon political and social history. It is possible for the historian concerned with such matters simply to throw in a few references to variable climate and the influence of the sea. But how much clearer and simpler to borrow from the geographer his classification of the four types of air-masses likely to invade the British Isles: the warm damp tropical maritime from the Atlantic, which often brings fog or heavy rain; the polar maritime, which usually brings periods of rain showers and sunny intervals; the polar continental which brings a cold, dry, biting wind, often provoking a 'temperature inversion' and fog; and the tropical continental, which brings dry, stable weather and occasional heat-waves.[12]

To describe the general physical geography of the British Isles, absolutely basic to an understanding of the processes of urbanisation and the processes of urban deterioration which are so critical in the last two hundred years of British history, what more economical method than to adhere to the geographer's classification of the country into three components: lowland, upland and highland?[13] In the lowland regions of the south lay the original agricultural wealth of England, while it was amid the mineral wealth of the upland areas of South Wales, the Pennines and central Scotland that the Industrial Revolution took place; the highland regions of central Wales and northern Scotland were steadily drained of their native rural populations and left to decay while the rest of the land was prospering; today, with the advent of new light industries, the movement of population is back to the lowland areas.

4 HISTORY AND PSYCHOLOGY

Consciously or unconsciously historians have always dabbled, amateur-ishly and haphazardly for the most part, in geography. Similarly in their discussions and analyses of the motives and actions of men and societies they have had to venture into the realm of psychology. Trevelyan, we have seen, believed that history remained literature rather than science by virtue of its need for deep insights into the minds of men. Later commentators have rightly remarked that so long as the historian continued to back his own psychological insights without reference to the discoveries of modern psychology he was producing, if not literature, certainly fiction. Because of their preoccupation with the biographical approach to history and the doings of great men, historians of Trevelyan's generation had to make frequent recourse to their psychological insights. Today no historian could write a biographical study without betraying something of the influence of Freudian and post-Freudian psychology.

Just how far the historical biographer should penetrate into the depth psychology of his subject is by no means a settled matter, even among those historians who are most receptive to the influences of the social sciences. For one thing the individual biography *in se* would not now normally be regarded as one of the most important forms for historical writing to take. Many of the greatest historical works of today have indeed been biographical in form; but in content they are almost always of the 'life and times' type; that is to say they use the biographical device to illuminate a far wider sector of human experience. If the main focus of attention in the biography is on the political and social achievements of the subject, on his relationships with various social groups, and with their reactions to him, there may be less need for detailed study of his own individual psychology than a purist might think. Further, many of the great contemporary biographies – Alan Bullock's *Hitler* is a supreme example – are concerned with men of quite extraordinary individual characteristics. Theories of psycho-pathology are almost all derived from the study of 'failures'; Hitler was no failure. The historian is concerned less with Hitler's private fantasies than with his huge destructive achievements. Even with more 'normal' figures, much of the detail which might be yielded through use (retro-spectively, of course, and therefore imperfectly) of some of the tech-niques of psycho-analysis may well prove more appropriate to the higher gossip than to an understanding of the major problems which exercise, or should exercise, the mind of the historian. Many of the nastier big men in history – the Nazis are a good example – are widely believed to have been defective in their sexual equipment. The same point is some-times even made about more conventional political leaders. The diffi-culties in finding hard evidence (as distinct from inspired conjecture) are, for the historian, immense; and even if he does find the evidence, how much further does this take him?

These are merely qualifications, not in any way rebuttals of the highly stimulating attempts which have been made to bring the resources of psychology to the aid of historical biography (some of which we shall examine in a moment). They are preliminaries to the statement of one simple point about the uses of psychology which is too often ignored. Although there is in practice no rigid line between the *individual* psy-chology which we have been discussing up till now, and the *group* and *social* psychology which must be of the utmost value to the historian, the distinction is one which should always be borne in mind. In brief, my argument will be that just as the individual biography is a less significant area of study for the historian than a society, or a sub-stantial segment of a society studied in totality, so individual psy-chology is less directly relevant to the needs of the historian than is group psychology. Individual psychology will provide illuminating details; social psychology may in some cases be a *sine qua non* of the intelligent analysis of certain historical problems. Where individual psychology can probably be of most significant utility is in helping to establish types of individual political leadership, of 'great man' activity, and in explaining aberrations in political behaviour.

Martin Luther was clearly a 'great man', in the sense of being a man whose actions did demonstrably affect the course of history. His stormy career has attracted legions of biographers, historical and fictional. Before the First World War one of the most distinguished of twentieth-century American historians, Preserved Smith, published both a biography and a collection of Luther's letters. He followed these up with an interesting paper, published in 1915, on 'Luther's Early Development in the Light of Psycho-analysis'. More recently the subject has been treated with greater sophistication by a practising psychiatrist, Erik Erikson, in his much-acclaimed book, *The Young Man Luther: A Study in Psycho-analysis and History* (1959) (on which John Osborne subsequently based his successful play). The book makes fascinating reading and in its discussion of such matters as Luther's childhood conflicts with his father, his 'anality', his 'lifelong burden of excessive guilt', undoubtedly makes a major contribution to our understanding of Luther. I have suggested above (p. 110) that there are vast tracts of history, even biographical history, where individual psychology is not a specially useful tool (though clearly some knowledge of psychology must replace Trevelyan's literary intuition): Erikson's study is a triumphant signal indicating the area of applicability of psycho-analysis to history. But it is a book by a psychiatrist bringing his expertise to bear on materials collected and collated by generations of historians. More interesting in many ways is Sir Lewis Namier's study of *Charles Townshend* (1964), the brilliant English politician whose erratic political behaviour has sometimes been regarded as a contributory cause of the American Revolution: a study drawn from a mass of unsorted manuscript material, but openly employing the categories of Freudian psychology, and showing how conflicts between Townshend and his father 'produced a mental attitude towards authority which he carried over into the field of politics'.

Nonetheless it is social psychology, out of all the social sciences, upon which the historian today is most likely to call. That this science may be regarded as a branch of sociology rather than as a branch of psychology only shows that history is not alone in having its demarcation difficulties. Here I shall deal only with the more manifestly psychological elements, returning again to some other major contributions furnished by social psychology when I look at the crucial problem of the relations between history and sociology.

Looking back over the human past, one obvious feature stands out: the amount of time, energy and human life which has been expended in that most destructive of all man's activities – war. Given his concern with the specific and the unique, the historian will no doubt continue to place great emphasis on diplomatic exchanges, political and strategic calculations and immediate social and economic circumstances. Yet some of the broader generalisations made by some historians – about, for example, the 'will to war' to be detected in European societies on the eve of the First World War – cry out for analysis in the light of the important studies of human aggression now being produced by the social psychologists. In general the works of Konrad Lorenz and his disciples demonstrate how nasty a creature the human animal is, and describe the conditions in which the nastiness is liable to break out in the form of large-scale violence or war; one such condition is overcrowding. The historian can demonstrate the rapidity with which urbanisation was taking place in hitherto relatively pastoral European countries in the years before the First World War; he can also show impressionistically, through a study of popular reading-matter, music-hall songs, modes and language of public protests and demonstrations, that there was something that can fairly be termed a 'will to war'. With the assistance of the theorists of human aggression he is enabled to suggest a correlation between the two, and, more tenuously, a possible explanation of the war as an objective fact. A final answer, of course, will depend very largely upon the historian's traditional methods of approach – an examination of the mechanisms by which the decisions which finally matter are arrived at, that is, an examination of final responsibilities for actual declaration of war.

In the past historians have been fascinated by the origins of wars; only recently have they begun to pay due regard to the question of the consequences of wars. In this realm, too, there is much to be learned from the studies of the social psychologists. The phenomenon of mass hysteria in the form of jingoistic patriotism has often been noted; with the assistance of social psychology it can be discussed in a more rigorous and less impressionistic way. The effects of bombing upon civilian morale is a matter of interest to both psychologists and historians. Most important of all from the point of view of assessing the long-term social consequences of war are the 'disaster' studies undertaken by certain social psychologists, which have assisted our understanding of the 'reconstructive' effect war can have, the desire to build anew and build better than before.

An understanding of the significance of group psychology for the historian, we have seen, underlies much of the work of Bloch and Febvre. Involvement in the problems of crowd psychology has led George Rudé and others into some fascinating work on the role of the crowd in various revolutionary upheavals, and in other disturbances.

Psychological insights into the effects of factory discipline, into the human consequences of creating a new emphasis on clocks and time-keeping, has brought a new qualitative element into the historian's assessment of the social consequences of the industrial revolution. The concepts of 'reference groups', by which people censor their activities or assess their standards of living, and 'relative deprivation' have helped to take some of the imprecision out of the traditional study of social conditions.

5 HISTORY AND ECONOMICS

The relationship of economics to history is rather different from that of the other social sciences; curious as it may sound, this relationship in many respects comes close to that between history and literature. Economics, after all, is the science (in the broad meaning of the term) of something which men actually do: even if the science did not exist, men would still make economic decisions, economic predictions and participate in the various forms of economic organisation which, in part, it is the economist's function to describe. Similarly the disciplined study of literature is concerned with something which men would also do anyway even if the disciplined study did not exist: compose poems, act out dramas, write novels and read them. Political science, or the discipline of politics, has, it is true many similarities to economics, particularly where it is concerned with generalisation about political structures. But political science covers a great range of other topics as well: it does not stand in simple relation to political history as economics does to economic history. Sociology clearly is an 'invented' science in the sense that in everyday life men do not make 'sociological' decisions or join 'sociological' organisations (the sociologist, of course, may study the stock exchange, or trade unions, particularly with reference to traditional and psychological influences upon their structure; but at base these organisations were founded for economic purposes).

The historian then is forced, whatever his period of study, to have some rudimentary knowledge of economics since so much of man's activity in societies is concerned with economic matters. In the same way a historian who seeks a thorough knowledge of any particular period must acquire a true familiarity with the literature of that period. In the earlier part of this century, a century much preoccupied with the economic problems of whole nations and with the economic needs of individual men, it is probably true that most historians did possess some basic knowledge of economics as the subject was then understood: in the amateurish atmosphere of the great British and American universities the subjects were in fact held to lie pretty close together, as we could see from the early career of J. H. Clapham.

However, economics in the last generation has become a much more complex and difficult subject, with economic theory heavily dependent on mathematics taking over from the old common-sense approach. On the basis of the arguments at the beginning of this chapter it should still be true that the historian today ought to acquire a basic working knowledge of modern economic theory. However, such counsels of perfection must always be tested against practical utility: if in fact the historian did try to acquire all the skills which he 'ought' to, he would have precious little time left for the writing and study of history. So again we come upon a necessary academic division of labour. We have already noted the evolution of the various sub-histories, of which economic history was one of the most important. Originally economic history was distinguished from other histories more by content than methodology; now, as Professor W. H. B. Court has put it, economic history is 'that part of history which requires a knowledge of economics for its full understanding'.[14] The question more and more economic historians are having to ask themselves is whether their primary loyalty lies to history or to economics: as a matter of academic convenience many university economic history departments now derive their main function from being a service department for economics. But whatever the immediate function, economic history remains a part of history, part of the attempt to increase that understanding of the past which is necessary to human society. In so far as the line between the economic and the general historian is not simply an educational and administrative device, the economic historian is a historian who has deliberately decided to study one part of history in great depth, that depth to be obtained primarily by use of economic tools. His conclusions must be served up in clear and intelligible form, for they may then be used by the general historian interested in the totality of human experience in any given period. More usually the general historian will himself be carried by the questions which he wishes to answer into territory where possession of certain economic tools will be necessary: he will then for specific, *ad hoc* purposes, need to acquire them.

In this section, therefore, we shall be concerned with two slightly different aspects of the relationship between history and economics. First of all we have the question of the borrowings which the general historian from time to time and the economic historian (of the traditional type) all of the time will have to make from economic science. Right away we come upon the question of the historian's use of statistics ('Il faut compter', as Lefebvre said), which often is a matter of more or less sporadic borrowing. I can myself recall that while wrestling with some conclusions which I wished to draw with regard to the quantitative consequences of the First World War for Great Britain, I literally shouted across the road to a colleague in the department of economics, who also happened to be a neighbour, so that he could quickly check my extremely simple mathematical premises. However, the question of the use of mathematics and statistics, though fundamental to modern economics, really does take us beyond economics and will be considered separately in the next section. Another obvious and absolutely inevitable borrowing is that practised continuously by any historian concerned with twentieth-century history: impossible to deal with such crucial circumstances as, say, the Wall Street Crash of 1929, the policies of the New Deal, or the world trading structure established after 1945 without a knowledge of the relevant economic theory. Even for historians who still prefer great men to the nameless masses, it would be difficult to find a single more influential twentieth-century figure than the British economist J. M. Keynes.

A much more interesting style of 'borrowing', however, is that adopted by Professor Thomas C. Cochran and his associates when they embarked upon a history of the Pabst Brewing Company. First they asked Professor Arthur H. Cole, the Harvard economist, to draw up a list of questions which the economist would ask of business records. According to Professor Cochran this list immediately suggested a number of problems not generally dealt with by historians, and produced some of the most interesting aspects of the history. Cochran has cited the specific example of the use made of the economist's concepts of 'location theory', as shown in this passage from the history as finally written:

> The most compelling locational advantage of Milwaukee over Chicago, Cincinnati, and St Louis was . . . the smallness of the population which restricted the company's home market. With all other factors favourable to large production and the growth of a shipping business, the Milwaukee brewers were forced into a contest for the national market in order to sell their surplus product at a time when their future rivals in the larger western cities were still content to sell at home.

Cochran himself deals with the objection that many traditional historians would make, that far from employing economic theory all he has done here is to use the historian's age-old standby 'informed common sense':

> The difference between the application of a well-structured group of related concepts, and the intuitive use of common sense is often subtle. The gain resulting from the more systematic procedures may appear mainly in the orderly presentation of the evidence and the explicitness of the conclusions. But granting the staggering problems of the

historian, even this gain would seem sufficient to justify the method. Researchers unequipped with the concepts of location theory might have seen clearly the paradox of the Pabst brewery location, but then again they might not.[15]

Different altogether from this fruitful idea of historical borrowings from economics is the question of the existence of two forms of new economic history deeply rooted in the methodology of economic science. First, a form which has already gained wide acceptance and which is concerned with concepts of economic growth and the study of national economic statistics in the aggregate. This kind of economic history was pioneered in the United States by Simon Kuznets: it was due to his initiative that in 1950 the International Association for Research in Income and Wealth decided to embark on a series of analyses of the evolutions in national income, national wealth, and their components, for various countries, and that in 1956 the Social Science Research Council (of the U.S.A.) created a fund to finance research on economic growth in various countries in the nineteenth and twentieth centuries. These initiatives have been developed in France by Jean Marczewski, who has coined the not altogether satisfactory description 'quantitative history', by Phyllis Deane in Britain, and by W. G. Hoffmann and J. J. Muller in Germany. This history, Professor Marczewski has told us, 'differs from traditional history in using a model consisting of quantified and interdependent magnitudes, the definition of which has its origin in national accounting'; it not only ascertains 'the past evolution of the various aggregates, it also seeks to explain it'.[16] Professor Marczewski finds the justification for the resort to national accounts in 'the growing interdependence of economic phenomena which is characteristic of the evolution of modern society'. But he makes no absurd claims for 'quantitative history': his reply to Professor Leontief's criticism that 'we cannot pass from the aggregative concept to the economic phenomena as they have been directly observed any more than we can turn an omelette into the whole eggs from which it has been made' is simply that no historical narrative 'can reflect the infinite complexity of the real world'. For Professor Marczewski the 'true origin of all history' is 'the appearance of new ideas and facts':

> There can therefore be no opposition, nor even competition, between quantitative and qualitative history. They represent nothing more than two distinct but complementary approaches, both equally indispensable to historical research.

'Quantitative' history is a type, perhaps the most important type, of economic history, itself only part of the totality of history. General historians will often wish to make use of the conclusions and discoveries of the historians of economic growth; but they will not themselves necessarily become familiar with the techniques employed by these historians.

More controversial, and in some respects more stimulating, is the form of economic history called, boringly, the 'new economic history', or, pretentiously, 'cliometrics', or, least offensively, 'econometric history'. Econometric history, Professor E. H. Hunt has written, can be considered to have three aspects.[17] The first actually differs only in degree from the approach long pursued by most economic historians: much greater emphasis is placed on statistical method and upon precision of definition and categorisation, and computers are enlisted to carry out calculations which formerly would have been impossible. As an example of this aspect, Professor Hunt cites some work of R. P. Swierenga on land speculation in nineteenth-century Iowa:

> Earlier attempts to assess land speculator profits were characterised by a reliance on non-mathematical techniques, the omission of certain key elements, vague definitions of what constituted 'profits', and the sheer impossibility of undertaking sufficiently large studies without the mechanical aids now available. Swierenga defined each term carefully, chose a sample area and prepared a data card for each parcel of land sold. Chronological details, prices, agents' fees and other data were punched onto the cards. After processing he was able to give precise figures of rates of return, broken down into year of entry, size of holding, and other categories.

The second aspect of econometric history, the enlistment of economic and statistical theory in order to reconstruct 'measurements which might have existed in the past but are no longer extant' – to use the words of a leading econometric historian, R. W. Fogel – is again a matter of degree rather than a complete break with older methods. Indirect quantification of a rather unsophisticated sort had been used, for example, in the standard-of-living controversy in the historiography of the British Industrial Revolution, or in tracing the expansion of a money economy in nineteenth-century Ireland through sales of Guinness beer. The indirect quantification of the econometric historians draws upon a much more sophisticated armoury: regression analysis, rent, input-output and location theory, hypergeometric distribution, and the von Neuman–Morgenstern utility index.

The third aspect of econometric history, the most distinctive and ambitious, is

> the use of the counterfactual conditional concept, starting with the premiss that we can understand the significance of what did happen only if we contrast it with what might have happened, and going on to quantify 'what might have happened'.[18]

The most famous exponent of the counterfactual conditional concept is

R. W. Fogel, who, in challenging the long-standing theory about the central importance of American railroads in the expansion of the American economy, constructed a model of the American economy as it would have been *without* railroads: the American gross national product in 1890 would, he reckoned, have been only 6·3 per cent lower than it actually was. The other outstanding piece of work in this canon is that of John R. Meyer and Alfred H. Conrad on 'The Economics of Slavery in the Ante-Bellum South', which effectively challenged some old theories about the uneconomic nature of slavery. Wild claims therefore have been made on behalf of the achievements, real and potential, of econometric history, often by those who have least direct knowledge of its operation. When Keith Thomas, of *Past and Present* and a distinguished student of the English Revolution, declared in the *Times Literary Supplement* that econometric history was sweeping all before it and would soon provide 'definitive solutions' to various historical problems, he was answered by Professor Peter Temin of the Massachusetts Institute of Technology, himself one of the most able of the econometric historians, who indicated the various limitations of this type of historical inquiry.[19] Again, then, more direct application of the techniques of economic science to historical problems can yield a rich harvest. General historians necessarily are familiarising themselves with the arguments and conclusions of the econometric historians; but that does not mean that they must all become econometricians forthwith. Finally it has to be stressed that in this section we have been concerned with economic history: that is, however valid the various approaches discussed here, they are irrelevant to vast tracts of the historian's territory. Statistics, certainly, can be applied to other sectors of human experience than the economic; to statistics we must now turn.

6 History and Statistics

The numeral revolution in twentieth-century historical study antedated the appearance of the modern computer: it was part of the reaction against the Whig political school and its classification of humanity into ill-defined groupings based on alleged ideological affiliations; this reaction in turn was part of the twentieth-century's sceptical treatment of the certitudes of its nineteenth-century predecessors: it was fostered on one side by Namier and his Tory school and on the other by Lefebvre and the economic and social historians. Many of the necessary calculations could be done by simple addition, subtraction, multiplication or division. Slowly historians weaned themselves away from such crass utterances as 'the people thought', 'a majority favoured', 'the king had wide support'; and endeavoured to answer 'how many people', 'what actual percentage' and 'which classes, and in which parts of the country'. One of the most interesting comparative statistics thrown up by Professor R. R. Palmer in his study of the 'Atlantic Revolution' was that in relative percentages there were more émigrés from the American Revolution than from the French: this was easily computed with pencil and paper by simple long division.

However, the development of the computer has made possible the processing of data which formerly would have filled several lifetimes. Marshall Smelser and William I. Davisson have summarised the virtues of the computer under two heads: first, the simple point that a computer can handle enormous quantities of fact at several million separate operations per second; second, the indirect point that in preparing his material for the computer the student is forced to ask precise questions.[20] Smelser and Davisson give the example of the inventories of estate in the records of Essex County, Massachusetts, for the years 1640–82, which can be reduced to 26,000 data cards which together contain all that can now be known of the wealth of the county in those forty-two years. Whereas the computer can print seven one-page tables and eighteen explanatory graphs, presenting this information in systematic form, in about ten minutes, a manual worker would have to spend at least 500 hours organising the material and making about 125,000 calculations.

Two basic questions were asked of the material: first, did the number of draught animals (horses and oxen) increase between 1640 and 1682? and second, did the number of ships increase over the same period? Then these sets of answers were integrated in one graph showing the increase or decrease of draught animals and ships on the same scale at five-year intervals. The number of draught animals was in fact shown to be decreasing, while the number of ships was increasing, demonstrating that the main population centre, Salem, was changing from a farm village to a commercial centre. This not very surprising conclusion no doubt was, on the basis of impressionistic evidence, known to historians anyway: such is often the way with elaborate statistical demonstrations; nonetheless it is still valuable to have concrete supporting evidence for a previously held thesis. Smelser and Davisson do give one example of how their statistical methods undermined another long-held thesis, that of the triangular pattern of trade out of the northeastern colonial ports, a thesis based on various fragmentary pieces of evidence such as the odd surviving ship's log book. By processing the data for every ship (instead of the distinctly non-random sample on which historians had previously depended) for two three-year periods, 1733–5 and 1749–51, the authors were able to suggest that an 'H-shaped' trade pattern was more in accordance with the facts than a triangular one.

Obviously economic facts and theories are most amenable to statistical treatment, but computers can be enlisted in support of many other sectors of historical analysis. The problems of historical demography will be considered in a separate section; suffice it to say here that informed discussion of population movement, births and deaths, fertility rates and immigration would not be possible without the means to process and correlate the complicated data which have been thrown up by detailed research among the relevant records. Some of the most critical work on the early nineteenth-century British House of Commons and the effects, or non-effects, of the Great Reform Act of 1832 has been done by Professor W. O. Aydelotte, who has penetrated behind the generalisations to a statistical study of economic, social and political affiliations of the Members of Parliament. Even a nodding acquaintance with the elements of statistics has brought greater precision to history. Historians are now aware of the danger of a promiscuous citation of 'averages', and indeed of the difference between an 'average' and a 'median' figure. They now have some idea of the type and magnitude of error which can be involved in the old impressionistic sample methods, and they are aware of which fluctuations are statistically significant and which are most probably due to random error. In introducing one of the most massively significant historical works to be published in the last decade Lawrence Stone has explained:

> Statistical measurement is the only means of extracting a coherent pattern from the chaos of personal behaviour and of discovering what is a typical specimen and what a sport. Failure to apply such controls has led to much wild and implausible generalisation about social phenomena, based upon a handful of striking and well-documented examples.[21]

7 SOCIOLOGY, ANTHROPOLOGY AND POLITICS

After taking so long to work back round to sociology, it may seem cavalier to lump into this section anthropology and politics as well. But, speaking of course from the outside as a historian, it does seem that although the balance of material studied differs in these three disciplines, the methods employed are essentially similar.[22] Here I shall most often speak of sociology, though some of the techniques discussed may more properly belong to the other disciplines, or to social psychology. Sociology embraces much of what, separately, is taught in social anthropology and politics: it does not seem desperately important whether psephology be strictly allocated to politics or be allowed to align with sociology. Certainly it is true that at the heart of all arguments about the nature of history lies the question of its relationship with sociology, a love-hate relationship resulting from ancestral coupling and feuding as intense as any which bedevilled the lives of the Forsytes.

The connection between history and sociology springs from the history of the two disciplines and from their subject matter. If Auguste Comte was the founder of sociology, he is also an important figure in the development of historical studies. Karl Marx was both a great historian and a great sociologist. Both history and sociology were and are concerned with the study of man in society: the difference, which in the end of course can be a fundamental one, is of approach. In the first instance it was the professionalisation of history which moved it apart from sociology, still at the end of the nineteenth century somewhat lacking in established scholarly standards. In the twentieth century it has rather been sociology, more and more sure of itself, and more and more sure that it was history that fell short of the desired precision, which has moved still further away from history. Yet until at least the very recent past there has been a continued and fruitful interaction between the two disciplines.

This interaction has been specially strong in France, where Émile Durkheim exerted a strong influence over generations of historians. The career of Durkheim (1858–1917) illustrates the way in which sociology only slowly established itself as an autonomous discipline. In 1887 a special course in social science was created for Durkheim to teach at the University of Bordeaux; and in 1896 he was elevated to the first Chair of Social Science in France. In 1898 he founded the periodical *L'Année Sociologique,* which was to have a tremendous influence on the later development of historical studies in France: among its most important contributors from the historical side later on was Lucien Febvre. When Durkheim achieved the eminence of a Chair at the Sorbonne, so great still were the resistances to new-fangled subjects that it was a Chair of Education. Not till 1911 was the title changed to Education *and* Sociology, the first time the tag sociology had been attached to any chair in France, although there were already such chairs in Germany and the United States.

Durkheim was preoccupied with the problem of the irrationality of human actions and with the question of collective consciousness, or group psychology. These concepts, we have seen, greatly influenced Lefebvre, Febvre and Bloch, while there was a direct train of influence between Durkheim and his younger contemporary (who outlived him by thirty-seven years) Henri Berr. Berr saw sociology as 'primarily a study of what is social in history'; its point of departure, he thought, 'must be the concrete data of history'. Durkheim he particularly admired for applying 'a precise, experimental, comparative method to historical facts'. But, Berr was clear, 'for all the importance and legitimacy of sociology' it was not 'the whole of history'. The historian, he said, in a classic statement of the differences between the two subjects,

> must give some attention to the individual peculiarities that make for the variations in history and that explain even the most general transformations of societies. And the more we study the most highly developed forms of societies, the more, perhaps – at least up to a certain level of development – does the 'individual' importance of what is distinctive grow, by very reason of the advancement of the societies.[23]

More interesting, however, is Berr's view, which, in a way, links the sociology of Durkheim with the history of Febvre and Bloch, that the approach to history through utilising contributions from social science, 'amalgamated through historical synthesis, must lead ultimately to psychology':

> The comparative study of societies must lead to social psychology and to a knowledge of the basic needs to which institutions and their changing manifestations are the response.

The greatest of all twentieth-century sociologists, and the one who has most significantly influenced historical study, is Max Weber (1864–1920). Weber, who was appointed Professor of Economics at Freiburg University at the age of thirty was a man of astonishing erudition who could read eight languages. His 'interests and skills' included law and economics, Biblical studies and the interpretation of religious doctrines, the land-surveying techniques of ancient Rome, medieval trading companies, the modern stock exchange, the comparative history of urban institutions, east German agriculture, the medieval origins of Western music, and conditions in the west German textile industry.[24] Flitting from topic to topic, constantly throwing up illuminating ideas, Weber coined concepts and produced basic studies of certain institutions which have dominated sociology and history ever since. From Weber originate the concept of the 'ideal type', of 'bureaucracy' and of the 'status group' as being as important a category as 'class'. He was the first to suggest the correlation between the Protestant ethic and the spirit of capitalism, the suggestion which so influenced Tawney; he was a pioneer in studying the importance of bureaucracy in the growth of the modern state; he virtually created urban sociology and the sociology of law. Like Durkheim he was specially interested in the non-rational foundations of human action: he invented the *charisma*, the 'magical', irrational quality which gives certain men the power to attract the loyalty and devotion of their followers. Most of this was served up in scattered articles, all of them appallingly written and, at times, extremely difficult to follow. As Weber's wife explained:

He was entirely unconcerned with the form in which he presented his wealth of ideas. So many things came to him out of that treasurehouse of his mind, once the mass was in flow, that many times they could not be readily forced into a lucid sentence structure. And he wants to be done with it quickly and be brief about it on top of that, because ever new problems of reality crowd in on him. . . . Therefore, much must be pressed hurriedly into long involved periods and what cannot be accommodated there has to be put into the footnotes. After all, let the reader take as much trouble with these matters as he had done himself.[25]

This is fine for a sociologist of genius (though it explains why Weber is more quoted than read): most historians would argue that only when their ideas make sense to their readers can they be sure that their ideas make sense at all.

Already during the period of Weber's greatest influence the lines between history and sociology were hardening. It became clear that sociologists were themselves engaged in two rather separate types of activity of which the second, and increasingly more usual, seemed a far cry from history. The first activity continued the traditions of Durkheim and Weber, the production of broad general formulations covering significant areas of human action and drawing upon historical material. This traditional aspect of sociology, it could be said, acknowledged an initial dependence upon history, though history in turn could, and frequently did, benefit from the syntheses produced by the sociologists. The second aspect of sociological study, which developed in the years after the First World War, was the detailed study of some very narrow area of human activity. In such studies the 'scientific' element could be much more pronounced, particularly as sampling techniques and questionnaires were developed in a manner which minimised subjective influences. Early examples of this style of sociological inquiry were the famous *Middletown* studies of the Lynds.[26] Since then smaller and smaller areas of study have been delimited: single educational institutions, even small controlled groups of human beings. It is this type of inquiry which for a time seemed likely to sever all links between history and sociology. Gone certainly was the dependence of sociology upon history; but the perceptive historian could see that if the organic connection between the subjects was now weakening, it was still open to the historian to borrow from sociology much as he borrowed from the whole range of other social sciences.

Not all sociologists were pleased with this notion of the historian borrowing from sociology. Some believed that the disciplines had now moved too far apart and that where the historian did affect the language of social science he merely exposed further his appalling inadequacy and ill-understanding. Others argued that the organic association still existed: that the individual research projects of the sociologist were a necessary part of the continuing wider aims of the subject; and that historians and sociologists should still strive to bring their subjects together. This wide issue will be considered in the next section. Meantime we shall concentrate on the borrowings which historians can and do make from sociology.

In the last generation probably the most important single improvement in the writing of history is the increased degree of precision. It would be a misreading of the way things in fact happen to attribute this entirely and directly to the influence of sociology or of the social sciences in general. Rather is it part of a general intellectual movement in which there has been increasing distrust of, on the one hand, the rotund pronouncements and facile generalisations of an older generation, and, on the other, of the elaborate hedging which in the end says precisely nothing at all, of that generation's successors. The problem has been vigorously stated by an ex-historian turned crusading sociologist:

> The language in which history is written is ordinary everyday language: and the type of explanations which historians offer is the type of explanations which people offer in everyday life. People in their daily life assume, without being aware of the fact, that they already know the laws of human behaviour and social interaction. They do not hesitate to offer explanations of why so-and-so has divorced her husband, of why someone has failed at university, or of why someone else has been so successful in business: nor do they refrain from enumerating the causes of racial tension, of industrial conflict, or of Britain's economic difficulties. They do not stop for a moment to consider that these questions might be problems for investigation for social scientists.[27]

Historians do now very definitely stop to consider this, and increasingly they are willing to profit from the fruits of the very necessary investigations conducted by social scientists. Certainly the questions of 'language' and of 'explanation' are critical. In their depth studies of 'human behaviour and social interaction', sociologists (including social psychologists) employ a much more precise descriptive language than historians have been wont to use. It is certainly a matter of common sense that historians should familiarise themselves with this language and be prepared to use it if thereby greater precision can be obtained. (The historian's problem of course is that the infinite richness of the human past is often not amenable to precise categorisation.) However it would seem reasonable that historians who write cheerfully about changes in the 'social climate' or revolutions in 'manners and morals' (a reputable enough phrase, since it has for certain periods of study the validity at least of contemporary usage) should be aware of the valuable distinction the sociologist makes between *folkways* and *mores*. Folkways are standardised practices, matters of dress, leisure habits, etiquette, which though observed as a matter of tradition and custom need not necessarily be observed by every individual; mores are patterns of behaviour upon which the survival of society is held to depend – they concern, for instance, the freedoms allowed to women, the usage of addictive drugs, attitudes towards 'crime' – and which are enforced by very strong social pressures, often amounting to legal sanctions.

In one fashion or another, usually in a most off-hand and impressionistic one, historians have had to cope with such fundamental data as shifts in population. Demography is now a highly developed social science in its own right, and also, in its historical aspect, a sub-branch of historical study. Historians are accustomed enough to using phrases like 'birth rate' and 'marriage rate' and for many of their purposes these rather blunt concepts are perfectly satisfactory. But should it be necessary to establish a real level of fertility then such concepts as *age-specific fertility* become necessary. This forbidding term means 'the number of children borne in relation to a woman's age, and this varies, being higher in the mid-twenties than in the mid-thirties, or indeed in the late teens, and very much higher than in the mid-forties'. And that, Mr Peter Laslett has told us, 'is only one amongst a whole series of new terms which we hope will come to have a place in the universe of historical discourse':[28]

> And for each term there is a corresponding statistic. Infant mortality, that favourite measuring-rod of welfare, should soon become a commonplace of accurate estimation rather than a matter of fragmentary and somewhat wistful guesswork. Expectation of life at birth; the chances of a woman being pregnant at the time of her marriage; the rate of illegitimacy; the size of families; the lesser (or greater) liability of gentlemen to die than craftsmen and peasants; movement of individuals from place to place about the country; perhaps, ultimately, their movement from position to position on the scale of social differences in England, the best graduated of all societies: all these and more are on the way to demonstration.

Depending upon whether he is simply attempting to draw a picture of the social structure of a particular community at a particular time (for purposes of comparison with the same community at a different point in time, or with some other community) or whether he is concerned to explain the actions of individuals in terms of their social 'class', the historian will rely to a lesser or greater extent upon the finer distinctions drawn by the sociologist. If a picture of society is desired there can be no question of classifying each individual three times over according to his *class*, *status* and *power*, very helpful concepts if the historian has the second problem in mind. In drawing a picture of a society the historian must settle for one rough classification into classes, estates or whatever term was *acceptable to the people living at the time the historian is studying*. But it is certainly important that any historian who finds it necessary to generalise about class should be aware of the more refined threefold categorisation.

In analysing social groups great assistance is to be had from what in sociology is termed *role theory* (involving Weber's 'ideal types' mentioned above), the idea, in the words of Professor Metzger, that

> Every society, in order to achieve its goals, requires its members to play standardised roles, these being assigned in the main on the basis of age, sex, class and occupation.[29]

Professor Thomas C. Cochran, whose application to historical study of other social science tools we have already noted, has made most effective use of role theory in such important pioneering works as *Railroad Leaders, 1845–1890: the Business Mind in Action* (1953). He has summed up in the following illuminating fashion:

> Role analysis applies to a central problem of the historian: What makes for permanence and for change? Sharply defined roles with strong defining groups make innovation more difficult, while loosely defined roles invite variations in behaviour. The difference in roles gives meaning to such clichés as 'a young country' and 'an old country'. In new situations social roles are still fluid; in old traditional situations they tend to be well defined. The American promoter on the unsettled frontier governed his conduct largely by expediency, while the Congregational minister in New England knew rather precisely what was expected of him.[30]

We have already mentioned the notion of the 'reference groups' by which people assess their role in society: periods of rapid social change are often marked by a change in the 'reference group' by which people judge their material standards. For example, in Britain during the First World War many workers were able for the first time to savour amenities hitherto enjoyed only by the middle and upper classes. Henceforth the workers would judge their satisfactions by a new reference: this in itself became a potent agent of social change.

Sociology made its declaration of independence late in the nineteenth century, and by the mid-twentieth century was in a position to look with some scorn upon the pretensions of history. Political science (or 'politics'), generally, was slower to make good its claims to autonomy. Up until the most recent past it was usual in both British and American universities for political science teaching to be included within the history departments. Where long-established departments of political science have existed it has often been difficult to determine how in fact they differed from departments teaching recent history. Charles A. Beard actually found his main remunerative professional employment, till he resigned from it after a political dispute with the university establishment, in the Department of Political Science at Columbia University.

The Gladstone Chair of Government at Oxford is currently held by a distinguished historian, Max Beloff.

Late in the day, however, politics has developed somewhat in the same direction as sociology. Again there are useful borrowings for the historian to make. Much attention in the 'Is history a social science?' debate has been focused on the question of public opinion polls. Undoubtedly opinion polls taken today will form valuable source material for historians in the future, but of course for the vast sectors of the past with which the historian is concerned there can be no question of quizzing the opinions of the dead. Where history has been beneficially influenced is through the insight recent polls give into electoral behaviour in general: it is a little less easy now for historians to deliver those fatuous judgements about 'the people thought this' or 'the electorate wanted that', which were pure guesses and pretty shoddy ones at that. Other techniques developed by the political scientists perhaps deserve more attention. Samuel H. Beer, for example, has developed some interesting techniques for measuring such difficult quantities as party cohesion.[31]

And so we are back with mathematics. While historians were in any case beginning to lisp in numbers in the inter-war years, it must be agreed that that vague movement has been greatly stimulated by the obvious successes of the social scientists in quantifying the sort of human and social material long thought not to be amenable to such treatment. Rather similar is the influence asserted by the social sciences in persuading historians to make greater use of 'models'. This elaborate term may in fact amount to little more than a couple of inter-related propositions which might be used as the basis of analysis of a specific problem. Such 'models' have long been familiar to historians. More ambitious projects, such as Crane Brinton's *Anatomy of Revolution* or Professor Hugh Trevor-Roper's 'general crisis' in the seventeenth century, have not so far received whole-hearted approval within the profession. But undoubtedly there is today a much greater willingness to play about with such generalising concepts.

8 Last Words

With great wit, Professor C. Vann Woodward has pointed out the frequency with which historians have met in solemn resolve to pay closer attention in future to the discoveries of the social scientists, and have then carried on exactly as before.[32] Professor Bruce Mazlish argues that all historians should undergo a training in psychology before embarking in their researches;[33] Mr Holloway thinks history and sociology should merge, that is that historians should become sociologists, not mere borrowers;[34] many others have suggested even more arduous courses of apprenticeship. It does seem a little curious that members of a society which enjoys the fruits of the simple principle of division of labour should now be proposing, in regard to the poor historian, to repudiate that principle. This is not to argue for obscurantism, but for the type of collaboration (where necessary) so fruitfully pioneered by Professor Cochran, who for his work on *Railroad Leaders* consulted economists, sociologists, political scientists and social psychologists. Division of labour is seen at its best in the University of Pennsylvania Norristown Project, an investigation into the social history of that town between 1900 and 1950, involving the co-operation of anthropologists, sociologists and historians. Thanks to detailed and quite technical demographic work one most significant central fact was unearthed: that essentially Norristown contained two populations, the long-term residents, and a constantly changing migrating group.[35] Some of the other interesting things historians today are doing will be discussed in chapter 6.

Before leaving this topic, however, we should perhaps just make the simple point that if history has imperfections, so indeed have most of the social sciences. Historians in earnest and laborious pursuit of the insignificant have rightly been mocked in the past; but some of their puny labours are made to seem positively significant compared with certain social science projects where vast statistical resources are brought into play in the interest of restating the obvious in the most obscure fashion possible. Among those sociologists who go in for model-building on the wider scale it is often to be noted that their handling of historical material is cavalier in the extreme; and one frequently finds a curiously naïve reliance on the sort of narrative source material which historians for fifty years have been viewing with grave scepticism. Two books of quite outstanding brilliance which respectively show these weaknesses are Stanislav Andreski's *Military Organization and Society* (1954) and William Guttsman's *British Political Elite* (1963). All important books have weaknesses; but social scientists should scrutinise themselves before denouncing the weaknesses they think they detect in the works of historians.

In support of his plea for a merging of history and sociology Dr Holloway approvingly quotes the advice of the great social scientist Robert K. Merton:

> The report of data would be in terms of their immediate pertinence for the hypothesis and, derivatively, the underlying theory. Attention should be called specifically to the introduction of interpretative variables other than those entailed in the original formulations of hypotheses and the bearing of these upon the theory should be indicated. . . .

The conclusions of the research might well include not only a statement of the findings with respect to the initial hypotheses but, when this is in point, an indication of the order of observations needed to test anew the further implications of the investigation. . . . One consequence of such formalisation is that it serves as a control over the introduction of unrelated, undisciplined, and diffuse interpretation. It does not impose upon the reader the task of ferreting out the relations between the interpretations embodied in the text. Above all, it prepares the way for consecutive and cumulative research rather than a buckshot array of dispersed investigations.[36]

And that is a perfect example of that to which history never has and never will aspire.

NOTES

1. *The Times* (London), 12 October 1968.
2. E. H. Carr, *What is History?* (1961) p. 69.
3. See W. H. Walsh, *An Introduction to the Philosophy of History* (1967 edn.) p. 41.
3a. Schmitt, *Fashion and Future of History*, p. 23.
4. *What is History?*, p. 84.
5. E. E. Evans-Pritchard, *Anthropology and History* (1961) p. 18.
6. In H. P. R. Finberg (ed.), *Approaches to History* (1962) p. 144.
7. *Times Literary Supplement*, 7 April 1966.
8. G. R. Elton, *The Practice of History* (1967) p. 27n.
9. W. O. Aydelotte, 'Quantification in History', *American Historical Review*, LXXI (1966).
10. Quoted in Stern, p. 360.
11. Stern, p. 347.
12. See, for example, J. B. Mitchell (ed.), *Great Britain: Geographical Essays* (1962) pp. 17–31.
13. Ibid., pp. 3–16.
14. In Finberg, *Approaches to History*, p. 17.
15. Thomas C. Cochran, *The Inner Revolution* (1964) pp. 20–3.
16. Jean Marczewski, 'Quantitative History' in *Journal of Contemporary History*, III 2 (1968) 179–91.
17. E. H. Hunt, 'The New Economic History' in *History*, LIII 177 (1968) 3–18. What follows draws heavily on Professor Hunt's model exposition.
18. Hunt, in *History*, LIII 5.
19. *Times Literary Supplement*, 7 April and 28 July 1966.
20. Marshall Smelser and William I. Davisson, 'The Historian and the Computer: A Simple Introduction to Complex Computation' in *Essex Institute Historical Studies*, CIV 2 (1968) 111ff. For Merle Curti's important quantitative work in *The Making of an American Community*, see below, pp. 197–8.

21. Lawrence Stone, *The Crisis of the Aristocracy 1558–1641* (1965) pp. 3–4. See below, p. 223.

22. For a closer look at anthropology, see Evans-Pritchard, *Anthropology and History*, and Keith Thomas, 'History and Anthropology' in *Past and Present*, xxiv (April 1963). Professor Evans-Pritchard seems to make little distinction between social anthropology and sociology.

23. Quoted in Stern, pp. 250–5.

24. Reinhard Bendix, *Max Weber: An Intellectual Portrait* (1960). See also the introduction to H. H. Gerth and C. Wright Mills (eds.), *From Max Weber* (1948).

25. Quoted by Bendix, p. 18.

26. R. S. and H. M. Lynd, *Middletown: A Study in Contemporary American Culture* (1929) and *Middletown in Transition: A Study in Cultural Conflicts* (1937).

27. S. W. F. Holloway, 'History and Sociology: What History Is and What it Ought to Be' in W. H. Burston and D. Thompson (eds.), *Studies in the Nature and Teaching of History* (1967) pp. 8–9.

28. In E. A. Wrigley, D. C. Eversley and Peter Laslett, *An Introduction to English Historical Demography* (1966).

29. Walter P. Metzger, 'Generalizations about National Character' in Gottschalk (ed.), *Generalization in the Writing of History*, p. 90.

30. Thomas C. Cochran, 'The Historian's Use of Social Role' in Gottschalk, pp. 109–10.

31. S. H. Beer, *Modern British Politics* (1965) pp. 257ff.

32. 'History and the Third Culture' in *Journal of Contemporary History*, iii 2 (1968) 23–35.

33. 'Group Psychology and Problems of Contemporary History', ibid., p. 177.

34. Burston and Thompson, p. 18.

35. Sidney Goldstein, *Patterns of Mobility 1910–1950: The Norristown Study* (1961).

36. Merton, *Social Theory and Social Structure*, p. 100; Holloway, in Burston and Thompson, pp. 17–18.

5 The Historian at Work

1 HISTORICAL SOURCES

PROFESSOR Barraclough's useful definition of history which we have already noted called it the attempt to re-create the significant features of the past on the basis of imperfect and fragmentary evidence. This imperfect and fragmentary evidence is the historian's 'sources'. A historical work is deemed scholarly and reliable according to the extent to which it is based on 'primary' sources, the basic, raw, imperfect evidence. The book the historian himself writes is a 'secondary source': the wider public, the journalist, the interested layman, the idly curious, when desirous of securing some information on a particular historical topic, and not having time to consult, let alone search for, the primary sources, will rely on this secondary account. Simplifying slightly, one could say that the historian at work is engaged in converting the scattered, difficult primary sources into a coherent, intelligible secondary source. Historians necessarily make great use themselves of secondary sources – the books and articles of other historians. It is a rule of good scholarship that when embarking on some topic of research the historian should master all the existing secondary material. Most textbooks, and one or two truly original and illuminating historical works, have been written entirely from secondary sources; but no historian could be regarded as fully trained and fully competent to interpret the past to others who had not himself worked in primary source materials.

The great achievement of the nineteenth-century German school was the establishment of the 'scientific' study of primary sources. At times the fetish for primary sources has proved destructive of genuine historical study. The discovery and printing of a new document has been held far above any discussion of the possible relevance of the document. Too frequently the critical question in deciding the acceptance and publication of a scholarly article is whether it parades a sufficient array of primary material rather than whether it makes any real contribution to historical knowledge. Nonetheless the difficult article with undigested wodges of primary documentation may provide fodder for a more imaginative colleague; the readable, airy article, all insights and no evidence, may provide a good read, and the necessary reputation for its author, but precious little for any one else to work on. Study of sources alone does not make history; but without the study of sources there is no history.

Probably the single most important development in twentieth-century historical studies is the broadening of our conception of what constitutes a historical source, together with the growth of new methods for handling new types of source. Trade or population statistics compiled by some governmental agency or by some interested private individual have long been accepted as important primary sources: recent advances in statistics have allowed for their more extensive and ambitious use by historians. The historian has learned to use the materials and, therefore, the tools of the archaeologist. Surviving factory installations, old brickwork, old machinery, are a valuable source for industrial history: we now, indeed, talk of 'industrial archaeology' to describe the systematic study of the remains left by an earlier industrial age. J. R. Green called the landscape a basic document; Michelet and Bloch tramped the French country-side in their search for primary evidence; historians now supplement the inadequate gleanings of their own eyes with the revelations about land forms and earlier patterns of cultivation revealed by aerial photography.

At a common-sense level the distinction between a primary and a secondary source is obvious enough: the primary source is the raw material, more meaningful to the expert historian than to the layman; the secondary source is the coherent work of history, article, dissertation or book, in which both the intelligent layman and the historian who is venturing upon a new research topic, or keeping in touch with new discoveries in his chosen field, or seeking to widen his general historical knowledge, will look for what they want. Of course many laymen interested in history will find the scholarly secondary work too forbidding and will turn to textbooks or popularisations. There is in fact a kind of hierarchy of scholarly acceptability among secondary sources, running from the academic monograph at the top to the sensationalised popular work at the bottom, to which in fact academics would not allow the title secondary source at all. The line between what passes muster as a secondary source (or secondary 'authority') and what has no authority can be seen from the bibliography of any important historical work: the books included are secondary sources; books omitted, though the author may in fact have read them, are *de facto* not acceptable as sources or authorities at all. The secondary source is itself dependent on primary sources: textbooks and popularisations tend to be dependent on secondary sources, or indeed upon other textbooks and popularisations. We shall return to this hierarchy shortly; meantime we must look in more detail at some of the more important types of primary sources. They too are often organised in some kind of hierarchy.

The informing principle behind this hierarchy is the idea that something which is handwritten, and of which there may be only one copy, is somehow more *primary* than something which is printed, and of which there may well be many copies. Behind this idea there lies the more fundamental and perfectly reasonable one that the historian who has searched around, travelled far, written the necessary ingratiating letters to secure access to a rare document, has put in more man-hours than the historian who has relied on printed documents obtainable in all the major libraries (I am not here referring to a printed edition of the rare document, but to, for example, a government paper which began life in print and in many copies). Possibly there is an element of the feeling that it is in the study of rare documents that the historian asserts his professional autonomy: printed papers are more readily open to inspection and use by scholars in other disciplines – economists, lawyers, sociologists – and indeed to the vulgar mob. At one stage in the development of historical studies it was held – and this is how the hierarchy arose in the first place – that a document written in a man's hand was more immediate to historical reality, closer to how it really was, than a document that had suffered the less direct method of production on a printing-press. This distinction is scarcely a valid one: a document written in one man's handwriting may be a genuine record of a transaction which actually took place, or a record in good faith of something the writer has seen with his own eyes, or it may be the record of a statement dictated by one man to another, or the record of a collective decision, or it may be a complete invention on the part of the writer. It will in any case yield answers only to certain questions; if what one requires is the final statement of government policy on a particular issue, the printed document may well prove a much more valuable primary source *for that particular topic*. Primary sources do not have an autonomous value entirely apart from the questions which the historian wishes to ask and the context in which he wishes to set them.

The accepted hierarchy of primary sources, nonetheless, can be seen in the bibliography of any substantial piece of historical scholarship. First the manuscript materials: thus, E. P. Thompson in the bibliography of his classic *The Making of the English Working Class* (1965) first lists various papers found in the Public Record Office in London: the relatively well-sorted Home Office Papers, of which he made special use of those catalogued as series 40 and 42; miscellaneous bundles of papers relating to the London Corresponding Society, food riots and other working-class topics found among the less well-sorted Privy Council Papers; and the Treasury Solicitor's Papers which (among a mass of material of no direct use to Thompson) contain some of the evidence, such as informers' reports, depositions, intercepted letters, from which the Crown briefs against State prisoners were prepared. In the Manuscript Room of the British Museum Thompson consulted the much-worked-over Place Collection, which includes Minute Books and Letter Books of the London Corresponding Society. In the Sheffield Reference Library Thompson used the Fitzwilliam Papers, where the relevant material for his study included part of the correspondence on public affairs of Earl Fitzwilliam, and reports from Yorkshire Justices of the Peace and other informants during the time when Fitzwilliam was Lord Lieutenant of the West Riding of Yorkshire. At a private country mansion, Rudding Park, Harrogate, Thompson consulted the Radcliffe Papers and made use of the correspondence of Sir Joseph Radcliffe, a Huddersfield Magistrate responsible for bringing Luddite agitators to trial. In the Nottingham City Archives Thompson consulted the Papers of the Framework-Knitter Committee.

Having listed and discussed his manuscript materials, Thompson then proceeds to the next level of the primary hierarchy: contemporary pamphlets and periodicals, discovered mainly, the author tells us, in the British Museum Reading Room and the John Rylands Library, Manchester. A historian concerned with similar problems in a slightly later period (Thompson is concerned with the late eighteenth century and early nineteenth century, when the governmental system was pretty rudimentary) would also include on this level (published) government reports and reports of parliamentary debates. The bound volumes of Acts of Parliament could also be included here. A diplomatic historian, having put private manuscript collections and archival material from the various embassies, state departments and foreign offices first, would, on the second tier, list published collections of foreign correspondence. Finally, the historian mentions the secondary authorities; in Thompson's case, such books as J. L. and B. Hammond, *The Skilled Labourer*, J. H. Clapham, *The Economic History of Modern Britain*, and I. Pinchbeck, *Women Workers and the Industrial Revolution*.

Certain materials do not fit neatly into the categorisation as primary or secondary sources; some are primary sources from one point of view, secondary from another. The outstanding instance is the autobiography. Often listed in bibliographies as a primary source, an autobiography often assumes the proportions of a secondary history of the times through which the writer has lived as well as a primary account of his own experiences and thoughts. Usually composed long after the events described, an autobiography will usually have to be treated with even greater circumspection than the more straightforward primary document. In somewhat similar case is the contemporary history, that is to say the history of events through which the historian has himself lived, a history which may have some of the eye-witness quality of a primary record. Actually contemporary histories fall into two types: those written in the normal, detached (as far as this is ever possible) fashion of any reputable historian writing about any period, and those written by actual participants in the events narrated. A. J. P. Taylor's *English History 1914–1945* (1965) would be an instance of the former; Clarendon's *History of the Great Rebellion* and Winston Churchill's volumes on the two World Wars are classic instances of the latter. *English History 1914–1945* is uniformly valuable as an authoritative secondary work by a distinguished professional historian; Churchill and Clarendon, when they deal with the wider sweep of events, are much less authoritative: they are not outstanding as secondary sources. They are of most value when dealing autobiographically with events with which they themselves were intimately associated; and where, demonstrably unreliable on detail, they nonetheless convey something of the atmosphere of the time in which they lived, something of the excitement of direct involvement, something of that quality of seeing events as they seemed to contemporaries which historians must labour for years to attain. The comment of the Tory elder statesman A. J. Balfour on Churchill's First World War series was apposite: 'Winston has written an enormous book about himself and called it *The World Crisis*.'

A further example of this kind of hybrid source is a work of contemporary politics such as Engels's *Conditions of the English Working Class* (1845). Engels was concerned to paint as black a picture as possible of working-class conditions and of the wickedness of their capitalistic exploiters. We cannot take his descriptive matter entirely at face value, though his eye-witness accounts, however critically they must be assessed (and all primary sources must be assessed in this way), stand as primary sources. Much of the book, however, is taken from newspaper accounts and from government papers, and in that sense is secondary: the historian must himself go directly to the sources from which Engels quotes and, in some cases, misquotes. But from the point of view of a rather different topic, *The Condition of the Working Class in England* is a most important primary source – that is from the point of view of the study of the development of socialist thought.

The example is instructive. Engels essentially wrote his book with a specific, definite purpose – the exposure of the evils of capitalism. He was not consciously writing a source book for the study of the history of socialism. The historian, however, does not take from the book what Engels wants him to take, he does not accept without reservations the picture presented by Engels, he does not regard it as a completely authoritative source for what it consciously purports to be about, the condition of the working classes in the early nineteenth century. But the historian does value the book in a manner that was not in Engels's mind at all. This gives us a further clue to the nature of primary sources. They are contemporary, of course; they belong to the period which the historian is studying. But just as important, they are not deliberately designed for the benefit of the historian. The primary source served a real purpose for the men who created it: their purpose is a quite different one from that of the historian coming along later. The Declaration of Independence was a masterly piece of political propaganda serving a tremendously important immediate political purpose: no doubt vague thoughts of posterity were in the minds of its framers, but it was certainly not written for the benefit of future students of the American Revolution. Magna Carta was designed to meet a specific political crisis in early thirteenth-century England: it was not drawn up so that future historians could learn about the assumptions of society at that time, though in fact historians do learn much along these lines from it. Domesday Book was compiled for very mercenary reasons by William the Conqueror, desirous of knowing the potential wealth of his domain: but it has proved a godsend to historians seeking all kinds of information about the structure of eleventh-century society.

On the whole it can be said that a primary source is most valuable when the purpose for which it was compiled is at the furthest remove from the purpose of the historian. (This is not absolutely true: the census-taker may most usefully be asking the same kind of questions as the historian wishes to, though in a most tantalising way he often does not.) The American Revolution could not be explained solely in terms of the Declaration of Independence: the historian has to beware of the rhetorical flourishes of such documents. Even more care is needed with the more literary kind of diary, or with a collection of letters of the type left by the eighteenth-century patrician Horace Walpole: Walpole was consciously writing for posterity, which does mean that he provides information on all sorts of topics that a less self-conscious observer might well have missed; but the historian has to be on guard for the moments when self-consciousness interferes with the immediacy of the reporting. The distinction I have in mind has been neatly summarised by the distinguished science historian Henry Guerlac, when he talks of 'intentional record' and the 'unwitting testimony' of official records and private correspondence. Essentially the special expertise of the historian lies in examining and assessing the 'unwitting testimony' of the past.

In considering his primary sources there are a number of questions which the historian must ask. First of all, is the document authentic, is it what it purports to be? Take for example a medieval charter apparently dated early in the eleventh century and purporting to make a grant of land from the king to a monastery. It is always possible that the charter was actually forged by the monks late in the twelfth century (say) in order to establish a right to the land. The document will still be of value to the historian as a genuine twelfth-century forgery which will tell him a good deal about that century, but he will have to be very circumspect in his use of it if his subject of study lies in the early eleventh century. To establish authenticity the historian will apply his technical expertise: he will be familiar with the characteristic forms of an early eleventh-century charter, the script used, the style of language, and the legal forms; if the charter in front of him departs from these he will on *internal* evidence suspect its authenticity. He will also have certain *external* evidence which he can apply: was the king actually in the part of the country where the charter was supposedly issued at the date when it was apparently issued; was he in the habit of making grants of this type; does this purported fact, in short, accord with other known facts? If it does not, the historian may well be on the track of a revision of hitherto accepted versions of events, in which case he has got a great deal more work in front of him; or he may decide, especially if the internal evidence suggests this as well, that the document is not authentic.

Once authenticity is established, that is, that the document was written by the person it says it was written by, at the time it says it was written, and with regard to the matters it purports to be about, the historian is concerned with the question of *reliability*. Certain other points have to be settled, of which the crucial one is: how did the document come into existence in the first place? Who exactly was the author, that is, apart from his name, what role in society did he play, what sort of person was he? What was his purpose in writing it? For example, an ambassador's report on conditions in the country in which he is stationed may be biased in various directions: if he is a Catholic in a Protestant country he may tend to exaggerate the evidence of a Catholic upsurge; he may send home the kind of information he knows his home government wants to hear; he may, as for instance Nevile Henderson, British Ambassador to Hitler's Germany was, be over-anxious to maintain peaceful relations between the two countries; when reporting on an ally he may give a hopelessly optimistic account, say, of the likelihood of unrest among the general populace. How far is Horace Walpole, a Whig aristocrat, reliable in describing the mainsprings of the 'Wilkes and Liberty' movement? Does a tax return give a fair account of real wealth, or will there not be a tendency on the side of the individual to conceal the extent of his possessions, on the side of the tax-gatherer to over-assess them? John Reed's *Ten Days that Shook the World* (1919) is an exciting on-the-spot account of the Bolshevik Revolution: but, in using it as a primary source, how can we be certain that in fact he ever left his hotel bedroom? These, and many others, are the sort of questions historians must ask all the time of their primary sources: they are part of his basic expertise.

Different areas of historical investigation bring up particular technical problems of their own. In general there is a broad difference in

the problems encountered by the medieval historian and those encountered by the modern historian. The medieval historian will have a
greater need of technical proficiency in palaeography, diplomatics and
philology. Many of the controversies in medieval history, indeed, centre
on the shade of meaning allotted to a specific passage in dog-Latin or
medieval French: we have already quoted from the Anglo-Saxon
Chronicle (whose original versions were in Latin) the phrase about the
state of religion in William the Conqueror's time being such 'that
every man who wished to, whatever considerations there might be
with regard to his rank, could follow the profession of a monk'. An
alternative translation, which gives a much narrower meaning, reads
'Christendom was such in his day that every man who so desired
followed what pertained to his order.'[1] All historians have at times,
as it were, to 'squeeze the last drop' out of the document in front of them,
to build as complete a representation of reality as they can on the
foundation of the very imperfect evidence in front of them (making
clear in their references just how imperfect this evidence is), or to
follow up the vague promptings of one particular turn of phrase (for
instance, when a suffragette magazine in Britain during the First World
War talked of certain events *threatening* to make women's suffrage a
live issue, this suggests just how far the excitements of war had for the
time being turned it into a dead issue).[2] But medieval historians, in
high degree, have the problem of making the most of minimal and
fragmentary evidence: here the discovery of one new document can
genuinely be of critical importance. Modern historians, as is often said,
suffer frequently from the converse problem of having too much evidence at their disposal, so that they have to develop a special expertise in
selectivity.

One particular type of source material which has given rise to much
interesting disputation is the imaginative literature left by an age or
generation. Right off we can make one obvious point: a novel or poem,
if it is a source at all, is a source for the period in which it was written,
not for the period about which it is written. In other words the novels
of Sir Walter Scott may tell us a great deal about the early nineteenth
century; but though Scott was undoubtedly historically minded, a
novel such as *Ivanhoe* will not tell us much about the twelfth century
that we could not better and more reliably find elsewhere, though it
might (and this is true of all great novels), through the author's
creative insight, suggest lines of inquiry which should be checked against
the other sources. We would pay more direct attention to a novel
written late in life by a writer drawing upon his own childhood many
years before and upon the memories of still earlier times passed on to him
then by his parents. Nonetheless, the use of imaginative literature has,
in quite recent years, fallen rather seriously into disrepute in the wake of

a spate of popular, chatty 'social histories' drawing their evidence, say, for social conditions in early nineteenth-century England almost exclusively from the pages of Dickens. Which takes us to one basic rule in the historian's handling of imaginative literature: for the concrete facts of everyday existence, wage rates, living standards, environmental conditions, he will prefer, if he can avoid it, not to take the word of a novelist, but will turn to government papers, statistical series, company records, trade union archives, private correspondence, houses still in existence from the era he is studying, or their remains (industrial archaeology). Once he has established the record from such sources, the historian may well use a vivid example culled from a novel or poem to *illustrate* (not *prove*) that record. Thus it is fairly easy to establish from bills of mortality, private diaries and the like the truly noisome conditions of eighteenth-century England: but *communication* with the reader may well be intensified by a judicious quotation from Fielding's *Tom Jones*. One of the most famous examples of a false trail having been established by a great creative writer lies at the door of no less a person than the Bard of Avon himself: Juliet was married to Romeo at the age of fourteen; her mother, as apparently the other ladies of Verona, had been married even earlier; Miranda in *The Tempest* was married at fifteen. Arguing from these and other plays, historians have deduced that the marriage age in Elizabethan and Jacobean England must have fallen consistently in this age range. In fact recent demographic research has shown that in that era the marriage age was higher, not lower, than at present: the commonest age of first marriage for women being at least twenty-two.[3]

If the historian has good reason for seeking elsewhere for the concrete facts of everyday existence, what he can derive from imaginative literature is an insight into the *mores* and the *folkways* of the period he is studying and into attitudes towards that most subtle but important topic, social class, or, for pre-industrial history, status. If he is to understand an age from, as it were, the inside, the essence of true historical thinking, he must saturate himself in the art and literature of that age. He must, in the words already quoted from G. M. Young, 'read and read until he hears the voices of the age speaking to him'. From this it will be clear that in writing of some particular period or topic a historian may, although his mastery of the literature is extensive, in the end make no direct reference to, or quotation from, any specific novel or poem. His reading will have shaped his understanding of his period, helped him to squeeze more out of his other sources, but it may not have given him one single piece of concrete information. On the other hand it may have done just that: the nineteenth-century social historian, suspecting from the fragmentary evidence of other sources (reform in the laws governing married women's property, for example, and the

speeches and articles written on this topic), that however little freedom
women may have had by today's standards, they were in mid-century a
little less unfree than they had been a generation or two earlier, might
well find his most specific utterances on this score in the novels of
Anthony Trollope. Such a novel as Trollope's *The Prime Minister*, too,
gives clear suggestions of the changing attitudes of aristocratic political
figures towards the rights of electors. This, perhaps, is no more than a
pointer, which the historian would have to verify from more conventional
sources. One striking pointer which, curiously, generations of historians
ignored, was Dickens's description (in *The Pickwick Papers*) of the
Eatanswill election. What reader, aware that the scene is set in the
1840s, could not at least begin to doubt the theory that the Great Reform
Bill of 1832 completely cleaned up the British electoral system? In fact,
as the leading authority on the period, Professor Norman Gash, has
pointed out, Dickens erred on the side of restraint when he described
the electoral malpractices of the time.[4]

One metaphor which comes readily to hand in this sort of discussion
is that of art and literature being 'a mirror of the age'. Like most such
metaphors this one begs more questions than it answers. The basic
notion involved is that of the *Zeitgeist*, the 'climate of the age'; a
useful concept, though one subject to constant abuse. If there is an
identifiable climate, it is the creation of a relatively small group in
society, the practitioners of the arts and their audience; the practitioners,
though, may well be responding to stimuli which spring from the state
of the wider society – intense religious conflict, buoyant economic
circumstances, imperial decline. A description of the 'intellectual
climate' of any particular age, derived largely from a study of the
creative artists and writers of that age, may very well be an important
part of historical study in that it contributes to our understanding of
that age. More than this, it is from ideas in the minds of men that much
of the stimulus towards social and political change originates: so the historian, concerned with the problems of change through time as all
historians are, must study the prevailing intellectual ideas of a particular age, the countervalent ideas being brought forward, and the
state of the conflict between two.[5] Finally it should be said that since the
highest achievement of any society is its creative art, the historian of
that society, though too often incapable of anything more than a
weary catalogue of names and titles, must be concerned with this creative
work in, as it were, its own right. The mirror of art, too, can be held
to the face of society, to see whether it lives and breathes, or is mori-
bund.

Occasionally in a bibliography a historian, after enumerating primary
and secondary authorities, will suddenly make an announcement to
the effect that actually the reader will learn far more about the period

by reading one or two good novels. Often this is a somewhat hypocritical gesture, designed to persuade the reader that the historian is not such a stuffy chap after all. No one could really learn more about a past age from a handful of novels than he could from one authoritative textbook. Yet undoubtedly the penetrating insights, the deep sense of social awareness of the gifted novelist can enable him firmly to grasp at least one segment of the age about which he is writing. The historian, and layman, who ignores the imaginative literature of the period he is studying is as foolish and incomplete in comprehension as the historian or layman who relies exclusively on such material.

Recent historians, well up in the current fashions, have tried to give a special primacy among primary materials to sources of a non-literary type: statistics of gross national output, demographic tables, aerial photographs, industrial archaeology. Yet the wisdom acquired by the traditional historian among his written sources is not to be lightly brushed aside: treat every fragment of evidence circumspectly; take nothing on trust. The newer types of source material are not, in absolute terms, more reliable (or less reliable) than the older ones: they are better for answering certain questions, but they still have to be approached with the traditional caution. Human errors creep into the compilation and recording of statistics; statistics do not in themselves provide answers – it is still the historian who must frame the questions, most usually in the light of the other types of evidence at his disposal. Aerial photographs of the village of Leighton Bromswold in Huntingdonshire reveal additions to the village as, from a survey plan of 1680, it was known to exist at that date. But as M. W. Beresford and J. K. S. St Joseph, two leading authorities on aerial photography, remark, these additions 'are capable of two interpretations between which only documentary evidence or excavation may some day arbitrate'. They sum up their own experiences in the following manner:

> Sometimes interesting photographs suggested profitable research among documents which might explain them; sometimes documents suggested profitable photographs. Some of the topics illustrated are well known to historians, and the only novelty lies in the clarity and comprehensiveness which air photographs can give. Still other topics, it is believed, receive a fresh contribution when the subject-matter is seen from the air. The function of the air photograph is not always that of making new discoveries, but of clarifying what is but partly visible on the ground.

They then speak of the 'documentary and the pictorial tool of research' working 'in alliance'.[6] What is said here is true of the relationship between all non-traditional sources and documentary sources: the historian must make full but critical use of every resource at his disposal, allocating no false primacy to any particular one.

Unhappily there are still reputable historians of today who wish to deny that those who work in non-traditional sources are in any authentic sense historians at all: this is to arrogate 'no documents, no history' into a fetish; to assert the supremacy of method over purpose. Every society has a past; every society has a need to know its past; and every society, in some form or another, has a recorded interpretation of that past. A history based exclusively on non-documentary sources, as say the history of an African community, may be a sketchier, less satisfactory history than one drawn from documents; but it is history all the same. It was in fact Collingwood who remarked that 'the enlargement of historical knowledge comes about mainly by finding how to use as evidence this or that kind of perceived fact which historians have hitherto thought useless to them.' Marc Bloch was a celebrated exponent of this doctrine, and today historians of Africa are making fruitful use of the evidence afforded by such disciplines as ethnobotany, linguistics, serology (the study of blood-groups) and the study of folk-lore.

Sources are basic; but they are many and varied. Occasionally an important new interpretative work is produced by a historian working exclusively from secondary works; but in general it would be correct to say that a truly great work of history will be rooted in the primary authorities. That certainly is the way in which historians themselves look at the matter. When H. G. Richardson and G. O. Sayles unleashed their devastating attack on the heresies of medieval history which they claimed had held the field since the time of Stubbs, they started out with that elemental hunting call which no historian could ignore:

> It is to the sources, to a representative assembly of texts at the very least – not, we may emphasise, a selection carefully chosen to bolster up some foregone conclusion – that we would direct the reader who would know the truth. And we shall have failed in our aim if we do not persuade some of our readers to look, or look again, at the sources. If with the aid of texts unknown to us or perchance misunderstood by us, they are able to confute us, none could more willingly submit to correction. We would, however, be spared the censure of those who may be moved to contradict without examining the texts we have cited in our notes.[7]

2 THE WRITING OF HISTORY

If the historian discover the most revealing of private source collections, what shall it profit him if he fail to communicate the significance of his find to his fellows? Not much. The historian at work, as Professor W. H. Walsh has noted, has a 'double task': 'He must do justice to his evidence and at the same time must do his duty by his readers.'[8] His readers in many cases may simply be other historians, but this does not mean that he can escape the problems which arise in the writing of history.

Certain basic problems of presentation, of course, are far from unique to the historian. In the first instance, as is pointed out in the early chapters of that indispensable work, *The Modern Researcher* (1957) by Jacques Barzun and Henry F. Graff, the historian engages in the common activity of making a report: his activity at this level is not different from that of an Inspector-General reporting back to the Czar of Russia on his tour of investigation, of an ambassador reporting home to his own government, of a newspaper reporter preparing his copy on the latest five-alarm fire, or of the chief medical officer reporting on the health of the population. 'History is easy: all the historian does is to ascertain the facts and report them.' 'Ascertaining the facts', we have noted, is a complicated business, but this favourite topic for discussion (and demolition) among teachers of historiography is wrong even in its supposition that reporting is easy. Once a corpus of facts has been ascertained the reporter, of whatever description, inevitably has a problem of *selection*. Does the newspaper reporter, detailed to cover a murder case, give the ages of all witnesses, does he give a full description of all the more interesting younger women in the case, or does he stop at the conventional 'pretty, twenty-two-year-old . . .'? As important to even the most simple report is the question of form: that is to say, the report *must be systematic* and orderly in presentation:

Facts and ideas in disorder cannot be conveyed to another's mind without loss and are hardly likely to carry much meaning even for the possessor. This is because the mind is so constituted that it demands a minimum of regularity and symmetry, even in the arrangement of toilet articles on top of a bureau.

In written matter, Barzun and Graff continue, 'the most frequent and visible failure of *form* is that which comes from wrong emphasis':

Organisation distributes emphasis in the right places. The mind cannot give equal attention to every part; it must be guided to those parts – of a sentence or a book – which it should attend to for a correct understanding.[9]

Common to every report, then, is the labour of organising facts and ideas so that the reader takes from it exactly the meaning which the writer intended to put in it. The undergraduate student may not in his history essay be making any contribution to historical knowledge, but he should at least be mastering the essential elementary principles of presentation.

However, that is only the start; the writing of history presents certain important problems of its own, many of which are encountered at every level of historical writing. Because of the intense richness and complexity of historical experience, the problem of selection is a particularly acute one. Having unearthed a wealth of biographical information on a hitherto unknown historical personage, the historian may be tempted to unload all he has discovered, thus distorting the significance of this personage relative to others mentioned in his account. Information provided for the sake of information is not really information at all: the historian must himself be aware of its significance and make that significance clear to his reader. The phrase 'it is important to note that . . .' is often a warning that the historian has a piece of information which he feels he'd better set down, but about the importance of which he is not really at all clear. As Dr Kitson Clark has remarked: 'One of the earliest and most painful lessons which a young researcher must master is that much that he has discovered with difficulty, and with some exaltation, will prove in due course to be of no significance and of no imaginable interest, and in the end will have to be left out.'[10]

The problem of form in historical writing is also peculiarly acute because not only must the historian represent the complexity of past experience, he must represent it in movement through time. The historian must achieve a balance between narrative and analysis, between a chronological approach and an approach by topic, and, it should be added, a balance between both of these, and, as necessary, passages of pure *description* ('setting the scene', providing routine but essential information, conveying the texture of life in any particular age and environment). When S. R. Gardiner wrote his great seventeenth-century *History*, he composed it year-by-year, completing his study of one year before he would even allow himself to turn to the documents he had amassed for the study of the succeeding year. Thucydides and the other ancients never departed from the strictly chronological approach. Diplomatic and political historians today often find the chronological method the most satisfactory one. On the whole, however, it can be said that any historical writer, whether at the undergraduate or the highest professional level, who reduced his subject entirely to chronological narrative would incur the grave risk of being accused of intellectual naïvety – though it is too easily forgotten that the establishment of the sheer chronology of events is one of the fundamental, and sometimes most difficult, tasks of the historian. However, generally speaking, straight narrative is the easiest form of historical writing save that it is not usually very historical. Its fault, as Barzun and Graff have pointed out with their usual incisiveness, is

that it mixes events great and small without due subordination, and that it combines into a parody of life incidents that occur only once with permanent truths about habits and tastes, character and belief.[11]

On the other hand it may be possible (contrary to the views of Barzun and Graff) to produce an excellent historical study based entirely on analysis by topic: Namier did this in his great eighteenth-century studies. Yet undoubtedly there is danger in the purely analytical approach, for it may easily forfeit the fundamental historical essence of change through time. Furthermore an analytical study spread over too long a period may seriously distort the objective reality of the past if it treats on the same footing material culled throughout the period on topics which may meantime have undergone significant change, as, for example, 'the merchants', 'Puritan attitudes', 'the constitution', or 'the price of corn'. In general, therefore, the historical writer will usually strive for the combination of narrative and analysis which best conforms to the requirements of his subject and to the requirements of form. One method, useful, if not always very elegant, is to alternate chunks of narrative with chunks of analysis: by and large this was the pattern of the older volumes of the *Oxford History of England*. Another effective technique involves breaking the entire chronological period of study into a number of sub-periods, chosen, not arbitrarily, but on the basis of some logic of historical development perceived by the historian in the course of his inquiry: then, within each sub-period the material is analysed topic by topic, one topic possibly being given primacy in one sub-period, while perhaps a completely new topic is introduced in a different sub-period. Christopher Hill's study of the seventeenth century, *The Century of Revolution* (1961), is a good example of this method at its most straightforward. The separate sub-periods taken are 1603–1640, 1640–60, 1660–88 and 1688–1714: within each sub-period he discusses in turn 'Economics', 'Politics and the Constitution' and 'Religious Ideas'. An effective compromise which keeps up the narrative flow throughout the book is that adopted by Asa Briggs in his study of Britain in the period 1780–1867, *The Age of Improvement* (1958), where the material is grouped round a succession of key concepts which form the chapter headings, with a flexible range of sub-sections within chapters allowing for a balance between narration and analysis. An early chapter, for instance, is fixed on 'The Impact of [the French Revolutionary] War'; there are later ones which in fact cover the same chronological period, the 1830s and 1840s, first from the aspect of guided political change – 'Reform' – then from the aspect of the nature of society at the time – 'Social Cleavage'. Denys Hay's *Europe in the Fourteenth and Fifteenth Centuries* (1966) adopts a tripartite design: the early chapters display and analyse the main social groups; the long middle section carries the narrative forward by outlining the main changes in political life; finally thematic unity, which political narrative always threatens to tear apart, is restored through a survey of the main unifying forces, religious, cultural and commercial.

Apart from getting his form, selection, narrative, analysis and descriptive passages right, the historian will bring to his writing certain ideas about the way things were likely to happen (and unlikely to happen) in his chosen area of study, and certain ideas about how to communicate these 'happenings' in a manner which both satisfies the demands of form and yet does not do intolerable violence to the complexities of his subject. Here we come up against the inescapable truth that history is the science of the mature, that it is not, at its highest levels, a subject for young minds (though young minds, naturally, may be readiest to open new approaches to historical study). We come close, too, to that mystique of historical writing to which the wilder social scientists take such exception. Let us remember that there are 'gifted' sociologists and 'gifted' physicists, as well as 'gifted' (and 'ungifted') historians; and that it is usually the plodders who are keenest upholders of the doctrine that intellectual eminence comes by hard work and observance of certain clear-cut rules. Richard Pares once defined history as 'a series of bright ideas'[12] (he also said that no one under the age of twenty-five should study history). One should perhaps make a distinction between the basic ideas which the historian through experience (and, hopefully, sound instruction) develops about how to give a tolerable representation of the complexity of the past, and the bright insights with which he illuminates his study. The two are intimately related certainly, for where there is no relationship it is open to the veriest tyro, operating in a complete void as far as historical knowledge is concerned, to coin witty aphorisms and coruscating generalisations which in fact have no foundation in historical reality. One of the results of the amateur tradition in British and American universities is that students are too often given high praise for wit and verbal felicity even when these gifts merely combine to produce complete historical nonsense. Here we shall look first at some of the basic ideas which the historian brings to bear on his writing of history, then at the question of 'bright ideas' and of 'generalisation' – a word, as usual, with many shades of meaning.

The historian must always be on the look-out for elements of continuity, for illuminating parallels and comparisons drawn between one age and another and one country and another; but essential to historical thinking, and therefore to historical writing, is the avoidance of anachronism, that is the importing into the past of concepts which only have reality in the present; equally the historian must not import into a study of nineteenth-century China standards of political and social behaviour which were prevalent only in the industrialising West. Because he is so conscious of the way in which the past is different from the present, the historian must also be conscious that the future will be different from the present. This, for example, is why, although we admire him so much on other grounds, we can be critical of Ranke as a historian when he accepts the Prussian national state as the ideal end of the historical process. The historian must always suppress the severe temptation to write as if the seeming reality of the time in which he is writing (a 'reality' which may instantly dissolve as events take a new turn) is an inevitable outcome of the historical processes he is studying.

Probably only an infinitesimal fraction of all practising historians have any kind of theory of causation worthy of the dignity of that title: but at least practised historians learn to avoid the naïvety of monocausal explanation, of *post hoc propter hoc*, or of indiscriminately listing a haphazard series of 'causal factors' (though too many middle-range professionals, perhaps, still do this). Very rightly, there has been a strong reaction in recent years against the kind of historical writing which argued that because somebody recommended a certain course of action centuries or decades before the course of action was actually taken, that person automatically becomes a 'cause' of the course of action: thus Wycliffe, without further thought, is a 'cause' of the English Reformation. Much bad so-called intellectual history is still written along the lines of 'so-and-so said it first, therefore he must be important', though the actual implementers of the Act, Revolution, or what have you may quite probably never even have heard of so-and-so. 'Ball-of-string' history of this sort is the easiest history to write. Lucien Febvre, who, we have seen, spoke of the 'multiplicity of profound causes', defined the three variables in historical causation as contingency, necessity and idea. Richard Pares thought there must be at least four or five independent variables: climate, war, religion, technology and science, and the 'condition of production'.[13] Some historians, no doubt, prefer instead to keep at the back of their minds the notion of the dichotomy between 'ideal factors' and 'material factors': Professor Herbert Butterfield in his *Origins of Modern Science* suggested that the development of modern science was inspired by the *idea* that natural phenomena were not unpredictable (though it is quite possible that this idea, part of what is conveniently called the 'Renaissance spirit', was inspired by material changes in conditions of production).

Even those historical writers who have no conscious thoughts on the principles of historical causation (the vast majority, one suspects) do have to be aware of the distinction between explanation and description (itself a useful, but inevitably less taxing, function) or, indeed, disguised narration. To say that a certain war *accelerated* improvements in the conditions of the lower orders may be excellent as a description of what actually happened, but it does not explain anything. Consider this passage from a widely used textbook of twentieth-century American history:

As for the war, it had raised the living standard of factory workers and built a powerful labor movement; it had created great shifts in popu-

lation and accompanying tensions. It had given a temporary bonanza to
the farmer, stepped up mechanization of agriculture, and brought the
plow to tens of thousands of acres of semi-arid prairie grasslands.
Much of this transformation had been painful, and led to further difficult adjustments in the twenties. War also had changed styles and
fashions, and molded consumer demands into new channels. In little
ways (such as in the introduction of wrist watches for men, shorter
skirts for women, and cigarettes for both) and in major ways that
involved basic shifts in the economy, it was changing the pattern of
life for most Americans.[14]

This is a splendid summary of changes which took place over the
period of the First World War, but, of course, it does not in any way
explain why the war should have brought such changes: although as
narrative it penetrates below the mere surface flow of events, it is nonetheless narrative.

'Bright ideas' are often an effective means of historical explanation,
both of *why* something came about, and of *what* something was. An example of the first is the notion developed in A. V. Dicey's *Law and
Opinion in England* (1902) of the *fait accompli*, that is to say the
notion that once something is done by a government, however little
advance support there may have been for the action, it will generally
gain the approval of the populace at large as a *fait accompli*; opinion
research conducted more recently by political scientists has provided
empirical validation for this 'bright idea'. Marc Bloch developed the
fertile notion that the traditionalism inherent in peasant societies was
basically due to the manner in which young children were mainly in
the company of their grandparents, since working conditions kept their
mothers and fathers out most of the day. An example of the second sort
of bright idea, explaining *what* something was, is Maitland's brilliant
elucidation of the meaning of *sake* in the medieval phrase *sake and
soke*: though the word has practically gone out of existence, it still
appears in what must be its medieval sense, as Maitland pointed out, in
the phrase 'for my sake'. Bright ideas in another form often spring from
the historian's function as communicator, from his search for form at
its most economical and elegant, and from his desire to arrest attention
for a particularly important point. The test to be applied here is whether
the bright idea is designed purely for literary effect, or whether it
throws genuine light on a genuine problem. Sometimes the attempt at
elegance, the effort to arrest attention, collapses into the same meaning-
lessness which tends to afflict the cautious historical writer who seeks
never to give a precise evaluation of anything, never to give one thought
preponderance over another, never indeed, to have any thoughts at all.
A metaphor, intelligently and aptly used, can be a great aid to communication and understanding. But equally metaphors can be used to

conceal meaning, or lack of it. When the reader encounters a torrent of tortured metaphors he may well suspect that the historian himself no longer quite knows what he is talking about. The protracted metaphor is usually to be distrusted: a specific incident between two powers may, if the writer has a liking for particularly hackneyed metaphors, be likened to a match being held to a fuse; but it will be unwise to endeavour to liken certain other events to the heaping of gunpowder, or to the temporary extinction of the fuse, or to the adding of petrol, or what have you: here the metaphor takes over from the historical events, and it is not often that the pattern of history follows that of a true metaphor. Often metaphors are simply neutral: they do little harm, but they don't really say anything either. Here is a quotation within a quotation where it is hard to say which is feebler, the absurd metaphor or the would-be balanced, though in fact meaningless, assessment of it (*what* exactly is 'exaggerated', and how much is a 'modicum'?):

'All the cards in the hand of her (France's) post-liberation destiny', says . . . (Mr R. Mathews in *The Death of the Fourth Republic*) 'had been dealt by April 1945; it only remained for time to play them.' Such a view, though exaggerated, does contain a modicum of truth.[15]

All the great historians have been masters of the telling phrase, of neat incapsulations or brilliant paradoxes. Sometimes these are of very limited and specific application, as for instance Professor Esmond Wright's justly famous comment on John Adams: 'He carried his rectitude like a banner: and he stopped now and then to salute it' (*The Fabric of Freedom 1763–1800* (1961)). More often they verge on the twilight land of the historical generalisation: 'Chamberlain's virtues were worse than Baldwin's vices', for instance, though completely specific in its terms, does offer a general statement about two entire Prime Ministerial careers. But, of course, bright ideas can be much more general than that. We can proceed on up an ascending scale towards such famous apophthegms as Lord Acton's 'Power tends to corrupt, and absolute power corrupts absolutely.' Such statements, of course, are not uttered in the same spirit as the formulation of a scientific law. Alan Bullock has pointed the matter up clearly:

When Marx says 'The history of all hitherto existing society is the history of class struggles', Marxism as a system stands or falls by the truth of such a generalisation. Its only interest in history is to produce such generalisations. But when Professor Namier says 'The relations of groups of men to plots of land form the basic content of political history', it does not matter whether this is only partially true. It does not invalidate his investigation.[16]

There is a world of difference between these 'bright ideas', these *ad hoc* generalisations, as it were, and the systematic use of generalisation to bring order to the chaotic world of history, to draw history nearer to the orbit of the social sciences. Much heavy weather has been made of the problem of generalisations in the more normal sense. Rightly it is pointed out that there are 'regularity' generalisations which historians have usually avoided like the plague, and 'labelling' (or 'classificatory') generalisations upon which the historian calls every time he mentions 'revolutions', 'wars', 'the middle classes', 'liberalism' or any other category of events, persons or ideas. The problem to consider for the moment is that in writing history one must always be conscious of how often recourse is had to generalisation, and one must always be ready to check afresh the validity of each generalisation. The succession of bright ideas can quickly become a series of dim platitudes. Historians, benefiting from their contact with the social scientists, occasionally coin new classificatory generalisations of their own. Sometimes there is a tendency to confuse the inventing of a new label with the discovery of a new truth. But often new labels are needed before new truths can be perceived. For instance, in their valuable study of that most important phenomenon, the working-class Conservative in urban England, Mackenzie and Silver made the illuminating distinction between the 'secular' voter, who votes on a pragmatic assessment of his own self-interest, and the 'deference' voters, whose behaviour is governed by a belief that the upper class knows best: young people, they noted, tend to be 'secular' rather than 'deference' voters.[17]

Regularity generalisations we can leave aside as a non-problem as far as the normal writing of history is concerned. What is critically important, however, is the question of the theme, or thesis, which binds any piece of historical writing together. Partly this is again a matter of *form*: a disconnected series of gobbets of miscellaneous information and analysis, however interesting in themselves, is unlikely to do its duty by the needs of the reader. At the same time to impose some arbitrary thematic unity is to make the same, only more massive, error, as the perpetrator of the bright but unhistorical paradox. Usually an intelligently conducted historical inquiry will in fact reveal one or more themes upon which a report can be intelligently structured. In a shapeless piece of historical writing the fault is usually not simply one of presentation, but a failure in research, a failure in asking the right questions of the source materials. Most historical writing is of such a humble order that the basic theme is already implicit in the terms of reference which the writer has himself provided. Just after the Second World War the distinguished American scholar S. R. Graubard wrote a paper on 'Military Demobilization in Britain following the First

World War', a narrow but interesting topic, strung upon a natural tension between the good intentions of the British Government and the frustrations of the British soldier. Nonetheless the young Professor Graubard was not able to let well alone: he ended his article with some high-sounding platitudes about the British policy operating by 'trial and error' and (in ghastly mixed metaphor) about the experience gained having enabled the British Government at the time of writing 'to avoid at least some of the pitfalls which plagued similar efforts more than a quarter of a century ago'.[18] Nothing was thereby added to the value of his historical account. A similar case (among multitudes) is that of Miss Pauline Gregg's *The Welfare State* (1967). Again this social history of Britain in the period 1945 to 1960 would seem to have a natural unifying theme in 'the welfare state', as a concept whose meanings and implications can be explored through the various events of the period. In fact the title proves to be a false one, masking a disconnected series of essays, each an individual primer of miscellaneous (though valuable) facts. To make up for the lack of thematic unity and the lack of analysis (there is also, it may be said, even a lack of any sense of chronological development), the author supplies a few little homilies on the mass media, crime and the uses of leisure. It is a common human weakness to want to make a point, to be remembered for some bold affirmation: but a relatively trivial piece of historical writing does not cease to be trivial because some grandiose conclusion has been tacked on to it; and there is as wide a difference between a moralising homily and a critical historical evaluation as there is between copy-writer's rhetoric and an authentic estimate of historical significance (two things which are also sometimes confused).

All this brings us back to the business about moral judgements in history; for it is always easier to dish out praise and blame, and thus to seem to be offering more than mere narrative and description, than it is to provide analysis of motive and assessment of circumstance. Moral judgements, we have seen, cannot, and need not be, avoided. Certain phrases used by the historian inevitably carry moral overtones: phrases like 'religious persecution', 'military atrocities', 'faction', 'sinister moves'. But the best historical writing will be that where the evidence marshalled by the historian speaks for itself: where it is not necessary for the historian to add his own thunderous denunciations. The best advice on all these points is this: when you have finished, stop.

3 SOME TECHNICALITIES

The actual process of turning the 'raw' primary source materials into a finished piece of history offers some further special problems of presentation. A solid academic monograph is often distinguished by the frequency with which the ordinary broad type gives place to long passages in that forbidding small type which signals a direct quotation from (usually) a primary source; for the reader it is rather like driving along one of those foul British motorways where every so often one's progress is curbed by the sign 'Road narrows'. Yet to my mind those excellent counsellors Barzun and Graff fail us when they recommend that quotations 'must as far as possible be merged into the text'. In general it is true, as they say with all the force of the italics at their disposal, that *'quotations are illustrations not proofs'*; but, remembering the special difficulties of 'proof' in historical study, it is far from being always true. Quite often the whole burden of a particular phase of a historian's argument depends upon the text of a new document which he has discovered, or upon a new significance which he has seen in certain sentences in a well-known document. In such cases he must give his quotations the prominence of indentation and separate type: the last thing he wants to do is to merge this vital material with his own potentially inept text (as he will admit if he has due humility – an earlier generation of historians had the irritating habit of writing their books as, in essence, a paraphrase of what they conceived to be the basic documents for their topic, 'merging' reliable authorities, dubious authorities, and their own errors and prejudices into one undifferentiated whole). Frequently there is no better means at the disposal of the historian for conveying a sense of period, a sense of understanding from the inside, than by an unadulterated direct quotation from a contemporary source. Even where the quotation is simply illustrative, its illustrative value will stand out all the more clearly for being given the dignity of proper presentation. In this present book of mine the reader will find many quotations served up in this special dignified way, as for example on pages 124, 125 and 126. Here I am, of course, anxious, for reasons I hope made clear in the text, to cite the views of important writers with whom I am not myself in entire agreement. To merge these quotations, to 'make their knowledge my own',[19] as Barzun and Graff stipulate, would patently be absurd. How, finally, one 'merges' a poem, a folksong, or a couple of lines of dialogue from a television programme, all of which could legitimately be cited as *illustration* or even as *proof*, these authors do not say.

However, there can be no doubt that, as always, they have a point. Clearly a technique of presentation which is necessary in an academic monograph may be much less suitable for other levels of historical writing; and of course it is open to abuse by the writer of an alleged scholarly monograph. There is all the difference in the world between the deliberate full-dress citation of a long quotation for some definite historical purpose, and the mere stringing together of a miscellaneous collection of such quotations in the hope that the end product will pass for a kind of history. When one comes to the undergraduate essay, or the work of historical popularisation drawing exclusively upon secondary authorities, there will usually be little justification for the indented quotation, save perhaps in the case of a particularly striking and important passage with which the writer does not himself agree but around which he wishes to build up an argument, or of a genuine piece of primary material (no doubt culled from a secondary source). On the whole, quotations should be kept to an absolute minimum in both popularisations and undergraduate essays. The opinion that a case is somehow clinched by citing the direct speech of one or two authorities is as erroneous as it seems to be widespread: a silly unhistorical judgement is no less silly because it happens to have been once uttered by a once-eminent authority. The writer who embarks upon that dialogue with the reader which we have several times stressed as integral to historical writing must be sure that it is his side of the dialogue that he is expressing and not an assortment of ill-digested and misunderstood items culled from other people. 'Scissors-and-paste' is the contemptuous phrase we rightly apply to a piece of would-be historical writing which in practice amounts to little more than such an assortment.

Presumably before he even embarks on any historical work the reader has noted the name of its author: should he become specially outraged, he has at most simply to turn back to the title-page to detect the perpetrator of the outrage. When apprised by quotation marks or indentation that a certain passage is a quotation from some different source, the reader has an equal right to have that source identified. Above all where the entire thesis of a scholarly work is built up on primary materials, these materials must be fully identified to the reader so that he may derive at least some inkling of what trust to put in the interpretation placed before him. The easiest way to provide this necessary identification of both primary and secondary sources is a note at the foot of the page, or, less desirably, at the end of the chapter or of the book. Only fools scoff at the historian's footnotes and references. Significantly it was the absurdly complacent planners of the old *Cambridge Modern History* who thought they could do without footnotes – nobody could doubt *their* experts. We are wiser today: no work which claims serious scholarly attention deserves that attention unless it is equipped with the full apparatus of references, provided to enable the reader, if he wishes, to participate to the full in his side of the dialogue, and as a guide to future researchers in the same field.

And here we have the only true rationale for the rules governing this technical branch of scholarship: references are for use, not show; and they must be furnished in such a way that they are genuinely useful. Almost always there is some good reason for the finicky styles of presentation evolved by scholars: for example, if it has come to be accepted that a certain source is cited in a certain way, it is obviously sensible for all researchers to follow the same practice rather than introduce possibly confusing styles or abbreviations of their own. From the point of view of detailed scholarship it is often important to know whether a particular document cited is published or unpublished (that is, manuscript, or perhaps typescript): scholars therefore have adopted the convention of italicising (or underscoring) published materials, while printing unpublished ones in the ordinary way. However, more critically important is an understanding on the part of the historian of why he bothers to provide references at all. As he doesn't want to take up all his space with them he naturally endeavours to set them down in as economical a fashion as possible (hence the various Latin abbreviations, loc. cit., ibid., and so on, which we need not bother with here), but at the same time he must provide just enough information for another researcher to track down without difficulty the same reference. It is a *sine qua non* of the scholarly reference that it be honest. This is why some historians insist upon a golden rule that before any work is published all references must be checked. But there is, of course, a difference between the inaccuracy which is human, and wilful dishonesty (also, alas, all too human). If I confess that I do not myself go in for the systematic checking of my own references, I can add that I have had occasion to regret my own carelessness when endeavouring to follow up and take further some of my own previous researches, finding certain materials much harder to retrace than my own footnotes would suggest. The historian should always remember that his most dedicated reader may well turn out to be himself.

Earlier in this section I mentioned the case of the undergraduate essayist or popular writer citing a piece of primary material which he has in fact lifted from a secondary authority; this is a practice which sometimes is forced upon even the most rigorous scholars. What is called for in the appropriate footnote is a statement both of the primary source involved, and of the secondary source from which it was in fact lifted. If the remarks quoted are clearly those of a Foreign Secretary or Ambassador there is little point citing as the reference, say, W. L. Langer, *The Franco-Russian Alliance 1890–1894*: the reader wants to know *which* Foreign Secretary or Ambassador, and, of course, *where* and *when*. But, on the other hand, to blandly give as the reference 'Aerenthal, Austrian First Secretary in St Petersburg to Kálnoky of the Russian Foreign Office, 10 November 1892' would be to give the dishonest and misleading impression that the dispatch itself (as distinct from Langer's quotation of it) had been studied. The reference required by honesty and common sense would be something along the lines of 'Aerenthal's dispatch . . . etc. . . . as quoted by W. L. Langer . . . etc.'[20] The need for a footnote reference arises in cases other than where a direct quotation has been made. Most of the time the historian takes from his sources, primary and secondary, not whole phrases for quotation, but one single idea, or one relatively simple piece of information, such as a wage rate, a price increase, or a decision made in some court or council; but again, obviously, an appropriate reference is called for.

Valuable historical works have been written with much less in the way of scholarly apparatus than the foregoing paragraphs would seem to call for: they remain good books, but to the extent that they irritate the serious reader who asks (as serious readers of any historical work must constantly ask) 'how does he know *that?*' they are less good than they might be. Since scholarly apparatus is there for use, in the end only common sense can determine how elaborate an apparatus any particular piece of writing requires. Where absurdity marches in is when a book which is clearly nothing more than a mish-mash of other secondary authorities without pretence to original scholarship attempts to masquerade behind the trappings of scholarship. Whatever the level of the book the duty remains upon the author to identify, at the minimum, his direct quotations; but where the full scholarly apparatus is manifestly inappropriate, as for example in this book where I can make no pretence to having thoroughly studied all the works of Ranke, Gibbon, etc., all the issues of *Annales* etc., or every item that pertains to the philosophy of history, it is possible to provide the necessary information in the text and in a few brief references.

From there let us move logically to the question of bibliographies. In the preface to volume three of his *Economic History of Modern Britain* J. H. Clapham went on record against

> What in my heart I regard as the rather pedantic and ostentatious tradition of the formal bibliography in a book which contains footnotes.

Nothing could be more disingenuous: the compilation of a bibliography is certainly a tedious chore and one which, a book finally finished, any author can be excused for shrinking from; but often, sad though the thought may be, it is the single most useful service he performs. Clapham and his generation rode high in the supreme confidence that if they wrote a book, that book would be read. They were probably wrong even then: Clapham's *magnum opus* is now much more used as a work of reference than read cover to cover. Increasingly in a busy age one 'savours' books, even good ones – reads carefully passages directly relevant to one's own immediate interest, skiffs through the rest. But what one certainly does want is a bibliography (not as a sign of the author's worthiness as a historian, but as an aid to one's own further reading and research), and one does not want to have to scan through the footnotes to compile one – a labour which properly rests with the author. There are few sights more ludicrous than one of those converted Ph.D. dissertations which some publisher has been prevailed upon to bring out with the minimum of alteration save that, in the interests of economy, the one portion that might conceivably be of use to others, the bibliography, has been chopped off.

The roots of this controversy really lie in the two rather separate functions which a bibliography may be held to perform. Originally it was intended as a kind of adjunct to the footnotes: a final statement of the sources upon which a certain piece of historical writing claimed to rest. It was (and, in the realm of pure scholarship, still is) reckoned the most serious of crimes to mention in the bibliography a source you have not actually consulted. One would certainly agree with Clapham that there seems little point in the bibliography repeating exactly the functions of the footnotes: it might well serve as a guide to *all* the relevant literature known to the author even if he has not been able himself to consult every item (as for example in the case of a book published after he has gone to press). However, this is a technical point on which historians are not agreed; what is important is for the writer to be clear what kind of bibliography he is compiling – nothing is less useful than a bibliography which merely presents a random selection of books neither representative of what the author has himself consulted, nor valuable as a reliable guide to further reading (this, for instance, is the criticism one would be forced to make of that otherwise excellent textbook *Post Victorian Britain* by L. C. B. Seaman). One minor point: should a bibliography be annotated or not? The answer, as so often to such questions: yes, if the annotations can be done authoritatively and helpfully (as, say, in most of the volumes of the *Oxford History of England*). Too often, however, annotations merely take the form of smart-alecky comments on minor works, interspersed with eulogies of anyone who might be likely to review the annotator's own book, or, perhaps, offer him a job.

4 MONOGRAPHS, INTERPRETATIVE SYNTHESES, TEXTBOOKS AND WORSE

All who endeavour to write history encounter some of the same problems, but, as we have already suggested from time to time, there are obvious differences in the level of activity and intellect upon which different writers are operating. Professor Elton has drawn a rigid distinction between 'amateur' historians and 'professional' historians, including in the former category many who undoubtedly make a professional living out of history:[21] Professor Oakeshott has distinguished between 'practical' and 'pure' history,[22] a distinction which, in all conscience, I find quite meaningless. Here it is proposed to stick within the relatively safe bounds of activity already touched upon, bounds which allow for the obvious fact that one historian will often operate in many different ways, sometimes writing a monograph, sometimes a textbook, sometimes appearing on television, sometimes going fishing and merely cogitating on his subject, sometimes going to a football match and boring his companions with irrelevant pseudo-historical comments; sometimes, in short, he is more practical than pure, sometimes most professional in his amateurism, or vice versa. Not that I can claim any special validity for my own terminology. 'Dissertation', 'learned article', 'monograph' and perhaps even 'standard authority' are terms with a fairly clear and precise connotation. 'Interpretative synthesis', however, is totally vague, and does not in fact exist as an accepted term for any particular form of historical writing, though I shall endeavour to make it serve as such. To some people 'textbook' is a term of praise, to others one of scalding abuse: it has no universally accepted meaning as a descriptive category. 'Pop history' is written by historians of impeccable academic distinction, and by journalists of none: often the work of the latter comes much closer to meeting the minimum standards of 'good' history than does the work of the former. The scale I shall work through here is not one of excellence, it is one of numbers: I shall start with the form of historian's activity which commands the smallest audience and proceed towards those with the largest audience.

The first major piece of serious historical research which most would-be members of the academic historical guild (those who both teach *and* research in history) undertake is that directed towards the universally misnamed degree of Doctor of Philosophy, or for some other research degree such as (in the United Kingdom) the M.Litt. or B.Litt. Within academic circles there is some uncertainty as to whether postgraduate work of this sort is mainly intended as an apprenticeship exercise in the nature and techniques of historical research whose value in that sense may stand high irrespective of the importance of the end product as a 'contribution to knowledge'; or whether it must, in its own right, stand as a genuine contribution to knowledge. There can be no doubt that in the earlier years of the twentieth century some truly significant work emerged in the form of the doctoral dissertation, particularly in the United States, and in the countries of Continental Europe. For a long time there was no special emphasis in Great Britain upon the doctoral degree: many gifted men who embarked upon it preferred to present

their early conclusions in the form of learned articles, and their more
rounded ones in the form of books, without ever going through the
rather laborious formality of submitting a doctoral dissertation. Now
even in the United Kingdom the doctorate is beginning to take on the
status of union card for the academic profession which it has always
had in the U.S.A. In both countries more and more students are embarking on Ph.D. degrees, though it sometimes seems that there are not
always enough contributions to knowledge still to be made. Some
dissertations, certainly, though they may well have served a purpose in
providing a necessary training for the budding historian, are of so trivial
a nature that they are patently not a contribution to knowledge. Dissertations vary enormously, of course; but in general it is expected of
the candidate that his research be conducted in depth over a very narrow
and specific field so that the bulk of the work will in fact be in the
primary sources. It is expected that he will provide to a full, even
exaggerated, degree all the apparatus of scholarship. In Britain it is
widely accepted that such criteria necessarily mean that a successful
Ph.D. thesis will not automatically be suitable for publication: even
though it be an important contribution to a specific area of knowledge,
it will still be too narrow and too technical to interest anyone beyond
the narrow band of specialists (perhaps three or four each year) who
will wish to consult it in the university library where it rests, or even
purchase it on microfilm. In America, however, such is the pressure on
the young academic to publish at all costs, and such is the desire of
minor university presses to have something to publish, that quite often
the narrowest and most unilluminating of dissertations are immediately
reborn as books. It is an American scholar who has spoken of 'converted
dissertations . . . with their Germanic earnestness and bulk footnotes
magnified in book length format'.[23]

When wiser counsels prevail the dissertation will either serve as the
basis for one or more learned articles, or its scope will be extended
(more research, wider reading) and it will be published as a reputable
academic monograph; or both. Perhaps I could cite my own experience
here, which is not untypical save in that my Oxford B.Litt. dissertation
(originally aimed at what that ancient university prefers to call the
D.Phil.) was a particularly poor piece of work (a reasonable collation
of primary material, but not properly worked through, or linked up
with anything beyond the narrow frontiers of the topic itself). The topic
was 'The [British] Independent Labour Party, 1918–1932'. The completed work I never attempted (and would never attempt) to publish –
though it sells a few copies each year on microfilm. It was instead
served up in the following manner: the whole boiled down into one
learned article for the *Bulletin of the Institute of Historical Research*;
one chapter, plus a little extra research, incorporated into another, later

article for the *Scottish Historical Review*; three chapters incorporated into my published biography of *Clifford Allen* (1964), whose private papers had been my most important single source for my dissertation. Though I have now switched my interests almost completely away from British labour history, I still occasionally dabble in it, and my dissertation at least provides me with some kind of footing in that subject. It so happens that while I was writing this dissertation at Oxford, R. E. Dowse was writing one on exactly the same topic at London (this coincidence, I think, was largely due to the fact that the Allen papers had just then become available for consultation, a common factor in determining lines of research at this relatively elementary level). Taking rather more time over his labours than I had done, Mr Dowse succeeded in producing an infinitely better piece of work: some years later, having followed the accepted British practice by doing further research round the edges of his subject, he published a complete study of the Independent Labour Party from its origins in 1893 up to the present. One might well cite this book, despite its rather eccentric title, *Left in the Centre* (1966), as a model academic monograph.

Many monographs and many articles, of course, originate elsewhere than in a postgraduate dissertation. Sometimes a historian has an idea which he reckons if followed up will yield an interesting article: as his research proceeds he finds he has a full-length monograph on his hands. Sometimes he writes a monograph and finds he has certain fragments left over, interesting in themselves, but of a nature to disrupt the thematic unity of his monograph: so he works these up into learned articles. An article of mine published in the *English Historical Review* in 1964, 'Middle Opinion in the Thirties: Planning, Progress and Political "Agreement" ', began essentially as a by-product of my Allen biography; it has proved in the upshot to be a rather more important contribution to knowledge than was the biography. The essence at any rate of both the learned article and the monograph is that they deal with one single, clearly defined topic, and they are based on all the relevant primary source materials: their contribution to knowledge, at the least, is that they make available hitherto unknown, or little-studied, pieces of primary source material (this is to ignore for the moment that very important, and increasingly favoured, type of learned article which conveniently summarises and synthesises existing knowledge and research in progress in some topic of rather wider character than those suitable for monographic study from primary materials).[24]

Occasionally a monogaph will capture the attention of a wider audience than that normally expected – an audience made up of other students and specialists. Usually this means that there is some element of controversy in the work, academic or topical, that the element of interpretation which must exist in any piece of historical writing is specially pronounced. Every scholar, of course, whatever his devotion to the primary sources, makes use of the work of his predecessors. Most monographs simply add a little more knowledge along lines not inconsistent with those established by older workers. But from time to time the new material presented in a monograph completely upsets existing lines of thought within some broad field of study. It is therefore idle to try to erect any barrier between the monograph and the work of interpretation: all history is interpretation. But what I wish to move on to is that type of historical work, broader in scope than the monograph, which presents a new synthesis not based exclusively on the author's own primary researches, though these may indeed have played a key part. Into this category fall such works as Henri Pirenne's *A History of Europe from the Invasions to the XVIth Century* (1936) and R. R. Palmer's *Age of the Democratic Revolution* (two volumes, 1959 and 1964), a book which opens up a whole new perspective on the events of the late eighteenth century by making a comparative study of the 'democratical' (a contemporary term) revolutions on both sides of the Atlantic seaboard, in the smaller countries as well as the larger. Professor Palmer has himself suggested that the 'original concept' for a historical work of this sort 'does and should come from two altogether different kinds of sources – (1) the knowledge that workable bodies of information exist and (2) some general idea'. Palmer's general idea 'held in advance, was that there had been a "revolutionary era" in all these countries, not adequately perceived as a "culture-wide" phenomenon'. His two majestic volumes are a brilliant elaboration of this hypothesis, drawing both upon detailed primary researches of his own, and, naturally in such a broad topic, upon the researches of others. Professor Palmer, it should be noted, has stressed that terms like *culture-wide* do not appear in his book: 'Whether or not such terms have any utility in social science, history in my opinion should be written in the ordinary language.'[25]

Important historical works, whether primarily monographic or synthetic (truly great works of history are in fact like a series of monographs run together, the historian making a synthesis of his own best primary research), aspire to the title of 'standard authority'. There is of course no code to which one can refer to determine which books achieve this status, but there is a clue in Namier's aphorism about 'the great historian' being

> like the great artist or doctor: after he has done his work, others should not be able to practise within its sphere in the terms of the preceding era.[26]

A 'standard authority' is one to which every student and every researcher in the field *must* refer. Namier's great eighteenth-century studies, though challenged in certain aspects by other historians from Herbert Butterfield onwards, are standard authorities, because it was and is impossible for anyone to practise in the sphere of eighteenth-century political history in the terms which were current before Namier's great onslaught. The debilitating weakness of the eighteenth-century volume in the Oxford history (*The Whig Supremacy*, by Basil Williams) was that it attempted to ignore the completely new approaches opened by Namier. Standard authorities stand the test of time a little better than most works of history, but of course eventually they too require substantial revision. Stubbs's *Constitutional History of England* is a standard authority, because Stubbs carried through a successful revolution in medieval studies. Perhaps Richardson and Sayles, the most devastating critics of Stubbs and his disciples (witting and unwitting), are also standard authorities; no one certainly could work in their field without first mastering their contributions in it. Maitland indisputably is a standard authority. Pioneers often become standard authorities, while those who stick to the well-trodden pathways usually end up minor historians. Oscar Handlin, who pioneered the study of immigrant groups in the United States, has become a standard authority on that topic. Standard authorities are usually easiest to identify in such spheres as history of science, or Far Eastern history, where, on the whole, experts are thinner on the ground.

What is a textbook? Probably the best way of arriving at an answer is by reference to the aims and intentions of the textbook-writer. He is not, in the first instance, set to work by the combination of 'some general idea' and 'the knowledge that workable bodies of information exist', but rather by the belief that there is a need among students and those outside the immediate circle of the professional guild for a clear and relatively simple exposition of the basic elements of some historical period or topic. Much more overtly than the monograph or the interpretative synthesis, the textbook will be geared towards immediate utility. Though laymen may read it, the prime intention will be that it should live out its life within the confines of the educational system, serving children or students at various levels (it is here distinguished from the work of popularisation, which is aimed at the lay audience). Often textbooks are written by expert professional historians of the calibre of a Palmer or a Sayles; but some of the most expert textbook-writers have written little else (though one might approach them rather cautiously if they had *never* had experience of working in the raw materials of history). Textbook-writing is not to be shrugged off as an undemanding occupation: in fact it poses most of the basic problems to be found in all forms of historical writing – selection, form, the balance of narrative and description against analysis. Furthermore, in interpreting the great authorities to his relatively unsophisticated audience, the textbook-writer has to achieve a certain authoritativeness of his own. Much of the dialogue between writer and reader goes into suspension because what the reader is seeking is clear and precise guidance. Textbook-writers are sometimes accused of lacking imagination and creative judgement; in fact their function is to present a balanced view of competing hypotheses, not to back one thesis (whether their own, or derived from some greater writer) to the hilt. Too frequently, unfortunately, the attempt at this sort of balance issues in a kind of meaningless neutrality: 'President Roosevelt did much to restore confidence, though many were worried by the increase in Federal powers.' Inevitably, therefore, the more stimulating textbooks have strong overtones of the interpretative synthesis. Professor Briggs's *Age of Improvement* (see above, p. 145) is one book which neatly straddles both categories; so, in briefer compass, is Eric Hobsbawm's textbook of modern British economic history, *Industry and Empire* (1967), where the Marxist inflections provide both stimulus and thematic unity, but where the basic task of providing a solid minimum of reliable information is properly fulfilled. By stressing, as historians are only slowly beginning to do, the social aspects of war, Gordon Wright imparted a special character to his authoritative textbook of European history, *The Ordeal of Total War* (1968). Sometimes a historian who sets out to write no more than a textbook finds his deeper instincts taking over and he ends up with a work which, though still admirable as a textbook, is also genuinely a work of creative synthesis. One might summarise the criteria by which a history textbook (on, or approaching, the level of a university or college) ought to be judged, in the following manner. First, it should be informed by an understanding of the older standard authorities in the period; where there is genuine scholarly controversy something of this should be reflected in the book. Secondly, it should reflect the latest major discoveries by contemporary researchers. Some scholarly matters, obviously, are too technical or too trivial to have place in a textbook; but no textbook should present interpretations which clearly conflict with received opinion among informed professional historians. Finally, even a textbook should carry with it some of the stuff and excitement of history: history, we all know, is not a mere succession of dates, of kings and presidents; nor does it divide neatly into three-paragraph sections, each of equal length and each amenable to some incapsulating title, such as 'The New Monarchy', 'The Age of Transition', 'Normalcy', 'Appeasement'; the man who can approach past events with a complete air of neutrality has no sense of history.

Textbooks aimed at more junior audiences are something of a different case; their writing involves much greater understanding of educational psychology than most professional historians can pretend to.

All one can ask is that school textbooks, still being the main contact which the majority of people have with history as a discipline, should not do more violence than is absolutely necessary to historical reality as revealed by the best recent academic writers; they should at least avoid both the aridity and the jingoism mentioned in the opening chapter of this book.

The layman who survives his school textbooks and allows himself in later life to give free rein to that interest in history which, I have suggested, is intrinsic to many human beings, will probably seek works of more popular character than those discussed so far. (In that textbooks have, as it were, a captive audience, they tend to eschew the literary graces.) But the category 'popular work', or even 'pop history', is not more clear-cut than any of the others. In the past, works of the great historians received a wide sale; today publishers have again become increasingly aware of the marketable quality of history, and certain books of the most unimpeachable academic pedigree have reached best-seller class (one thinks, for instance, of Robert Blake's *Disraeli* or E. P. Thompson's *The Making of the English Working Class*). This is as it should be: one of the historian's functions is that of *communication*, however much embittered academics may scowl upon colleagues whose books sell too well. Within the world of history a development is taking place analogous to that in the social world whereby increasing freedom in sex relations has reduced the market for the professional prostitute. The cloistered academic now seems to be taking the living away from the old-style pop historian, usually a journalist or some other kind of professional writer. Most of the old-style pop history was pretty dreadful: over-dramatised; over-personalised; given to little circumstantial accounts of how a certain person thought at a certain juncture, or how a certain room was decorated, when clearly there is not a whit of evidence on which to base such conjectures. Worse, such histories were frequently conceived in the most shapeless of narrative styles, the authors clearly hoping that the absence of anything verging on historical analysis would pass undetected in the colourful accounts of courtships, massacres, murder trials, sexual morals, and the idiosyncrasies of kings and politicians, enlivened by occasional witticisms. Into such a category fall a plethora of books about Mary Queen of Scots and about many other episodes in the history of her benighted land;[27] into it also fall the so-called 'social histories' of Frederick Lewis Allen (*Only Yesterday* (1931)), Robert Graves and Alan Hodge (*The Long Weekend* (1940)), Malcolm Muggeridge (*The Thirties* (1940)) and John Montgomery (*The Twenties* (1957) and *The Fifties* (1965)) – most of these read like a porridge of newspaper headlines with the odd lump of cliché about the influence of Freud, Einstein or affluence. Now that academics are increasingly writing for the wider market, the standard of pop history has risen greatly. It is instructive to compare two recent social histories of the period since the Second World War – both written by journalists – with the books just mentioned: both John Brookes's *The Great Leap* (1966) (referring to the U.S.A.) and Harry Hopkins's *The New Look* (1963) (referring to Great Britain) have a genuine sense of analysis: things don't just happen, the authors make some attempt at explanation. However, America still suffers from a sharper line of demarcation between the academic historian, who still seems to find it hard to write decent English, and the pop historian whose great stock-in-trade is the colourful descriptive passage: paradoxically the result is that certain approved pop historians are wildly overrated in the U.S.A. Thus Americans tend to think highly of Mrs Barbara Tuchman because she is readable, whereas in Britain, where there is some expectation that historians should be readable anyway, there are serious reservations about Mrs Tuchman's lack of historical sense. On the other hand, one of the great pioneers in breaking down the barriers which grew up in the early twentieth century between the professional historian and the lay audience was Alan Nevins, a journalist who rose to the heights of the American academic profession. Such journals as *American Heritage* (in the U.S.A.), *Historia* (in Italy), *History Today* and *Purnell's History of the Twentieth Century* (in Britain) have been successful in combining popular appeal with a preservation of high academic standards. And one area of historical study at least, military history, has developed its own body of writers quite detached from academic life, whose expertise academics challenge only at their peril.

Good history can be written by non-academics (that is by journalists, businessmen, etc.), many of whom have at an earlier stage had a historical training, and many of whom are only too happy to turn to the hard slog of historical research. The biggest advantage, probably, that the 'guild' historian has comes from living with his subject day in and day out, and above all, from teaching it: he is constantly forced to examine his thoughts, to organise them coherently, to face the pitfalls of historical explanation, to iron out inconsistencies, to eradicate non-explanations, to appreciate the difference between flowery rhetoric and genuine historical narration. But as pop history moves from the printed book to the television screen, the professional historian will find that his professional expertise must dovetail with that of cameramen, editors and other technologists. Such television series as *The Great War, The Lost Peace*, and *The Life and Times of Lord Mountbatten* bring out again that history is a social activity: on the whole, despite some lapses (falsified film, excessive naïvety in handling social trends, over-abundance of empty rhetoric, lack of thematic unity) these programmes were responsibly made, and called upon some of the best academic advice. Their supreme virtue lay in making available a convenient, viewable selection from the marathon mileage of archive film material (newsreels, etc.) – itself an important primary source for the historian of the modern period. As with the older forms of pop history, such programmes will go on being made whatever the academic historian thinks of them: on the whole it would seem best for him to accept that they too are a form of history – and an important one – and that it falls well within his province to do what he can to ensure that they are as historical as possible. For teaching purposes it is also possible, as has already been triumphantly demonstrated, for academics to go direct to the film archives (as a serious researcher would have to do) in order to compile their own secondary films.[28]

5 THE PLATITUDES AND CLICHÉS OF HISTORY

In the main, opinion within the historical guild favours the use of everyday language in historical writing; the jargon-laden excesses of much social science exposition has seemed to point a salutary warning. But the historian is at all times involved in the use of proper names and classificatory generalisations which raise all sorts of complicated problems. Professor Louis Gottschalk has referred to the ambiguities and implied assumptions contained in such an apparently simple phrase as 'Columbus discovered America on October 12 1492.' A more refined version, which highlights some of the problems, though it does not overcome all of them, is suggested by Professor Gottschalk: 'On a day conveniently labelled "October 12 1492" a group of sailors captained by a man known in English as "Christopher Columbus" landed on an island which was apparently the one [today] called "Watling Island".' The historian's problem, again to quote Professor Gottschalk, is seldom 'the paucity of ready-made labels . . . but rather the accuracy and fittingness of the available ones'.[29] Most of this section will be devoted to 'historical semantics', to the problems of the use and abuse of the labels which the historian does not always know what to do with, but which he knows he cannot do without; abused, as they so often are, these labels become the platitudes and clichés of history.

One of the most usual causes of the historian's difficulties is the manner in which down the ages men go on using the same word for something which is in fact constantly shifting in meaning and significance. 'Revolution' is a classic and well-worn instance. In origin the word apparently derives from the ancient conviction that the revolving spheres of the heavens directly affected the actions of men. The critical moment when radical political change achieved recognition as a self-conscious political process has been fixed in fourteenth-century Italy, where frequent upheavals in the towns gave currency to the term *rivoluzione*. This usage, however, was slow in spreading; it appears in English only at the beginning of the seventeenth century, just in time, as it happened, for the 'revolution' of the 1640s. Yet the word could still be used in its literal sense of a return to a previous state of affairs (the wheel coming full circle): the restoration of the monarchy in 1660 was deemed by Clarendon a 'revolution'. Only in the eighteenth century did the word become established, in both Britain and France, in its modern usage.[30] Yet what truly is its modern usage? A significant change in political structure carried through within a fairly short space of time: that might be an acceptable definition in that it covers what are universally agreed to be revolutions: the French ones of 1789, 1830 and 1848; the Russians ones of 1917; the Mexican one of 1906. However, leaving contemporary usage aside now, historians are very free in their use of the word, detecting educational revolutions, scientific revolutions, social revolutions, and even historical revolutions. We come to a second problem in the use of classificatory generalisations: most are heavily loaded emotionally. When the historian wishes to make a point forcefully he brings in the word 'revolution'. In this inexact, emotionally loaded usage, of course, historians are only copying the practice of the common man. Marc Bloch ruefully remarked that while the 'reactionaries of 1815 hid their faces in horror at the very name of revolution . . . those of 1940 used it to camouflage their *coup d'état*'.[31] The word had become respectable, even praiseworthy; however, for the historian, the best rule is to be as sparing in his use of it as possible.

Much that might otherwise be sadly misunderstood about our ancestors is clarified if it is remembered that 'liberty' once meant privilege; the wealthy supporters of 'Wilkes and Liberty' were much more concerned for their own rights as solid citizens than for 'liberty', in the modern sense, for the masses. 'Democracy' is another word which has gone through many shades of significance. We like now to give it a pretty precise meaning: political and social rights for *everyone*. But as used from Greek times onwards it represented a trend, a tendency towards broader-based government, rather than any kind of mathematical formula. To the Greeks, as to Queen Victoria, who once expressed the fear that the country might 'sink down into a democracy', the word had a pejorative quality. A more modern phrase which gives rise to a good deal of historical controversy, much of it essentially centred on the problem of definition, is 'welfare state'.[32] As usual it was the Germans who had a word for it: *Wohlfahrtsstaat* – used to describe the Bismarckian social insurance system of the 1880s. But although the term 'welfare budget' was sometimes applied in Britain to the Lloyd George budget of 1909 (more frequently and more aptly called 'the people's budget'), the phrase 'welfare state' was not used at all in English till the

1930s, when the classical scholar and historian Alfred Zimmern used it to point a contrast with the Nazi Power State. Its first appearance in print came during the Second World War in Archbishop William Temple's *Citizen and Churchman* (1941), and it was in fact the interest in social reform engendered by war which gave the term wide currency. In Britain the term tended to be associated with the 'universalist' principle in social legislation (welfare to everyone, whether rich or poor); on the European continent it was associated with the centralised direction of social policies. However when the word reached the United States in the late 1940s it assumed a much less thorough-going connotation (though still used as a term of abuse by the American Right). Some historians, mostly American, have attempted universal definitions for the phrase, but the social historian of the contemporary period, while, as always, interested in interrelations and comparisons, must accept that in practice it means different things in different countries.

The trouble with 'welfare state' is that it is a recent coinage which is still very much on the lips of politicians and publicists, and of many others who have no very clear idea what it means, save that they feel rather strongly about it. At the opposite pole there are labelling-words like 'sake and soke' or 'hide' (a quantity of land) that have gone altogether out of usage. Medieval historians have a good deal of difficulty with words which not only have gone out of existence but, in the process, have moved from one language to another – from, often, dog-Latin to medieval French. How to find a suitable rendering in modern English for a word in medieval French which is really a bad rendering of something originally in Latin is a fine problem. Translation, indeed, is another great source of imprecision in the handling of labelling generalisations. The Latin word *servus* became *serf* in West European usage, and *serf* is the word historians use to describe the unfree peasantry of medieval Europe; since the condition of the Roman *servus* was much different, historians reserve for him the term *slave*, though, as Marc Bloch has said, the term which is thereby transplanted into a Roman environment did not come into existence until about the year 1000, when it was used to describe the markets of human flesh where captive Slavs seemed to provide an example of a complete subjection by that time unknown in the West. 'The device', said Bloch, 'is useful, as long as we confine ourselves to extremes. In the intervening gap, where must the slave give way to the serf?' *Serf* is also widely used as a translation of the Russian *Krepostnoi*, though, according to Bloch, 'the so-called Russian serfdom had almost nothing in common with our medieval serfdom'.[33]

A curious double difficulty is embedded in the French word *ouvrier* (which today means workman) and its eighteenth-century English equivalent, manufacturer. At the time of the French Revolution *ouvrier* included what we would now call manufacturers, and manufacturers included what we would now call *ouvriers*: 'The English term has gone up in the world and the French one down.' The same historian[34] points out that '*Sans-culottes* is a political not an economic description: it could include a wealthy brewer . . . and exclude a valet or a footman.' Similar and even more difficult problems arise with the English term *radical*. By derivation the word ought to mean someone who wishes to carry through a reform 'from the roots'; in practice in nineteenth-century Britain it was a description adopted by men who sought reform in the direction of economic liberalism, but who stopped well short of anything which smacked of socialism. However defined, and the definition must vary with the period and groups studied, the term is certainly a political one; it does not define a social group, though most radicals were in fact middle-class.

The golden rule with a word like 'radical' would seem to be to use it as contemporaries themselves used it; yet contemporaries are not always as clear in their categorisation as the historian would like. Most of the older works on that interesting nineteenth-century British movement of protest, chartism, saw it as falling across a clear divide between 'physical force chartists' and 'moral force chartists', a rough-and-ready distinction which chartists themselves employed at the time. But modern historians have not really found it terribly helpful: the 'moral' appeal could often be a prelude to the assertion of 'natural liberties' by a show of force; violent language often concealed a complete reluctance to resort to force. On the whole, a sociological distinction between chartists of the relatively prosperous artisan class, and the 'hunger chartists' of the depressed factory areas has seemed a more fruitful distinction.

'Geographical abstractions' can be a peculiarly confusing type of label. It is hard sometimes to appreciate that the political map which we know, the labels we use and the boundaries we recognise, had no meaning during many centuries in the past. 'Great Britain', the entire island which includes the three separate countries of England, Scotland and Wales, is a term which still gives difficulty, many English nationalists and many foreigners preferring simply to say England; and the adjective 'Great', quite wrongly, is often taken as having imperialistic implications. Coined by the Romans from a native word, 'Britannia' was used throughout the Anglo-Saxon period, the 'Major' ('Great') coming in to point to the distinction from Lesser Britain – Brittany in northern France. The term entered into (more or less) regular modern usage with the proclamation in 1603 of James VI of Scotland as James I of Great Britain.

Trickier terms, as Denys Hay has explained, are 'Europe' and 'Christendom': 'There is no doubt', he writes, 'that we have had too much *Europe* about our history, too little *Christendom*.' It is true that Christendom as a unifying idea was long in emerging; but up to its clear emergence in the tenth century its alternative was not Europe, which did not receive acceptance as the only framework for politics and culture until the seventeenth century. Professor Hay admits that it may be necessary to talk of 'the history of Europe' in an earlier period:

> A series of books, or a series of lectures has to have a general title, and it is legitimate . . . 'to trace the medieval ancestry of Europe'. But that is what one must do – not treat the modern grouping of countries as the basis of the past. In the eleventh century even fewer men than today concerned themselves about the larger unities; but those who did thought in religious terms and if we wish to penetrate their world we must do something similar – that it was not religion as we now know it makes the problem all the more difficult and exciting.[35]

The modern mind seeks to impose not only 'geographical abstractions' on the past but abstractions covering entire social systems and entire eras of human activity. 'Feudal' and 'feudalism' are words the historian cannot do without; but they were, of course, unknown to those who lived under the so-called 'feudal system'. As Bloch explains in *The Historian's Craft*, the words 'were originally legal jargon, taken over from the courts of the eighteenth century by Boulainvilliers, and then by Montesquieu, to become the rather awkward labels for a type of social structure which was itself rather ill-defined'.[36] Labels like 'the Middle Ages' and 'the Renaissance' take us into the confused world of historical periodisation. The idea of a 'Middle Age' between the splendours of classical antiquity and the modern revival of the classical and humanist outlook was actually developed in the period of the Renaissance itself,[37] and was popularised by the historians of the Enlightenment, though it is usually accepted that the terms *ancient, medieval* and *modern* were invented by Pousin of Friège in his book *Feodium*, published in 1639, and advocated by Christopher Cellarius or Keller (1634–1701) of the University of Halle. We have to use these labels since we need to have organising ideas and classificatory generalisations, otherwise history would simply be a disordered flood of undifferentiated information. Choosing the title for a book or series of lectures is often a critical matter, almost ranking with those matters of *form* which we discussed earlier: ideally the title should represent the main organising idea, the theme upon which the properly unified work is being strung. Furthermore the title is an important element in the dialogue between historian and reader. Denys Hay has told us ruefully how his *From Roman Empire to Renaissance Europe*, first published in 1953, came to be republished as *The Medieval Centuries* (1964): he had intended that the original title should convey the essential principle that history deals with change through time; but in fact many prospective readers assumed that the central theme was the influence of the Roman world on the Renaissance, and some booksellers even stocked the book on their ancient history shelves.[38]

Medieval historians like to point out that the concept of a 'century' as signifying one hundred years has no meaning till after the Renaissance. How far it is justifiable to talk of the 'century of Pericles', 'the art of the thirteenth century' or 'the twelfth-century Renaissance' must be left to ancient and medieval historians to determine. The use of centuries to achieve a rough periodisation of the modern era is less asinine than has sometimes been assumed, since the modern mind is itself receptive to the idea that with a new century new ideas and new aspirations are in order. Ideas obviously do not clock forward on a kind of chronometer geared to the changing centuries, and interesting new perspectives have been opened up by historians deliberately seeking to break through long-accepted chronological frames. Yet it would be a rare pedant indeed who would wish to deny all meaning to such a phrase as 'the trouble with British politicians in the 1920s was that they looked at twentieth-century problems through nineteenth-century eyes'. The phrase is a neat summary, of great value provided the historian does not make it an excuse to burke his proper duties in the matter of elucidation and explanation.

And that is the text for some final reflections. 'The hall-mark of the historically minded person', to quote Denys Hay once more, 'is an itch for the concrete, a desire to get behind generalisations to the facts upon which they are based and to establish an almost physical relationship with the texture of earlier times.' Many of the well-worn labels and generalisations, unhappily, stand as barriers between the historian and his reader on one side and the real texture of the past on the other. Despite the wit which has been lavished on the demolition of such hoary old standards as 'the rise of the middle classes', it is too soon to say that this locution has now disappeared from the vocabulary of historians and their students. The trick to be used here, and whenever such phrases come to hand, is to switch on the mental television set, to endeavour to visualise the concrete realities implied in the phrase. Is it an entire class which is 'rising' (becoming wealthier? more influential?) or just certain members of it? Is the result that what was once a 'middle class' now becomes a 'ruling class', or does it just assert a right to have more influence than it previously exerted? Middling men in any given age and social structure are of course always going up in the world (and often down), whether as single spies or in battalions. It will not be *the* middle class which is 'rising' throughout the centuries, but *different* middle classes in different centuries. In a brilliant exposure of 'The Vocabulary of Social History' Alfred Cobban cited the example

of Langeois, Intendant of Montauban at the beginning of the eighteenth
century, who was the son of a Farmer-General and the grandson of a
second-hand clothes-dealer of Paris: 'Is this', asked Cobban, 'the rise of
the old rag and bone merchants?'[39]

Two final dangers to good historical writing should be mentioned:
the high-falutin' phrase, and the non-quantity. The first covers such
familiar friends as 'the workers wanted *economic* as well as *political*
freedom'; 'there was greater *toleration* of Catholics and dissenters';
'women achieved *emancipation*'. Old friends certainly, but what do we
really know about them? What is an economic freedom, or, for that
matter, a political freedom? The phrase may be valid as a heading, but
isn't it better to go on and explain in concrete terms (wages, living
conditions, etc.) what exactly the workers wanted? If known, that is; if
not known, then: historian, beware! What was it like to be a tolerated
Catholic? Could one live a completely normal life? or a reasonably con-
tented life if one kept strictly to oneself? or was one in danger of having
one's windows broken at regular intervals? What did it mean for a
woman to be 'emancipated'? did this condition apply to all women, or
only to some of the more conspicuous ones? did it mean having the vote?
getting equal pay? going alone into pubs? These are matters of the
texture of life which the historian must get at, and should not conceal
behind the fine-sounding phrase which is often far feebler in effect than
the elaborate and even cumbersome explanation which deals in realities.

The non-quantity occurs when labour unrest is explained to us through
the information that the price of corn has gone up to 180s a quarter.
We have no idea how much corn there is in a quarter, what the
'normal' price was, and what this rise meant in terms of the amount of
bread which a working-class family could purchase. Scattered throughout
our histories we have assessments of the influence of certain books based
on the number of copies sold, descriptions of how the population of a
town grew to a certain size, estimates of the total number of men involved in a certain riot. Such statistics are meaningless unless we are
given something to measure them against: how many copies did such
books normally sell? how many people could read, anyway? and so on.
The historical writer must encompass the concrete reality: the isolated
statistic, the fine-sounding verb, the hackneyed label, and the sweeping
generalisation all run through historical prose like the proverbial dose of
salts, emptying it of all true sustenance.

NOTES

1. See Garmonsway (ed.), *The Anglo-Saxon Chronicle*, p. 219.
2. Arthur Marwick, *The Deluge: British Society and the First World War* (1965) p. 102.
3. Peter Laslett, *The World we have lost*, pp. 81ff. The ages suggested by the plays may, however, have been relevant to a small, wealthy minority.
4. Norman Gash, *Politics in the Age of Peel* (1953).
5. For a triumphant example of what a historian can achieve in this respect, see H. Stuart Hughes, *Consciousness and Society* (1958).
6. M. W. Beresford and J. K. S. St Joseph, *Medieval England: an Aerial Survey* (1958) p. 5.
7. H. G. Richardson and G. O. Sayles, *The Governance of Medieval England* (1963) p. vii.
8. W. H. Walsh, 'Colligatory Concepts in History' in Burston and Thompson, p. 80.
9. Jacques Barzun and Henry F. Graff, *The Modern Researcher* (paperback ed. 1962) pp. 229–30.
10. G. Kitson Clark, *Guide for Research Students Working in Historical Subjects* (1960) p. 31.
11. Barzun and Graff, p. 233.
12. *The Historian's Business*, p. 6.
13. Ibid., p. 9.
14. Frank Freidel, *America in the Twentieth Century* (1960) p. 218.
15. Gordon Wright, *History of Modern France* (1959) p. 529. This, it should be added, is a Homeric nod: Professor Wright's book is a brilliant piece of historical synthesis.
16. Alan Bullock, in Hans Meyerhoff (ed.), *The Philosophy of History in Our Time* (1959) p. 296.
17. R. H. Mackenzie and A. Silver, *Angels in Marble* (1968) pp. 161–91.
18. S. R. Graubard, 'Military Demobilization in Britain following the First World War' in *Journal of Modern History* (1947).
19. Barzun and Graff, p. 289.
20. W. L. Langer, *The Franco-Russian Alliance 1890–1894* (1929) p. 277. Professor Langer is one of the most distinguished American historians in the strict professional tradition.
21. *The Practice of History*, pp. 16–17.
22. In *Rationalism in Politics* (1962) p. 153.
23. Leonard Krieger, in *History*, ed. John Higham (1965) p. 288.
24. E.g. D. K. Fieldhouse's indispensable survey of 'Imperialism' in *Economic History Review*, second series, XIV 2 (1961).
25. R. R. Palmer, in Gottschalk (ed.), *Generalization in the Writing of History*, p. 66.
26. L. B. Namier, 'History: Its Subject-matter and Tasks', *History Today* (1952).

27. The criticism does not apply to Lady Antonia Fraser's splendid *Mary Queen of Scots* (1969).

28. On the whole question of 'video-history', see my article in the *Listener*, 1 May 1969, and the correspondence which followed, 8–22 May. See also J. B. Krieger, 'The Historical Value of Motion Pictures', *The American Archivist*, xxxi (Oct 1968), and B.U.F.C., *Film and the Historian* (1968).

29. Louis Gottschalk, *Understanding History* (1956 ed.) p. 17.

30. See Denys Hay, 'Geographical Abstractions and the Historian', *Historical Studies*, ii (1959) 1ff., and sources there cited.

31. *The Historian's Craft*, p. 172.

32. Charles I. Schottland (ed.), *The Welfare State* (1967) is a useful collection of readings.

33. *The Historian's Craft*, pp. 159–60, 163.

34. Alfred Cobban, 'The Vocabulary of Social History', *Political Science Quarterly*, lxxi (March 1956) p. 14.

35. *Historical Studies*, ii 13.

36. Pp. 169–70.

37. This is the general tenor of, for example, Vasari's Prefaces to his *Lives of the Artists* (2nd edn, 1568). See paperback selection (1965), translated by George Bull, pp. 25–47, 83–93, 249–54.

38. Denys Hay, *The Medieval Centuries* (1964), preface.

39. *Political Science Quarterly*, lxxi 8.

6 *The Contemporary Scene*

I THE THIRTY YEARS' CRISIS IN HISTORICAL STUDIES

THE great virtue of taking a cool look at several hundred years of historiography is that it brings out the frequency with which historians have fought the same battles, suffered the same attacks from the outside, undergone the same doubts as to their status and purposes; throughout all this, historical study has on the whole achieved greater breadth and greater sophistication. The present 'crisis in history', part of the larger 'crisis in the humanities' (reflected a few years ago in the attention lavished on C. P. Snow's thesis of the Two Cultures), looms large in the eyes of those who spend a good deal of their time telling others how they ought to write history, rather less in the actual writing of history. In fact this crisis is merely the latest phase in the long history of tension generated by the very nature of history, and the conflicting demands made upon it, shaped, inevitably, by the great upheavals of the Second World War, and the rapid acceleration of technological advance since the 1940s. In the United States there was already a sense of crisis when in the thirties 'new' historians and relativists on one side, and straight-line professionals on the other poured the burning oil of academic scorn upon each other's pretensions while nervously insisting upon the social or the intellectual value of their work. In Britain, where pragmatic distrust of theorising about what the historian was and what he should be doing remained strong, there was scarcely any awareness that there was a crisis. Thus when the heart-searchings did finally penetrate the insular British consciousness in the fifties and sixties the effect was all the stronger.

The Second World War and its aftermath has coloured approaches to history in two specific ways. First, a serious challenge has been raised to the continued acceptance of the principles of genetic relationism (or 'historical geneticism' or, in its most acceptable usage, 'historicism') which in all the squabbles of the twentieth century had been the unconscious basis of every historian's thinking. Continuity was the historian's stock-in-trade: he made his living by showing that everything was connected to everything else; believing that 'the nature of everything is entirely comprehended in its development' (Professor Barraclough's excellent definition of the genetic or historicist outlook), the historian explained an institution or an idea by tracing its ancestry. But the tremendous upheaval of war made the notion of continuity look a bit sick, suggested, indeed, a rent in the 'seamless web' of history. Certainly there has in recent years been a fashion, perhaps it is no more than that, for stressing the abrupt nature of certain phases of historical change, the 'discontinuities' instead of the 'continuities'. Such an emphasis seems to underlie, for example, Professor Hans Baron's *The Crisis of the Early Italian Renaissance* (1955), Professor Elton's *Tudor Revolution in Government* (see below, p. 185), Professor Trevor-Roper's 'General Crisis of the Seventeenth Century' (see below, p. 195) and Professor Peter Gay's *The Enlightenment: an Interpretation* (1967). Secondly, the whole power balance of the world has changed since 1940: European primacy is ended once and for all; new attention is focused on Africa, South America and the Far East. The fact that the historical development of these regions had for centuries proceeded entirely separately from the European developments upon which historians formerly concentrated reinforced the challenge to the historicist concept of history as a unified interconnected process. More simply it created a fashion for historical study of the various regions which had now come into prominence.

Technological advance had an obvious influence on methodology, bringing to the historian's aid computers and other techniques discussed in chapter 4. It also served to stimulate a further most salutary fashion for the study of the history of science and technology. More important, it created a deep sense that the contemporary world of technological achievement was fundamentally different from all past ages, again emphasising the discontinuous in history, and indeed calling in question the relevance of the historical study of these past ages. Here, certainly, was a new doubt for those who had always relied heavily on a functional justification for history; some professionals renewed their rejoicing over this further demonstration of the uselessness of their subject. If the central arguments of this book be correct, however, it can be seen that however immense the 'great mutation' of the twentieth century, the essential necessity for the study of earlier centuries is not thereby obliterated. Indeed the very phrase is a historian's one; only through our knowledge of the remoter past are we in any condition to assess the nature of the 'mutation' taking place in our own time.[1]

The First World War had dealt the final blows to certain nineteenth-century absolutes; yet the historians of the inter-war years emulated their statesmen in seeking refuge from reality. A useful but elementary idea was elevated into a fine-sounding and fashionable creed of 'relativism'; there was much noisy turning from politics to social and intellectual history. In general a vaguely liberal tone prevailed: dynastic politics and secret diplomacy had brought war; surely rational policies could avert it for the future. Before the Second World War then, despite Freud, despite Namier and despite Durckheim, Bloch and Lefebvre, there was still a strong residual sentiment in favour of belief in man's essential rationality, an acceptance that wars and revolutions came about because of certain conscious decisions by certain key men, or at any rate through lack of conscious planning to avert such upheavals. A second World War and a full exposure of Nazi atrocities drained away most of that residue. Since 1945 there have been historians of all brands and varieties – more than ever before: but if there is one element which now characterises the whole profession, even those with a legitimate interest in the deeper regularities of human behaviour, it is a fuller appreciation of the force of the irrational, of the complexities of human psychology, and of the importance of the unexpected in history. Along with the boons of social science, historians have now increasingly enlisted the assistance of modern literary criticism, with its understanding of literature as a revelation of the irrational mind at work. Apart from his biographical technique of research, this is a form of understanding associated, in the English-speaking world at least, with Sir Lewis Namier, and his, as we have noted, is one of the dominating presences in contemporary historiography.

The Second World War affected the writing of history in more specific ways. German historiography in particular bore the mark of a second and still more catastrophic military defeat. Friedrich Meinecke's *German Catastrophe* (1946) voiced a repentance for his own concentration on political ideas; he argued that Germany had taken a wrong road in the nineteenth century when, instead of developing and extending her justly celebrated cultural tradition, she had turned towards the glorification of the political state. Having formerly kept up something of the bold self-confidence of Ranke, Meinecke now fell under the shadow of Burckhardt's deep pessimism. A younger compatriot of Meinecke's, an authority on the German Reformation and the author of an astonishingly wide range of books, Gerhard Ritter, has told us of the imprint left by events on the later editions of his short biography, *Luther: His Life and Work*. In the preface to the 1959 edition he remarks that although the central sections of the book have not been much altered since the first editions of 1928–9, the introduction and conclusion had to be more extensively rewritten:

> The original plan of this book, made shortly after the end of the First World War, emphasised Luther's importance as a national hero, as the central figure of German culture, with a vigour which I today feel to have been exaggerated. The catchword which was coined at that time – 'the Eternal German' – has been cut from this edition. . . .

Professor Ritter then explained how his theological understanding of Luther had been deepened by his participation in the struggle of the German Lutheran Church against the Nazi regime in the thirties:

In retrospect I feel that my book reached full maturity in the third and extensively revised edition which appeared in 1943. The world catastrophe which we had already sensed then and which broke on us in 1945 brought Luther's ideas of the hidden God and the twilight of world history home to us Germans with remarkable actuality. This led me to rewrite the introduction almost completely in the fourth edition (1947).

It was not necessary for a country to undergo formal defeat for the perspectives of her historians to be radically altered. Charles Carrington, author of quite the best single history of the British Empire, has explained how the plan for his book on *The British Overseas* took shape during 1937. His intention, thwarted by the coming of war, had been 'to display the growth of the Empire and the emergence of the Commonwealth Ideal from the point of view of the British pioneers'. He proposed to find out who they were and what they supposed themselves to be doing. In the 1930s it seemed as though answers could be found since 'the Empire-Commonwealth seemed to have surmounted an obstacle, to have reached a stage of equilibrium and to be moving steadily on a course which might be charted'. By the time the book was completed in 1949 the entire appearance of the Empire had altered, so that the later chapters 'revealed doubts and uncertainties that had not been evident in 1937'.[2] At London University the Professor of the History of the British Dominions in Asia became Professor of Oriental History. The change was symptomatic of a whole trend away from the study of imperial relations towards the study of individual regions and nations, seen as far as possible from the standpoint of the indigenous inhabitants rather than from that of their Western conquerors.

Much of the scepticism of the war and postwar generation of historians was particularly destructive in character, but undoubtedly it fulfilled an important task in drawing attention to the prevalence of the sort of platitudes and clichés discussed in the previous chapter. Alfred Cobban, a leading British authority on modern France, in addition to his gentle but telling irony against the softer forms of social history, suggested what might be done in the way of creating a truly rigorous social history, informed, but not dominated, by the concepts of the sociologists, in his *The Social Interpretation of the French Revolution* (1964). J. H. Hexter (b. 1910), an American authority on seventeenth-century England and author of the standard biography, *The Reign of King Pym* (1941), became peculiarly well known as a scourge of the pretentiousness which reached full flowering in the thirties, but which, of course, has continued in one form or another ever since. Hexter, with Cobban, has been one of the most deflating commentators on windy talk about the 'rise of the middle class'. Flatulent use of the word 'factor' was another Hexter target:

In the nineteenth century, the word 'cause' in either its noun form or its verb form would have done the work done by 'factor'. . . . But somehow, 'cause' got into trouble with the philosophers and the scientists and was dropped by all the best and some of the less good clubs. The work the word had been doing had to go on being done, however, since everyone found it necessary to go on talking about the species of relations which 'cause' had formerly designated. So 'factor' was slid into the slot which 'cause' had once filled in the vocabulary of rational discourse, and this made everybody very happy. Thus the human mind progresses – sideways.[3]

Hexter was also one of the first to expose the fatuities of the sub-world of the sub-histories, economic, intellectual, social, etc., which he grouped collectively as 'tunnel history'.

However it is more important to stress the constructive work which has taken place since 1945, leading to what Professor John Higham has referred to as the 'renewal' of the 1950s.[4] Without doubt the lead has come from the United States: indeed it was in great measure due to the controversies of the 1930s that the American Social Science Research Council instituted two inquiries into the nature of historical study, issuing in *Bulletins* 54 and 64, which, if somewhat laboured at times, are nonetheless essential reading for anyone interested in the problems with which this present book attempts also to deal. From the early fifties onwards historians no longer fenced with the social sciences; they confidently borrowed what served their purpose and just as confidently rejected what did not. This does not mean that the crisis in history has come to an end: in the nature of the subject there will always be controversy drawn out by the conflicting demands the discipline has to meet and the varying styles it has to accommodate. Whatever may be happening within the charmed circle of the academic guild, it is clear that most of the refinements of approach have yet to penetrate to the other levels of the historical industry; certainly news of them has not reached the ears of most of history's critics.

More than this: whatever changes may be made within history, this cannot affect the growing ascendancy in the modern world of the scientific disciplines, and the growth in popularity of those social sciences – sociology and economics in particular – which have a more immediate and self-evident relevance to the problems of contemporary society and of securing gainful employment within that society. In 1964 Dr J. H. Plumb edited a significant little book on *Crisis in the Humanities* (with which, incidentally, he included sociology and economics). In his own exploration of 'The Historian's Dilemma' Dr Plumb attacked the dying but still insidious (when pushed to extremes) creed of historical relativism, which in a manner typical of the confused purposes to which the word is put, he called 'historicism'. Dr Plumb's own remedy for the nihilism and social impotence of current history was a reassertion of *the idea of progress*:

> If this great human truth were once more to be frankly accepted, the reasons for it, and the consequences of it, consistently and imaginatively explored and taught, history would not only be an infinitely richer education but also play a much more effective part in the culture of western society.

Though few historians would accept the specific unifying element suggested for historical study by Dr Plumb, this suggestion does go to the heart of matters preoccupying the younger historians of the 1960s: the desire to give history some sense of purpose beyond mere fact-grubbing and the destruction of myths, the desire to reassert the totality of history.

In the inter-war years certain historians had sought refuge from the fragmentation of historical studies in one unifying element now increasingly denied to them: Marxist-Leninism. Shortly we shall look at one or two historians for whom Marxism, used imaginatively, has continued to be a valuable tool of analysis; but the crude Marxism by rote of an earlier period has certainly disappeared from all but the most lumbering efforts of the party hacks. The grand denunciation of those meta-histories of which Marxism was the prototype was unleashed in Karl Popper's *The Poverty of Historicism* (1942): a somewhat over-dramatised account whose main effect was to give currency to yet another meaning of historicism – and one which is very far from the original German or Italian.

All through debate and counter-debate, crisis and renewal, the essential continuity in the development of historical studies was perfectly clear. The first volumes in the *Oxford History of England* series, published in the thirties, had reflected both the broadening and the fragmentation of historical study of the period: separate chapters were written as though the author was in turn intellectual historian, political historian, diplomatic historian, economic historian, social historian, imperial historian, and art historian. The most successful work in this mode was Sir Robert Ensor's *England 1870–1914* (1936); the very neutrality of the title expresses Ensor's unwillingness to find a unifying concept for his work: the separate tunnels (in Hexter's usage) are brightly lit, exciting to travel along; but what is definitely lacking is the sense of historical totality. The general editor of the Oxford series was Sir George Clark (b. 1890), appointed Regius Professor at Cambridge in 1944: like Ranke and Stubbs in the nineteenth century, Clark found a unifying theme in politics and government; his inaugural address at Cambridge included a much-quoted statement to that effect:

> It is in public institutions that men express their will to control events, and therefore it seems to me that historians will go wrong if they try to

resolve political and constitutional history into other elements, just as our practical men will go wrong if they follow the current fashion of treating 'cultural' interests and activities as if they could be altogether separated from the affairs of states. The history of institutions must in some sense be central.

Clark had himself done, and continued to do, important detailed work in areas conventionally delimited as 'economic' (as in his *The Dutch Alliance and the War against French Trade 1688–1697* (1923)) or 'social' (as in his *Science and Social Welfare in the Age of Newton* (1931)). His words were spoken in 1944: twenty-two years later the general editor of the highly regarded *Longmans History of Europe*, himself a historian of broad social and intellectual interests, made much the same point:

> The desire for political power is the motor which drives men to public action. . . . It is . . . the politically dominant, a small fraction of the total population at most times . . . who are largely responsible for the cultural qualities of an age.[5]

And it is, of course, the 'cultural qualities' which are handed on and transmuted from age to age, thus forming an important stream in historical development. One of the best short appraisals of the renewed emphasis on politics as a synthesising element was penned by S. T. Bindoff, whose own early researches had been in economic history.[6]

This then was the legacy of the straight-line professionals of the inter-war years: an awareness of, often a deep specialist interest in, the newer subject-matter of history, but in the last resort a common-sense un-willingness to accept any dogmatic theorising as to the primacy of any one element in historical study and a natural rallying to the obvious centrality of institutions and political activity. The heirs to this legacy, strongly coloured by the disenchanted scepticism of Sir Lewis Namier, I shall term the 'modern empiricists': the leading historians of today who, when it comes to high-level theorising on the philosophy and the methodology of history, on the uses of sociology and the virtues of co-operative research, see much and say little; but who, with astonishing energy and application, get on with the main task of the historian – writing history.

2   THE MODERN EMPIRICISTS

In so far as this book is a history of history, its aim is to present an impression of the development of historical studies, not to provide a catalogue containing the names and potted accounts of all the great or

noteworthy historians. Accordingly this chapter is not intended as a
Who's Who of contemporary historiography. For obvious reasons the
missing names will now stand out even more clearly than the omissions
from earlier chapters: however, since in everyday life I am a specialist
in contemporary history, I have become resigned to this particular
occupational risk; I have tried at any rate to avoid the supreme impertinence of dropping the names of those whose eminence and importance
are undisputed, but about whom, through my own ignorance, I am
precluded from making anything but polite noises. In the third section of
this chapter I propose to look at some of the particular approaches to
history which have characterised the last thirty years, and at some
of the men (American and European) who exemplify these approaches; in
the fourth section I shall consider the modern Marxists, and also some
of the reactions among a still younger generation which represent the
latest stage in 'crisis and renewal'. Here, under the convenient grouping 'empiricists', which by definition is no grouping at all, I propose
to discuss four important British historians and one Italian.

Traditionally in Great Britain the primacy in historical studies was
assumed by the University of Oxford; in actual practice since the
Second World War a clear ascendancy has rested with the University of
Cambridge, formerly held in greater esteem for its contributions to the
physical sciences. In general both undergraduate and postgraduate study
at Cambridge has been more coherently and systematically organised
than at Oxford: Cambridge has had a far greater share of what one
might call elder statesmen of history (men who have not only written
on their own account but who have developed whole schools of loyal
disciples), running by subtle shifts from G. M. Trevelyan, G. N. Clark
(whose absolute injunction that the historian observe the first com-
mandment of always checking his references has apparently been en-
graven in the minds of all who have heard him speak on this point) and
Herbert Butterfield, to G. Kitson Clark and Geoffrey Elton, and to
Sir Denis Brogan (who has uniquely combined an expertise in French
and American history, and who has sponsored much research in British
social history), J. H. Plumb and E. H. Carr. In short, if history is an
industry, industrialisation has gone much further at Cambridge than
at Oxford.

George Kitson Clark (b. 1900) and Geoffrey Elton (b. 1921) present
important points of contrast. Elton, though he has written on European as well as on British history, is unmistakably identified with a thesis,
the 'Elton thesis' on the 'Tudor Revolution in Government'. Kitson
Clark, though a profound influence on the study of many aspects of
British nineteenth-century history, is not associated with any one
important thesis. He does, however, stand out as a kind of elder statesman of that gentle revision of early nineteenth-century British history

which has been in motion now for a generation. Typically, as a professional, his own major contributions to knowledge have appeared in the form of papers delivered to learned societies or as articles in the learned journals. His earlier researches were concentrated on Britain in the period following upon the Great Reform Act of 1832, a period long bedevilled by the notion of the rise to power of the 'middle class', a rise assumed to have been consummated by the 1832 Act. The great vehicle of middle-class influence in the 1830s and 1840s was the Anti-Corn Law League: historians had tended to take at face value the assertions of the League that the main opposition to repeal of the protectionist Corn Laws came from the great landed interests, the aristocracy and the squirearchy; and further that the landowners exerted undue influence upon the tenant farmers in persuading them to vote for protectionist candidates. Going behind the polemical statements of the League to the contemporary documents, Kitson Clark showed that it was the tenant farmers, operating on a tiny economic margin, who were most strongly in favour of protection, and that some of the violent agitation of the period sprang from suspicion on the part of the tenants that the candidates supported by the landowners were not sufficiently committed to the principle of protection. In the wider context of the power structure of British society after 1832, Kitson Clark's discoveries suggested that real power in fact still rested with the landowners, and that, as he put it in a later summary, 'the actual repeal was carried through by the head of one aristocratic party because he believed it to be desirable, with the assent of the other because, at least, he believed it to be expedient'.[7]

Though a revisionist historian and proud of it, Kitson Clark has always upheld the worthy professional (and empiricist) tradition of giving due honour to the dead, recognising the continuous development of historical studies rather than exaggerating each revision as a revolutionary break. Trevelyan, Clapham and Halévy are mentioned with deep respect, their ideas developed and refined, rather than 'revised'. But if the links with the past are strongly forged, so also are those with the rising generation. Indeed Kitson Clark's peculiar claim to our attention lies in the vast wealth of first-rate scholarly research sponsored under his aegis: in this respect his record comes closer to that of some of the great modern American scholars than to his British contemporaries, who have not generally shown the same interest in creating an inspired discipleship (Namier, of course, did just that). In the general approach inculcated into his disciples, Kitson Clark, naturally, represents very well the shape historical study has assumed since 1945: politics remain as an organising element, but meticulous investigation is conducted into what Clark (not altogether felicitously, I believe) has called 'background'. The empirical approach at any rate is stressed:

The old bland confident general statements about whole groups of men, or classes or nations ought to disappear from history; or if something of their sort must remain, and it is difficult to say anything about history or politics or society without making use of general statements, they must remain under suspicion, as expedients which are convenient, possibly necessary, for use at the moment, but are not the best that we shall be able to do in the way of truth.[8]

History 'described entirely in terms of the relationships between important individuals at the centre of politics' is history 'without background, and therefore obviously questionable'; but, he says, history without background is 'better than history with a false background provided by well-worn general phrases about whose general accuracy no one has ever bothered to think'. The point here is particularly relevant to some of the history written in the twenties and thirties when it was too often believed that the wish to write cultural and social history would father that very history, without the necessary recourse to hard labour in intractable source materials.

Many of those once supervised by Kitson Clark now occupy important academic positions throughout the English-speaking world, having in their own right made highly significant contributions to nineteenth-century historical inquiry: H. J. Hanham (Harvard) has written the standard work on *Elections and Party Management in the Age of Gladstone and Disraeli*; D. C. Moore has written a number of important articles on the Reform Bill crisis, and K. B. Nowlan an authoritative book on the question of the repeal of the Irish Act of Union; Royston Lambert (for a time an important consultant on government policy towards the Public Schools) is the author of the standard life of *Sir John Simon*, an important contribution to the history of public health; G. F. A. Best and James Cornford (both Professors at Edinburgh University) are the standard authorities on, respectively, the history of the Ecclesiastical Commissioners and on the social and economic affiliations of the Conservative Party at the end of the nineteenth century – the latter a topic which has been fraught with the sort of easy generalisation denounced by Kitson Clark.

Meticulous research into the realities behind the facile generalisations may well, Kitson Clark has admitted, be 'disheartening': the existing picture may be broken up 'so that nothing can be seen as a whole'; it may 'lead to a kind of historical nominalism with innumerable accidentals and no universals'. A willingness to face boldly up to this risk has been the hallmark of the modern empiricists, and a source of discontent both to humanists like J. H. Plumb and to the current generation of younger historians. However, it is also a characteristic of the modern empiricists that they have not shirked the responsibility of providing works of synthesis, and Kitson Clark has to his credit two invaluable studies of the nineteenth century, *The Making of Victorian England* (1962) and *An Expanding Society: Britain 1830–1900* (1967). The opening chapter of the former book, entitled 'The Task of Revision', is itself a masterly short essay which in vivid and trenchant style highlights many of the 'bright ideas' which have informed the work of this generation of historians. Students are warned against the hazard of accepting that just because the case put by one side in a historical controversy seems coherent and cogent they are thereby exempt from checking on what the other side had to say. Particular reference is made to the way in which historians offer a sweeping explanation as to why one side won a certain election (this has happened frequently in American historiography) – the explanation being that offered by some party orator in the aftermath of victory or defeat, which is no substitute for detailed study in the local records. We are warned against easy attribution of an economic motivation in politics by the reflection that 'a wealthy man in an important position is very likely to have a good many different economic interests and consideration for one of them might easily seem to work for the destruction of another'. Honest indignation, Kitson Clark remarks, has sometimes 'lent enthusiasm to research and imaginative force to the work that has resulted'. But, he continues, 'indignation, however honest, is a dangerous passion for historians'. The most important task of historical revision is 'to rescue real men and women who have been shrunk by historians into the bloodless units of a generalisation, or have become the ugly depersonalised caricatures of partisan legend or modern prejudice'. One other 'curious habit' sometimes adopted by historians to the detriment of history is identified by Kitson Clark:

> They are inclined to assume that certain things are important in certain centuries, and when they occur in the wrong centuries they are at liberty to leave them out or play them down because they want to talk about other things. Thus by the tradition of writing history religion is important in the seventeenth century, but in the nineteenth century interest should concentrate on democracy, nationalism, industrial development and the social question.

Picking up the threads from Halévy, Kitson Clark has himself stressed the importance of Christian religion in stimulating men to undertake reform in early nineteenth-century Britain. Here Kitson Clark is very much at one with the modern empiricists in the emphasis they place on the appeal of the irrational: he has himself written that 'in order to understand the springs of action it is important to try to understand the emotions, the irrational feelings, the prejudices, the experiences which form men's minds'. Typical also of the modern empirical approach is the simultaneous acceptance of the need to quantify, to submit to the 'discipline of arithmetic', and recognition of the limits beyond which arithmetic cannot be pushed: 'If a mistake is made in the premises of the calculation or in the identification of the units to be counted, the resulting figures can be simply a source of error.' Finally Kitson Clark, along with many others, has insisted upon the value of popular literature as a guide to contemporary preoccupations in all their oddity. Kitson Clark is one of the very few Englishmen to write about the nature and methods of history. His *Guide for Research Students working in Historical Subjects* (1960) stands comparison with Barzun and Graff's *Modern Researcher*. His *The Critical Historian* (1967) is conceived very much in that excellent British tradition which recognises that history does have utility and that accordingly our history must meet the most exacting critical standards. A man's life and mind, whether he likes it or not, says Kitson Clark, is invaded by 'the results of history, or what purport to be the results of history, as opinions coloured by beliefs about history':[9] we must therefore try to get as near as possible to the reality of history as it actually happened.

The emphasis placed by G. R. Elton, present holder of the Chair of Constitutional History in the University of Cambridge, upon the *discontinuous* character of Tudor administrative history has already been mentioned (see above, p. 175). The 'Elton thesis' was first adumbrated in the late forties in the pages of the learned journals; the fullest statement appeared in *The Tudor Revolution in Government* (1953), and further refinements have appeared in a steady flood of learned articles and in *The Tudor Constitution: Documents and Commentary* (1960). According to a tradition established by Victorian historians, 1485 was a key date in English history when, following upon a century of civil war and social disintegration, Henry VII, succeeding to the throne by right of conquest, proceeded to establish what J. R. Green called the 'new monarchy', developing quickly into the 'Tudor despotism' of Henry VIII. The straight-line professional historians of the early twentieth century, led by A. F. Pollard (1869-1948) – founder of both the [English] Historical Association (1906) and the Institute of Historical Research – had endeavoured to replace this by a more evolutionary view, stressing on the one side that many of the characteristics of the 'new monarchy' were in fact inherited from Henry VII's immediate predecessors, Edward IV and Richard III, and on the other that medieval methods persisted far into the Tudor period. For this somewhat soft-edged interpretation, 'ball-of-string' history at its best, Professor Elton substituted a version which accepted continuity as between Henry VII and his predecessors, but postulated a 'Tudor revolution in government' in the 1530s; a revolution which equipped England with a modern, national bureaucracy which could function, and provide political stability, irrespective of the personal qualities of the king or his deputies – medieval government, of course, was subject to breakdown whenever a weak king succeeded to the throne. Although the particular thesis relating to administrative developments in the reign of Henry VIII is clear, coherent and consistent, Elton is a complete empiricist in his insistence that the motor of historical change is 'individuals working in a somewhat unorganised and haphazard manner'. Elton in fact gives tremendous weight to the actions of one particular individual, Henry VIII's Secretary, Thomas Cromwell, whom he describes as 'the most remarkable revolutionary in English history'. The Elton thesis is a monument of constructive scholarship: as with all such theses it has been subjected to intensive attack. The emphasis on the personal contribution of Thomas Cromwell must seem excessive to many historians; and it would seem reasonable that the heavy stress on discontinuity in the 1530s, the 'revolutionary' view, might yield to some accommodation with the evolutionary view and its acceptance of certain fairly evident elements of continuity (in particular, the considerable administrative achievements of Henry VII). But a return to Pollard's ball-of-string is unlikely.[10]

Though deeply versed in economic, social, literary and military matters – what Kitson Clark would call the 'background' – Professor Elton is clear that what counts for most is 'the condition, reconstruction, and gradual moulding of a state – the history of a nation and its leaders in political action and therefore the history of government in the widest sense'. These words are taken from the preface to his textbook *England Under the Tudors* (1955), a fine example of the difficult art discussed in the previous chapter. In this instance Elton was presented with the problem of whether he should simply summarise the current orthodoxy or present his own important but controversial theories: he tells us that 'confronted with a choice between writing what I think to be true and repeating what I believe to be doubtful, I could not but choose the former'. He has some wise words to offer on the eternal problem of periodisation and the use of historical labels. Though 'modern' and 'medieval' seem to be meaningless terms, 'one cannot do without them': his usage implies respectively 'more like what came after' and 'more like what came before', without, he adds, 'prejudice as to what it was that came before and after'.

Elton is very much in the straight-line professional tradition, openly contemptuous of the would-be innovators of the thirties, metahistorians, and the sociologically orientated younger generation. His *The Practice of History* (1967) is the most eloquent statement of what, if I may be permitted to invent yet another label, might well be termed the up-to-date hard-line professional position. Significantly the first task Elton sets himself is to establish the *autonomy* of history: it may occasionally borrow, but essentially it has a developed professional expertise all of its own. He then presents a distinction between the *professional*, 'truly understanding an age from the inside', and the *amateur* who 'shows a tendency to find the past, or parts of it, quaint'. Acton, Trevelyan and G. M. Young are all ranked as amateurs. Elton is a resolute defender of the minute research of 'those who crawl upon the frontiers of knowledge with a magnifying glass' and of 'the young student who labours on what may seem a narrow or petty subject and attempts to master the techniques of study which it can teach', though he adds that one may reasonably be dubious of a mature scholar who has not progressed beyond this stage. He puts the 'apprenticeship' argument for the Ph.D. succinctly when he remarks that 'except for examiners, who are paid for it, no one needs to read Ph.D. dissertations'. He also repudiates E. H. Carr's attempted relegation of the editing of a text to a low level of historical activity.[11] It should be noted that Elton is a brilliant and vivid stylist, obviously concerned with the communication element in historical writing. With Macaulay he shares a concern for keeping up the narrative flow of his historical writing and in his own *Reformation Europe* (1963) he has presented a form of historical narrative 'thickened by the results of analysis': that is to say, instead of the conventional interlarding of bouts of narrative and bouts of analysis, there is continuous narrative with analysis incorporated where internal logic demands it; for instance, the point when Charles V becomes involved in war with the Turks is the point where a brief analysis of Turkish despotism is introduced. Elton, like Namier, is a Tory historian, only more so: he is tough, unsentimental, interested in actions rather than thoughts and ideals; while he clearly demonstrates that there was no 'Tudor despotism', he defends the authoritarian nature of Tudor government much as Namier defended the jobbery of eighteenth-century politics (part, no doubt, of 'truly understanding the age from the inside'); there is an over-readiness, perhaps, to come down on the side of the winners in history.

These two distinguished Cambridge historians are better known inside the historical guild than outside it. There can be no doubt that in the public mind *the* historian in Britain today is A. J. P. Taylor, formerly Tutor of Magdalen College, Oxford, now Librarian of the Beaverbrook Library. A first-year student of mine at Edinburgh University who not only knew the names of no other historians, but was scarcely aware that the writers of history have names, was conscious of having seen Mr Taylor on television. His performances in front of the television cameras on serious historical topics, without notes and without visual aids, were indeed unique. Mr Taylor's reputation is, of course, a world-wide one. He was born in March 1906 in Birkdale, Lancashire, and educated at the famous Quaker boarding school, Bootham, Yorkshire, and at Oriel College, Oxford, where in the 1920s there was no systematic teaching of nineteenth- and twentieth-century history, though this was the period when the study of the diplomatic origins of the First World War was coming into fashion. Taylor's own first interest was in that nineteenth-century working-class movement, Chartism, but as a routine part of the historian's apprenticeship he went to Vienna to learn German. His first idea for research there was to study the relationship between the 1848 upheavals in the Austrian Empire and British radicalism, but it was soon apparent that this was much too ambitious a project. In any case the great Austrian scholar A. F. Pribram, whose *The Secret Treaties of Austria-Hungary 1879–1914* had been published at the end of the war, and who subsequently produced the classic (if dull) diplomatic history *England and the International Policy of the Great Powers 1871–1914* (1931), was keen that he should take on some diplomatic topic. Eventually Taylor lighted on the idea of a study of *The Italian Problem in European Diplomacy*, which called for research in the Paris and London archives as well as in those of Vienna. In all respects this is a model scholarly monograph: the period studied is short, the topic clearly delimited and studied in great depth from an impressive array of primary materials; the presentation is detached, almost antiseptic. Only in the annotations to the bibliography did the scathing Taylor wit come properly into play. Taylor's first university appointment was at the University of Manchester, where Namier held the Chair of Modern History; his monograph was published by the University Press in 1934. Four years later there followed a further monograph, *Germany's First Bid for Colonies, 1884–1885*: again there was the same impressive mastery of extensive source materials, principally the German, French and British diplomatic documents, along with the Granville Papers; now, however, Taylor had a novel and stimulating thesis to advance – that Bismarck's bid for colonies was designed to provoke a quarrel with Britain in order that he could draw closer to France. The thesis, though not universally accepted in all its implications, still stands today as a significant contribution to the understanding of late nineteenth-century imperialism, which is increasingly understood by historians as the outward projection of European conflicts rather than as a purely economic phenomenon. The argument is presented with great verve and cogency; and the book ends in what was soon to be recognised as characteristic style: Bismarck, said Taylor,

> left an unfortunate example to his successors, who imitated his unscrupulousness without possessing his genius. Short of a run of Bismarcks, there is perhaps something to be said for government by gentlemen, even when they are such incompetent muddlers as Lord Granville and Lord Derby.

Taylor was later to write a biography of *Bismarck* (1955) which took to its furthest length the stress on the unexpected and the fortuitous in history which lurked behind all the work of the modern empiricists: Bismarck was presented not as a statesman with a fully worked-out policy for the creation of a German Empire, but as a brilliant opportunist with a remarkable facility for turning events to account. In shattering the familiar textbook stereotype Taylor again did an enormous service to historical study, though on balance recent evidence suggests that there was a greater element of forethought and planning in Bismarck's policies than Taylor allowed for. In between Taylor published three important textbooks, *The Habsburg Monarchy, 1815–1918* (1941), *The Course of German History* (1945) – characterised by a strong anti-German colouring verging on war propaganda, yet again a useful corrective to the liberal diplomatic histories of the inter-war years – and the famous *The Struggle for the Mastery in Europe, 1848–1918* (1954); and a number of thoroughly professional learned articles mainly related to the 'special subject' which he taught at Manchester on diplomacy at the beginning of the twentieth century when the 'Mediterranean problem' was a matter of particular concern.

There can then be no question about Taylor's qualifications as a complete professional historian. To his thorough technical grounding he has added the personal quality which distinguishes the great from the lesser: 'feel', 'intuition', or – as Namier said of his younger colleague – 'green fingers'. This quality is most apparent to the present writer in Taylor's *English History 1914–1945* (1965), since that book covers a field in which I have myself done a certain amount of primary research. I can only record that on first reading *English History* I was struck over and over again by the manner in which Taylor had managed to express, with the utmost lucidity and regard for the objective reality of the past, thoughts which I had myself struggled through pages and pages to express. I imagine that other students in other fields have found the same thing in regard to other books of Taylor's. This quality, naturally, is not necessarily one to endear Taylor to his earnest and hardworking colleagues. Taylor's own favourite book is the published version of his 1956 Ford lectures in the University of Oxford, *The Trouble Makers: Dissent over Foreign Policy 1792–1939* (1957). In the preface he explains that although he has sometimes treated the Dissenters 'lightly, even critically' the book nevertheless deals with the Englishmen whom he most reveres; and he adds the hope 'that, if I had been their contemporary, I should have shared their outlook. I should not have been ashamed to have made their mistakes.' Although in general Taylor's work is characterised by a scepticism and distrust of theory similar to that found in the other modern empiricists, his political sympathies incline to the Left, and he was a leading member of the most important of all

British radical movements since the Second World War, the Campaign for Nuclear Disarmament.

Taylor in fact is a man of diverse interests and gifts. As well as being a professional historian of the highest order, he is a gifted journalist and a striking television personality. The manner in which the various activities are kept apart is not always appreciated by his professional colleagues. He is very much in the tradition of the straight-line professionals in denying to history any special social utility of the sort postulated by this book (however, as we have noted, the greatest artists are often those who pay least heed to the needs of society): he likens the study of history to the study of poetry and music.[12] In fact, although in a review of Eric Hobsbawm's *Industry and Empire* Taylor stated his historical philosophy that 'things happen because they happen', in a subsequent review of Richard J. Ullman's *Britain and the Russian Civil War 1918–1920* he remarked:

> Works of history sometimes point a contemporary moral. This one does so. It is that foreign intervention is not a good way of promoting democracy. Perhaps Mr Ullman wrote with one eye on Vietnam.[13]

Dotted throughout Mr Taylor's extensive writings, many of which, in the manner of Maitland, offer pregnant and thought-provoking suggestions for new lines of inquiry, are the fragments of a philosophy of history in the second-level sense of the term. In essence it is the empiricist one, stressing the irrational, the unpredictable, the unique. Here are two quotations, long because it is not possible to improve upon the way in which Taylor puts things. First, one on *communication*:

> No historian is ever likely to depreciate the value of 'research'; but there has been something wrong with a profession which made this the sole, as well as an essential qualification for office and promotion. What used to be called 'vulgarisation' is now equally the duty of the professional scholar. Tired metaphors and flabby sentences should be as unforgivable in a historian as a faulty reference or an inaccurate quotation; and it would be no bad thing if academic promotion were open only to those who could hold listeners or win readers. For, although history may claim to be a branch of science or of politics or of sociology, it is primarily communication, a form of literature. No historian is worth his salt who has not felt some twinge of Macaulay's ambition – to replace the latest novel on the lady's dressing-table. It is to the credit of English history at the present time that some historians have felt this ambition and a few have even accomplished it. The historian has to combine truth and literary grace; he fails as a historian if he is lacking in either.[14]

And one on *scepticism*:

> The historian assembles data and is even more aware than the physical scientist how inadequate his data are. Much of the evidence on which

we could base our knowledge of the past has been destroyed or never was recorded. We guess from the few remaining fragments much as a geologist reconstructs a prehistoric monster from a single bone. Even at the present time, when thousands of trained experts are engaged in assembling and analysing the statistics of economic life, experts and governments have only the vaguest idea what has happened and no firm idea of what is likely to happen. There is little chance therefore of our reaching any very solid conclusions about early times when no reliable figures existed and there is not much information of any other kind. The only safe generalisation we can make about man's record was propounded by Anatole France: 'He was born. He suffered. He died.' History is the great school of scepticism.[15]

Taylor is the greatest twentieth-century exponent of the history defined by Richard Pares – history as a series of bright ideas. The trouble is that history, as the past, does not always unfold as a series of breath-taking paradoxes: the uncomprehending ambitions of men and societies, which Taylor understands only too well, do not always conform to neat literary formulations. Taylor has not in fact shown great originality in his choice of topics for study: the early preoccupation with diplomatic history, fashionable in Europe in the thirties, has given way to a broadened approach in which, as with Elton, the political theme re-mains central. As an Englishman first, then as a European, Taylor has shown no interest in other parts of the world. But Taylor has brought to his historical writing a style and manner of presentation unequalled in his own time, but very much of his own time. There are no long, rotund periods: the sentences are short, and hard and bright as diamonds, admirably fitted, despite the qualifications made above, to the tragic comedy of human frustration which Taylor relates. No one has resolved the problem of integrating analysis into narrative more successfully. Finally Taylor, in common with Shakespeare, Burns, Dickens and most other great literary practitioners, is an immensely witty writer: unhappily to many mean spirits it is incomprehensible that history seriously studied can be fun: Taylor shows that it *is* fun.

The most controversial of all Taylor's books, of course, is *The Origins of the Second World War* (1961, reprinted with a new introduction, 'Second Thoughts', in 1963). Since I propose to discuss the controversies over the origins of the Second World War in the next chapter when I turn to 'Problems in History', it is only necessary here to make a few points relevant to Taylor's place in the development of historical studies. *The Origins of the Second World War* is in many ways a throw-back to the style of diplomatic history with which Taylor began his career; it is not as copiously supplied with references as the complete scholarly monograph should be, but essentially it is a work built up from the documentary sources. Should a new edition of Fritz Stern's excellent *Varieties of History*, or a similar work, be planned, there could be no stronger candidate for inclusion than the foreword, 'Second Thoughts', added to the 1963 edition. The canons appealed to throughout are those of Ranke and Maitland, the former's pomposity replaced by Taylor's own updated pungency. The achievement Taylor claims is that of the straight-line professionals of the thirties, the destruction of legends, performed not as 'a vindication of Hitler', but as 'a service to truth': 'My book should be judged only on this basis, not for the political morals which people choose to draw from it.' Furthermore, says Taylor, 'it is no part of the historian's duty to say what ought to have been done. His whole duty is to find out what was done and why.' Taylor emerges very clearly as, in the non-party sense of course, a Tory historian. He is concerned as ever to stress the significance of contingency and accident as against advance planning – Hitler 'exploited events far more than he followed precise coherent plans' – and this theme is reiterated (to my mind rather tiresomely) throughout the text of the book. Early in chapter 10 there is a revealing passage where Taylor refers to the widely held view that 'Hitler was a modern Attila, loving destruction for its own sake', but, says Taylor, with an interesting swing towards historical Whiggism, 'his policy is capable of rational explanation; and it is on these that history is built'. 'Human blunders', he continues, 'usually do more to shape history than human wickedness. At any rate this is a rival dogma which is worth developing, *if only as an academic exercise*' (my italics). The book is indeed a most stimulating 'academic exercise', forcing a reappraisal of previously held convictions by all students in the field. But it is not a complete study of its topic: in particular, the 'Tory' emphasis on diplomatic sources means that the extremely important social, cultural and economic developments of Nazi Germany have been completely left out of account. Taylor's short, neat reply to his most profound critic on this score, Dr Tim Mason, is well worth extensive quotation:

> Of course historians must explore the profound forces. But I am sometimes tempted to think that they talk so much about these profound forces in order to avoid doing the detailed work. I prefer detail to generalisations: a grave fault no doubt, but at least it helps to redress the balance. . . .

After suggesting that perhaps he should have called the book 'The Origins of the Outbreak of War in 1939', Taylor admitted that this might seem a trivial topic. However,

> historians spend much of their time on trivialities, and some of them believe that only by adding up trivialities can they safely arrive at generalisations. Take care of the pence and the pounds will look after themselves. This is an old-fashioned view. But I am an old-fashioned hack historian.[16]

The first sentence recalls Bury; the last recalls that a young contemporary has referred to him as 'the last of the prima donnas'. 'Tory', 'Whig', 'hack', 'prima donna', and, throughout, a 'trouble-maker' (in his own sense of the term): Taylor is all of these. But no reader of his *English History 1914–1945* can think him unaware of the recent developments and fashions in historical study.

This combination of awareness of the contributions to be made to historical study by the social sciences and an emphasis on the traditional subject-matter of history characterised the most celebrated of Italian historians in the generation after Croce, Frederico Chabod (1902–60). Chabod studied at Berlin under the great German master Friedrich Meinecke, and his early work on Machiavelli and the Renaissance, published in the 1920s, reveals clearly the interest in intellectual history which was developing at that time. He did have some success in breaking through the split between political and cultural history which was beginning to characterise Italian historical writing, his aim in regard to Machiavelli being, as he put it, to present him 'as the expression, almost the synthesis of Italian life throughout the fourteenth and fifteenth centuries; and see reflected and clarified in his thought, as it were in its essential outline, the age-long process of development which leads from the downfall of the old, Communal freedom, to the triumph of the princely, the absolute State'. Otherwise much of his writing was of the conventional type, concentrating on political, diplomatic and sometimes religious themes. His aim was the highly professional one: to elucidate obscure points, to banish myths, rather than to open new approaches or new areas of study. In the postwar period, however, Chabod received a special acclaim for his *Storia della politica estera italiana dal 1870 al 1896* (1951). This is diplomatic history of a broad, almost sociological character, with a mass of intricate detail on the social and political 'background' (*pace* Kitson Clark), and a depth analysis of the psychology of those who formulated Italian foreign policy.

If however we move back to Oxford and to a rather younger historian, we can move away altogether from diplomatic history, in however modern guise, and on towards a historical attitude which touches closely upon that most characteristic of the present younger generation of historians. Hugh Trevor-Roper (born 1914), Regius Professor of Modern History in the University of Oxford since 1957, is the only contemporary British historian who comes anywhere near to rivalling Taylor as a public name. Curiously a much-heralded television encounter between the two men over Taylor's *Origins* proved, as Mr D. C. Watt has written, 'one of the least effective confrontations ever staged'. Trevor-Roper's range is as extensive as that of Chabod: he began his professional life as a student of seventeenth-century England, and he has had a special mastery of that century ever since, spreading his empire far beyond the confines of the British Isles. In September 1945 Trevor-Roper, as an Intelligence Officer with the victorious Allies, was given the task of scotching the various dangerous rumours which were circulating about the fate of Hitler by tracking down the exact circumstances of his death. It was a unique opportunity for a historian, whose work is sometimes somewhat idly likened to detection: here the scent was hot, but incredibly convoluted. Trevor-Roper's brilliant reconstruction, *The Last Days of Hitler* (1947, and many subsequent editions), was a classic; and it remains a standard authority unshaken by the fragments of evidence that have since come to light. Subsequently Trevor-Roper was responsible for scholarly editions of various important Nazi documents – for example, *Hitler's Table Talk* (1953) and the *Bormann Letters* (1954). He thus developed a reputation in a second field of study: Nazi Germany. Recently he has published a study of medieval history, *The Rise of Christian Europe* (1965), a series of lectures delivered at the University of Sussex, and broadcast over B.B.C. television in 1963. Throughout, Trevor-Roper has shown an interest, unusual among British historians, in historiography. He is general editor of the New English Library series, *The Great Historians*, and is himself editor of the volume containing the abridgement of Gibbon's *Decline and Fall*; he has also edited *Macaulay's Essays* and he is the author of one of the very rare significant discussions of Ibn Khaldoun, the fourteenth-century Muslim historian, and his *Muqaddimah*.

Trevor-Roper was twenty-six when he published his biography of *Archbishop Laud* (1940), a sympathetic but far from uncritical study of the Conservative High Churchman, set firmly in the context of the complicated social and religious circumstances of the time. The book has remained the standard work on its topic and upon attaining a majority was in fact republished. It was abundantly clear that the young Trevor-Roper had opened his ears to the Weber thesis of the interdependence between Calvinism and the rise of capitalism. Yet the first controversy in which he became deeply involved, and with which he is still inextricably associated, was with Weber's greatest English disciple, R. H. Tawney. This controversy, too, we shall leave over till the next chapter: suffice it to say here that while Tawney, in a kind of Marxian analysis, had sought to explain the conflicts of the seventeenth century in terms of a 'rising gentry', Trevor-Roper postulated a 'falling gentry': much of what Tawney had written was indeed open to the gravest criticism, but Trevor-Roper's counter-arguments did not in this case find widespread acceptance among historians. However, he did put forward one very fertile idea which, much argued over and qualified in detail, has held the field in Civil War studies ever since: this is that the social and economic conflicts which finally issued in the Civil War can best be seen as a polarisation between a corrupt, high-living 'Court' at one end and the 'Country' at the other, peers and gentry who had not obtained the spoils of office, men of Puritan outlook, censorious of the standards of the court. One of the many merits of this typology is that it uses the very language of the seventeenth century instead of introducing entirely anachronistic concepts of class.

Historians, I have said once or twice, must be, and are, willing to borrow from the social sciences. Trevor-Roper has established a certain eminence in his sensitive and entirely pragmatic use of such borrowings. Though he has long since shaken off the obvious crudities of the Weber thesis, there remains a continuing interest in sociological synthesis: historians, however, 'should recognise the limits of sociological or theoretical interpretations and admit that there are times when political parties and political attitudes are not the direct expression of social or political theories or interests, but are polarised round political events'.[17] From his investigations of English society in the seventeenth century he turned to Scotland and the Continent, developing a comparative study of Weber's dynamic duo, Calvinism and capitalism. Two relatively short papers heralded his new discovery, a 'general crisis' throughout Europe in the middle decades of the seventeenth century (the discovery, of course, was not entirely new: the distinguished French historian Roland Mousnier had already written of much the same phenomenon, though the two historians differed greatly on certain points of detail, and E. J. Hobsbawm had written of a 'general economic crisis'). Trevor-Roper has not developed his thesis into a full-length study but it forms the central theme of an important recent collection of essays (the essay is perhaps the typical Trevor-Roper format) published under the title *Religion, the Reformation and Social Change* (1967). Among the various aspects of the general problem studied is 'The European Witch-craze of the Sixteenth and Seventeenth Centuries' – very much a fit subject for a historian belonging to the age of Freud and Hitler, Durkheim and Febvre. Trevor-Roper noted that persecution of 'witches' was more prevalent in Scotland and on the Continent than in England, and he endeavoured to show the manner in which the craze related to the rise and decline of the main intellectual and social movements of the time. Likening the craze to twentieth-century anti-semitism he has, as most historians of his generation would be inclined to do, warned against any facile belief in a steady human progress towards greater rationality.

Yet in some sense Trevor-Roper does share with J. H. Plumb a desire to see the idea of progress placed at the centre of historical inquiry. He finds the Enlightenment historians particularly congenial: his notorious rejection of the idea that there can be any African history seems to be based on a broader philosophical basis than the Ranke–Elton line that there can be no history because the traditional written materials of the

historian are missing. Life in 'dark countries and dark centuries',
Trevor-Roper says, provides subject-matter for anthropologists and
sociologists, but not for historians: history

> is essentially a form of movement, and purposive movement too. It is
> not a mere phantasmagoria of changing shapes and costumes, of battles
> and conquests, dynasties and usurpations, social forms and social dis-
> integration. If all history is equal as some now believe, there is no
> reason why we should study one section of it rather than another; for
> certainly we cannot study it all. Then indeed we may neglect our own
> history and amuse ourselves with the unrewarding gyrations of barbar-
> ous tribes in picturesque but irrelevant corners of the globe: tribes
> whose chief function in history, in my opinion, is to show to the
> present an image of the past from which, by history, it has es-
> caped. . . .[18]

The explicit attack here is upon Rankean historicism, the idea of every
age being 'equal in the sight of God', of, as it has been wittily put, all
ages having been 'born free and equal'. No doubt something of the
same sort was being said at the beginning of the century by James Harvey
Robinson. Trevor-Roper's especial strength is that he has brought an
iron-hard intellectual apparatus, and some impressively original work, to
bear on his statements about the nature of history. He has the proper
professional respect for diligent research, honestly carried out: but he
has frequently pointed out the difference between creative research and
mere pedantry. Trevor-Roper is a provocative writer and sometimes a
somewhat violent controversialist. He is a key figure in the post-1945
'renewal' of history in Great Britain, but he is openly contemptuous of
many of the fads and fashions of our time. In particular he has defended
European history against the growing preoccupation with African,
Asian and Latin-American history:

> The new rulers of the world, wherever they may be, will inherit a
> position that has been built up by Europe, and by Europe alone. It is
> European techniques, European examples, European ideas which have
> shaken the non-European world out of its past – out of barbarism in
> Africa, out of far older, slower, more majestic civilisations in Asia; and
> the history of the world, for the last five centuries, in so far as it has
> significance, has been European history. I do not think we need make
> any apology if our study of history is Europa-centred.

3 New Styles and Stylists

We may perhaps distinguish between two interconnected aspects of
historical writing in the period of crisis and renewal: the overall style

of thought which characterises almost all historians, be they leftist or rightist, progressive or conservative, be they drawn to diplomacy or to literature or to sociology; in short-hand fashion that style might be described as a rational acceptance of the fact of irrationality. It has coloured the great mainstream works of history discussed in the previous two sections, the work of such solid authorities as Pieter Geyl, the eminent Dutch historian, and of the hosts of professional monograph writers. It has also led historians to take a more thorough interest in the nastier forms of human activity, witch-hunting or anti-semitism, for instance; or to turn towards the 'failures' in history, as did Carl E. Schorske in his study of the *German Social Democrats 1905–1917* (1955) or James Joll in his history of *The Anarchists* (1964); or to stress the failings of well-intentioned progressive movements as in A. J. P. Taylor's *Trouble Makers*, or in Richard Hofstadter's *Age of Reform* (1955): significantly Hofstadter remarks that his study of the populist-progressive tradition is much more critical than it would have been if written fifteen years earlier. Apart from the overall approach, however, there is the question of the way in which in the recent period certain particular approaches towards history have become fashionable. Here I shall look first at some of the more recent types of 'social science' approach, at some of the co-operative ventures which have been mounted, at the various pieces of 'numeral' research which certain historians have presented, and at some of the new sub-histories which have developed, particularly at historical demography and urban history. Then I shall look at certain approaches which have arisen directly from the historical conditions of the twentieth century: pre-occupation with science and technology, and with the non-European parts of the globe. Thirdly I shall glance at the triumphant reoccupation of the marcher lands that lie between history and literature; and at the new developments taking place in the study of ancient history. Finally I shall consider a style of history which has often reaped the well-deserved scorn of other professional historians, yet which seems to have also staged something of a revival: I refer to biography.

The co-operative Norristown survey has already been mentioned; clearly history cannot claim any special credit for this fascinating project, in which it was certainly no more than equal partner with the social science disciplines. However there can be no doubt as to the standing of Merle Curti, Frederick Jackson Turner Professor of History in the University of Wisconsin, and author in the forties and fifties of various front-rank historical works, including the standard *Growth of American Thought*. Assisted by Robert Daniel, Shaw Livermore Jr, Joseph van Hise and Margaret W. Curti, as also by the Numerical Analysis Laboratory at Wisconsin, Professor Curti undertook a historical study in depth of Trempealeau County, Wisconsin, with a view to illuminating two major historical controversies: the possibility of objectivity in history, and the validity of Turner's proposition that the open frontier had promoted democracy in America. The resulting volume, *The Making of an American Community: A Case Study of Democracy in a Frontier County* (1959), was, Curti explained, genuinely a collaborative work though it was in no way a collection of discrete essays: 'Each chapter, whether the first draft was written by me or by a collaborator, was prepared as part of a general scheme of treatment and directed by me.' He could not in the end claim that the work was 'completely objective', nor, of course, that Trempealeau was necessarily typical of all frontier counties; but he could very reasonably state that

> our operational approach to specific testable units of larger problems, combining as it has the traditional historical approach with certain social science methods, has yielded a higher degree of objectivity than we could have otherwise attained.

Among the points illumined by the study were, first, that despite traditional views as to the extreme poverty of Polish immigrant groups (a view which the authors were at first prepared, on the basis of their traditional researches in the literary sources, to accept), calculation of the median values of real and personal property showed that the Poles in fact were 'nowhere near the bottom of the economic scale'; second, that the common impression that the foreign-born, once settled on American land, were more likely to stay put than the native-born was without foundation; and, third, that there was no question of increasing concentration of capital and increasing misery – the rich in fact became 'somewhat richer' while the poor 'became a good deal less poor'. Conceiving of democracy as involving such processes as 'Americanisation' and 'multiple leadership' (and here obviously a subjective element comes in), Curti believed that their investigations did support the main implications of the Turner thesis: 'The story of the making of this American community is the story of progress towards democracy.' The first appendix to the book is a superb guide to the methodology employed by Curti and his associates, a godsend to innumerate colleagues and those who are mystified by the use of machines in the study of history. But the book is very much that of a historian: the quantitative methods are seen as having 'very usefully supplemented the traditional historical methods'.

The notion of quantitative study serving as supplemental to 'traditional' methods, and indeed to many other methods which are just as new as quantification, is a central one in much of the historical inquiry of recent years. Professor Lawrence Stone[19] and Professor G. E. Aylmer, for example, have both made great use of numeral analysis, complete with pages of statistical tables, to develop important lines of inquiry into English history in the seventeenth century. Dr Henry Pelling has used quantitative methods for his pioneering study of the *Social Geography of British Elections 1885–1910*, though he has, in a fine phrase, referred to 'the historian's customary process of assembling the evidence, however fragmentary and inconclusive, and making the best of it'.[20] Quantification is not the only supplemental benefit derived from social science; Professor David M. Potter has explained how in preparing the series of lectures delivered at the University of Chicago in 1950, and subsequently published as *People of Plenty: Economic Abundance and the American Character* (1954), he was 'assailed by misgivings as to the validity of the whole concept of "national character"'. As a historian, he tells us, he became 'embarrassed' to discover 'that the most telling contributions . . . came from cultural anthropologists and social psychologists rather than from my fellow historians'. The book itself is a most impressive example of a work, set in a genuine historical context, which integrates materials from history and from these two social science disciplines. One other important and characteristic example may be cited. Boyd C. Shafer's *Nationalism: Myth and Reality* (1955) is a brilliant exposition of certain principles which the author enunciates at the outset: although a historian, his study of nationalism made it 'not only enlightening but imperative to draw upon the findings of other social sciences' – which he lists as psychology, anthropology and biology. Shafer confesses to his amateur status outside history, but states his belief that 'historical work may be enriched by the findings of other disciplines'. Sometimes, of course, social scientists object to this amateurishness: historians should either become social scientists through and through or not trespass at all, is the argument. Actually Shafer's work is authoritative precisely because of his twenty-year immersion in the historical literature of nationalism: had he used the time instead to study psychology, anthropology and biology he would presumably not have been able to develop his encyclopedic understanding of nationalism as a historical phenomenon.

The modern study of historical demography was pioneered by Louis Henry of the French Institut National d'Études Démographiques, who developed new techniques for using parish-register material, particularly that known as 'reconstitution' where full details on a *sample* of families are compiled. In England, E. A. Wrigley, D. C. Eversley and Peter Laslett have been employing the method of 'aggregation', using material sent in by diligent researchers working in various parts of the country. Mr Peter Laslett's essay drawing upon these researches, *The World We Have Lost* (1965), was not received with universal acclaim by academic critics, but undoubtedly Mr Laslett has performed an important service in publicising the possibilities of this type of research. Although Laslett is optimistic about the 'objective' quality of this work, he stresses the importance in it of the 'exercise of the historical imagination'. Historical demographers have been particularly active, naturally enough, in the study of the 'population explosion' of the eighteenth century. Although no completely validated conclusions have yet been established, sufficient work has been done by Professor K. H. Connell, Professor J. T. Krause and many others to throw into disrepute the thesis which associated rising population with a falling death rate which in turn was associated with improved medicine, environment, etc. It is now pretty certain that whatever was happening to the death rate, there was in the middle and later eighteenth century a very definite rise in the birth rate; not to put too fine a point upon it, people were copulating earlier and oftener. Scholars of originality and imagination have been at work long enough for demography to have fallen under the sway of the Iron Law of Historical Tedium: many prentice hands are now grubbing at their separate little parish registers, carefully transcribing information onto data cards, then feeding the cards into a computer. But however inadequate an apprenticeship this may be for the young historian, there can be no doubt as to the exciting prospects for a fuller understanding of many aspects of the past opened up by the accumulated results of this kind of detailed investigation.

One new approach to history which probably more than most characterises historical thinking in the 1950s and 1960s is urban history. The interest in urban history has in part been due to the external stimulus of contemporary concern over the problems of the city; but its real roots lie in the recent internal reorientation of historical study. It is in fact an offshoot of historical demography. In fulfilling what Asa Briggs, a pioneer urban historian in Britain, calls 'the need to examine in detail social structure and change in the most meaningful units that historians can discover', it avoids the sterility of the traditional economic and social sub-histories. It provides, in the 'city', a convenient focus for comparative study between different societies, and it meets the current desire of historians 'to revise and rewrite national histories in the light of fuller knowledge of local relationships and pressures'.[21] In France the demographic stimulus to the study of urban history came from the Institut National d'Études Démographiques, while important contributions were also made by the long-established interest of French scholars in historical geography and by the *Annales* school. Numbered among the most influential members of the very varied French school of urban history are Adeline Daumard, Pierre Goubert and Louis Chevalier. In America and, subsequently, in Europe, the Chicago school of urban sociology has been a strong influence. From his work in immigrant groups Professor Oscar Handlin has moved into the main stream of urban history, and in 1963 he, with John Burchard, edited the important collection of studies *The Historian and the City* (1963). Urban history represents in unique microcosm the colossal range of source materials and of methodologies upon which the contemporary historian calls: census statistics and data processing at one end; the critical study of novels and poems at the other.

The reasons for the boom in the study of science history and history of technology are obvious. A generation or so ago science history was almost the exclusive monopoly of a few specialists who confined themselves to the internal development of science, paying little attention to social and cultural influences. Outside this specialist school there were only two other approaches: the economic histories, which presented somewhat bald catalogues of scientific and technological innovation without any very satisfactory explanation of how these came about or how they were related to the wider context; and the Marxist accounts, which had the great merit of stressing the social relations of science, but which were often rather facile in their insistence upon the dependence of scientific advance upon economic imperatives. Science history is now a much more sophisticated subject, involving on the part of the historian both an understanding of the scientific theories he is discussing and of the processes of historical causation and change:[22] both of these qualities are to be found in high degree in the work of the dean of contemporary science historians, G. C. Gillispie.[23] Much of the most interesting work in the history of technology, however, is now being done by researchers whose starting-point lies in the refined techniques of contemporary economic history. The progression of David Landes of Harvard University, from his *Bankers and Pashas: International Finance and Economic Imperialism in Egypt* (1960) to his present enviable position as an accepted authority on technological innovation and industrial change, based on his brilliant chapter in volume six of the *Cambridge Economic History* (1965), is instructive. One indication of the growing acceptance at all levels of history teaching of the importance of the history of science and technology is to be found in that excellent series edited by Bruce Mazlish of the Massachusetts Institute of Technology, 'Main Themes of European History': of the first half-dozen volumes two were concerned with the rise of science and with the development of technology. Similarly one of the first volumes in the 'Problems and Perspectives in History' series was the *Origins of the Scientific Revolution* by Hugh F. Kearney.

It would be tedious to list the names of the leading authorities in the various areas of non-European history which have become very fashionable in the last generation. What should be emphasised is the successful attempt which historians are making to get away from the old Western orientation: to see other civilisations from the inside and on their own terms, rather than merely as passive recipients of the 'impact' of Western colonisation.[24] Among British and American historians there

has, too, been something of a reaction against the notion of the unique-
ness of the British imperial experience, a reaction against the idea that
on grounds both of efficiency and morality the British were somehow
superior as colonisers to, say, the French or the Spaniards. One particularly interesting work by an English historian is D. K. Fieldhouse's
The Colonial Empires (1967), which adopts the broad comparative approach.

For the past few years British historians with no great sympathy for
the bigger innovations in historical study have been arguing that the
numeral urge has spent itself, that sociological history is now *passé* and
that the fashion-conscious should turn to that kind of history which is
characterised by its close association with literature. Actually the
'literary' approach has been in full swing in the United States for some
years now, for almost as long as the social science approach in fact; in
some cases, as for instance with certain urban historians, the quantitative and literary approaches go hand in hand. Nonetheless one of the
leaders in the movement back towards literature has also been one of the
most wittily sceptical commentators on, as he sees it, the historian's
periodic infatuation with the social sciences: C. Vann Woodward's *The
Burden of Southern History* (1961) contains an impressive plea that
historians seek a deeper understanding of Southern history through the
serious study of Southern literature:

> This is no plea for the relaxation of the severe limitations of the his-
> torian's discipline, nor for his borrowing the novelist's license. But
> once the historian abandons an old and false analogy with the natural
> sciences and sees that his craft employs no special concepts nor cate-
> gories nor special terminology, he will admit that he attempts to
> 'explain' history in the same way he explains events in ordinary life –
> his own as well as that of his fellow men – and with much the same
> language, moral and psychological. He should then acknowledge that
> Southern men of letters have advanced many of the aims he shares.

One portent into which much was read by those anxious to predict a
new direction for historical studies was the creation in the early sixties
of a new Chair at Harvard in History and Literature: the first incumbent,
John Clive, had written a model work combining the disciplines of
historical and literary criticism, *Scotch Reviewers: the 'Edinburgh
Review' 1802–1815* (1957). Another portent was the founding at
Indiana State University of the interdisciplinary journal *Victorian
Studies*. Certainly a new and often rich vein was being opened up. I. F.
Clarke's *Voices Prophesying War, 1763–1984* (1966), a fascinating study
of the war novel, brought out clearly both the orientation towards war
of Edwardian society, and the overwhelming impact of the Great War
in making impossible further romantic speculation about future wars.
Wallace Martin's *A. R. Orage and the New Age* (1966) opened new in-

sights into the 'cultural awakening' which immediately preceded the Great War. This particular labour was completed by Samuel H. Hynes's enjoyable study of *The Edwardian Turn of Mind* (1968); the bridge between history and literature was also complete, for Hynes is in fact a Professor of English.

Another important bridge constructed in recent years is that across the gulf which opened earlier in the century between 'ancient' history and 'modern' history. The lead in a new approach to the classical world was given in the nineteen-twenties by the Russian-born scholar Michael I. Rostovtzeff (1870–1952). Arnaldo Momigliano, one of the most distinguished among the later generation of ancient historians, has described the reactions of his contemporaries to the publication in 1926 of Rostovtzeff's *Social and Economic History of the Roman Empire*:

> We were accustomed to books on ancient history where the archaeological evidence, if used at all, was never presented and explained to the reader. Here a lavish series of plates introduced us directly to the archaeological evidence; and the caption of each plate really made us understand what one could learn from apparently insignificant items.[25]

Today some of the most exciting historical work is being done in the territory once delimited as 'the classics', and the more forward-looking historical journals and history departments are welcoming research and teaching in ancient history as a vital part of the study of history.

Now we turn to a branch of history which has often been spurned by the professionals: biography. Sir Lewis Namier, it will be recalled, pioneered a 'biographical approach' to history whereby a complete picture of a particular political structure was built up on the basis of a vast number of individual biographies of individual politicians. But this is not the kind of biography one usually has in mind. Namier, though he did leave a biography of Charles Townshend, expressed in classic terms the objections which can be raised against the conventional biography as a form of history. It was, he suggested, a lazy and easy form, having an obvious shape based on the birth, development and death of the subject of the biography. The biographer, Namier argued, could, without necessarily observing the critical standards of the scholarly editor, simply serve up the information contained in the private papers of his subject, while relying on secondary sources for 'background'.[26] There can be no doubt that many biographies are written to just this specification, so that they correspondingly do not rate very highly as history. But a moment's reflection shows just how necessary to historical study the writing of biography is, and may help to explain how in this age of quantification and advanced literary criticism so many of the major historical works of our time have in fact been cast in biographical mould. Without biographies of Christopher Columbus, Martin Luther,

George Washington, Joseph Stalin, vast areas of history would remain
totally obscure. In twentieth-century British historiography no gaps
are more yawning than those left by the absence of authoritative lives
of J. Ramsay MacDonald and Winston Churchill: the young historians at present at work on the authorised biographies of these Prime
Ministers, David Marquand and Martin Gilbert respectively, are assured,
when their labours are completed, of an important place in twentieth-
century British historiography. Reference has already been made to one
of the most important and authoritative works in the entire bibliography
of twentieth-century European history, Alan Bullock's *Hitler: A Study in
Tyranny*. Equally all twentieth-century British historians, who welcomed
the first two volumes of his *Life and Times of Ernest Bevin*, im-
patiently await the third volume, which will clearly be indispensable to
any rounded appraisal of that most important period when the first
Labour Government to have real power was rebuilding British
society and facing an unprecedented power situation abroad. One of
the greatest of the American straight-line professionals, S. E. Morison,
having written the official history of American naval operations during
the Second World War, returned to an earlier interest in biography,
producing a number of outstanding naval studies, including *Christopher
Columbus* and *Paul Jones*. One of the most distinguished of present-day
Oxford historians, Robert Blake, has confined himself almost exclusively
to the field of political biography: his *Disraeli* (1966) was one of the great
publishing events of the decade. A slightly younger historian, F. S. L.
Lyons, received much professional acclaim for his biography of the
Irish parliamentary leader, *John Dillon* (1968).

These in their various ways are works of traditional biography, using
of course all the insights of modern psychology; books whose essential
rationale is that their subjects are in themselves men of manifest historical importance. More recently, however, certain historians have been
using biography as a kind of focal device where an individual, often
himself of relatively minor importance, is cited as a 'type', or as a
useful 'lead-in' to problems of wide historical significance. Two strikingly successful examples of this kind of biography are James Joll's
studies of three *Intellectuals in Politics* (Marinetti, Rathenau and Blum)
and Klaus Epstein's *Mathias Erzberger and the Dilemma of German
Democracy* (1959).

4 MODERN MARXISM: THE PRESENT GENERATION

A quarter of a century has passed since the end of the Second World
War. Major historical works are many years in the making. Some historians publish their most characteristic contributions to knowledge at

thirty, others at sixty. Although it is possible to offer some tentative generalisations about historical writing since the 1940s, there have been within the same period many short-term movements in different directions; as with the study of contemporary history, it is not easy to say which short-term movements may achieve the status of long-term trends. So quickly do things move in our own time that one morning's new dawn may be the next day's fixed orthodoxy. What is pie in the sky in Great Britain may be old hat in France or America. The problem is not perhaps a very real one. My purpose in the historiographical sections of this book has been to stress the essential continuity in historical study. No scheme of periodisation will conceal the recurrent debates which go on in every age among historians themselves and between historians and their critics. I have called this entire period of historical inquiry one of 'crisis', while at the same time referring to Professor John Higham's considered opinion that, in the U.S. at least, the early fifties marked a period of 'renewal' in historical study. The two descriptions are not mutually exclusive: crisis often leads to renewal. However my own view would be that Professor Higham is a little too optimistic: historians have by no means faced up to all the criticisms (outlined in the opening chapter) which from time to time are made of their activities; many are still at heart deeply uneasy and troubled about the state of their profession. I propose in this chapter to look at certain movements of opinion among historians which run on rather further than the essentially conservative position established in the years following the Second World War. In the main I have tried to avoid attaching political labels to historians, since one of the great achievements of the development of historical studies has been a growing ability among historians to counteract their own political biases. The post-Namier empiricist movement in historiography was, however, a 'Tory' movement in its distrust of ideology, in its emphasis on the unpredictable, and in its scepticism about the possibilities of human control of human destinies, and in its insistence on the concrete quantifiable fact. Throughout the entire period a number of historians have seen such approaches as so completely negative as to take all purpose out of the study of history.

Marxism offered one possible means towards meaning in history. Actually the works produced by the handful of leading British Marxist historians are so subtle and penetrating in their historical analysis that it is hard to see that they differ greatly from the style of historical study fostered by the *Annales* school, or indeed from that of many other historians concerned with the *totality* of historical experience. However it would be churlish not to agree that a remarkable lead in the movement away from the main tenets of the Tory empiricists has been given by a group of English historians who are happy to style themselves Marxists. At the furthest extreme the empiricists seemed to be arguing that 'things happen because they happen' (a phrase actually used by Mr A. J. P. Taylor): the Marxists, and of course many others, have sought to show the meaningful interconnectedness of events. Their particular achievement, perhaps, has been to bring 'the people' back into history; not in the old vague romantic way, but in a manner which makes exhaustive use of every available source and every new methodology.

To be strictly accurate in placing Christopher Hill (b. 1912), currently Master of Balliol College, Oxford, one should record that his reply to the query 'Are you a Marxist historian?' is 'You define Marxist historian.' His first major intellectual interest was in the seventeenth-century metaphysical school; he found Marxism a helpful tool in his critical analysis of their poetry. In the forties his general historical writings on the seventeenth century took a somewhat crude Marxist standpoint, but the books published in the fifties and sixties – *Economic Problems of the Church* (1956), *Puritanism and Revolution* (1958), *Intellectual Origins of the English Revolution* (1965) – will undoubtedly hold a permanent place in the historiography of the English Revolution. While not a 'present-minded' historian in the absurd sense of the 'new' historians, Hill insists upon the social function of history: he has devoted his scholarly career to the study of the seventeenth century because he believes this 'century of revolution' to be crucial in the modern development of society. He has a certain scorn – shared, it may be noted, by Trevor-Roper – for history as a sterile academic exercise. Battles as destructive in their own context as those of the Great Civil War have been fought over the origins and history of that war: Hill has consistently had before him the objective of presenting a new synthesis to replace the older conception of a 'Puritan Revolution', long since the victim of many destructive forays. Echoing Marc Bloch, he has called for a history embracing 'the total activity of society'. Repudiating the more recent reading of the Civil War as merely a squabble among the ruling classes, he has insisted that 'the evidence still suggests that in 1640 there was a real popular hostility to the old regime whose depth and intensity needs analysis and explanation.' He has pointed out that 'Marx himself did not fall into the error of thinking that men's ideas were merely a pale reflection of their economic needs': the worst excesses of economic determinism have been perpetrated by later writers, many avowedly non-Marxist. 'The connections of religion, science, politics and economics', Hill has himself explained,

> are infinite and infinitely subtle. Religion was the idiom in which men of the seventeenth century thought. One does not need to accept the idiom, or to take it at its face value, to see that it cannot be ignored or rejected as a simple reflex of economic needs. Any adequate interpretation of the English revolution must give full place to questions of religion and church government, must help us to grasp the political and social implications of theological heresy.[27]

The *Intellectual Origins of the English Revolution* turns altogether away from economics, and indeed from Puritanism. The introduction is a brilliant piece of high-level historical thinking which again might well meet the needs of any would-be historiographical anthologist. Hill begins by remarking (such have been the advances made by proponents of the comparative approach) that it is no longer heretical in 1965 to suggest the validity and fruitfulness of comparisons and contrasts between the English and French Revolutions. Yet agreement continues that the English Revolution had no intellectual origins: it just happened, in typical muddled English fashion. Hill is able to quote his own earlier opinion that 'there was no Jean-Jacques Rousseau or Karl Marx of the English Revolution', before going on to insist that in fact there can be no revolution without ideas. Hill warns against the purely economic-determinist view; he warns against its strange descendant, the Namier method, with its too-ready assumption that 'the ideas which swayed men and women in the past can be dismissed as hypocrisy, rationalisations, or irrelevancies'; he warns against the danger, to which historians of science are prone, of giving marks to some scientists for being 'right' and of dismissing others for being 'wrong'; and he warns against the ball-of-string school of intellectual history – he is, he says, sceptical about pedigrees of ideas, A influenced by B, who got his ideas from C, and that explains action Z: 'It is always easy', he concludes, 'to contruct chains of causes once you know what you have to explain.' But these are negative points: what lies at the centre of the *Intellectual Origins* is a positive conception of the place of ideas in the historical process:

> Ideas were all-important for the individuals whom they impelled into action; but the historian must attach equal importance to the circumstances which gave these ideas their chance. Revolutions are not made without ideas, but they are not made by intellectuals. Steam is essential to driving a railway engine; but neither a locomotive nor a permanent way can be built out of steam. In this book I shall be dealing with the steam. . . .
>
> It seems to me that any body of thought which plays a major part in history – Luther's, Rousseau's, Marx's own – 'takes on' because it meets the needs of significant groups in the society in which it comes into prominence. . . .
>
> Men . . . do not break lightly with the past: if they are to challenge conventionally accepted standards they must have an alternative body of ideas to support them.

The more obviously Marxist character in the historical thinking of E. J. Hobsbawm (b. 1917), at present Reader in History at Birkbeck College, London, is apparent in such essays as his 'General Crisis of the European Economy in the 17th Century', which is an analysis of 'the last phase of the general transition from a feudal to a capitalist economy'.[28] His special interest in 'the people' is shown in *Primitive Rebels: Studies of Archaic Forms of Social Movement in the Nineteenth and Twentieth Centuries* (1959), *Labouring Men* (1964), which is about the 'working classes as such' rather than about the labour organisations and movements upon which many more conventional historians have concentrated, and *Captain Swing* (1969), written in collaboration with George Rudé. No textbook is a more flawless example of total history than Hobsbawm's *The Age of Revolution 1789–1848* (1962), from its opening chapter, 'The World in the 1780s', a superb piece of socio-historical scene-setting, to the carefully chosen illustrations which really do contribute to the text. 'The first thing to observe about the world of the 1780s', writes Hobsbawm,

> is that it was at once much smaller and much larger than ours. It was smaller geographically, because even the best-educated and best-informed men then living . . . knew only patches of the inhabited globe. . . .
> Humanity was smaller. . . . To take one illustration from the abundance of statistics about the physique of conscripts upon which this generalisation is based: in one canton on the Ligurian coast 72 per cent of the recruits in 1792–9 were less than 1·50 metres (5 ft 2 in.) tall. That did not mean that the men of the later eighteenth century were more fragile than we are. The scrawny, stunted, undrilled soldiers of the French Revolution were capable of a physical endurance equalled today only by the undersized guerillas in colonial mountains. . . .
> Yet if the world was in many respects smaller, the sheer difficulty or uncertainty of communications made it in practice much vaster than it is today. . . . To be within reach of a port was to be within reach of the world: in a real sense London was closer to Plymouth or Leith than to villages in the Breckland of Norfolk; Seville was more accessible from Veracruz than from Valladolid, Hamburg from Bahia than from the Pomeranian hinterland. . . .
> The world of 1789 was therefore, for most of its inhabitants, incalculably vast. Most of them, unless snatched away by some awful hazard, such as military recruitment, lived and died in the county, and often in the parish, of their birth: as late as 1861 more than nine out of ten in seventy of the ninety French departments lived in the department of their birth. The rest of the globe was a matter of government agents and rumour. . . .

George Rudé's work on the eighteenth-century crowd has already been mentioned. His collaborative work with Hobsbawm, *Captain Swing*, rescues the great and moving story of England's last agrarian rising, that of 1830, from the oblivion to which an exclusive interest in the development of the state, and an exclusive preoccupation with the winners in history, had consigned it.

E. P. Thompson (b. 1924), who is Reader in Labour History at the

University of Warwick, has achieved world fame with his *The Making of the English Working Class* (1965), though criticism from straight-line academics has not been lacking, particularly over Thompson's handling of his central thesis, the growth of a specifically 'working-class consciousness'. Most critics failed to notice that apart from being a masterly vindication of creative Marxism his book is also a classic vindication of the values of history as against the sterilities of the narrower social scientists. Thompson insists, as many historians have long implicitly accepted but never so well expressed, that class is a 'historical phenomenon' not a 'structure' nor a 'category', 'something which in fact happens (and can be shown to have happened) in human relationships'; class is a 'historical relationship' with a fluency which 'evades analysis if we attempt to stop it dead at any given moment and anatomise its structure', a relationship which 'must always be embodied in real people and in a real context'. Class happens 'when some men, as a result of common experiences (inherited or shared), feel and articulate the identity of their interests as between themselves, and as against other men whose interests are different from (and usually opposed to) theirs'. The book, eight hundred pages long, is a treasure-house of fascinating information and deep historical insight, informed by Thompson's immense erudition in all aspects of the creative literature of this period (and indeed of many others) and his profound understanding of the current preoccupations of psychologists, social psychologists, and other social scientists. Where economic historians were content to assess the quantitative gains of the Industrial Revolution, Thompson sensitively explores the qualitative losses, an exploration which he has subsequently taken further in some sparkling studies of the effects of factory discipline. Violence, he says, was done to '*human nature*'; for there was 'a violent technological differentiation between work and life'. It is 'neither poverty nor disease but work itself which casts the blackest shadow over the years of the Industrial Revolution'.

Implicitly Thompson alludes in an earlier chapter to the celebrated thesis of the great French historian Élie Halévy that the spread of Methodism had saved England from revolution in the early nineteenth century. Thompson's analysis is a good deal more subtle than that of Halévy, showing how Methodism could act both as an agent of the *status quo*, and as an agent of inspired political protest. Typical of a particular style of historical writing of which Thompson is a master is the fascinating but deeply serious passage in which he illustrates the 'obsessional Methodist concern with sexuality' which reveals itself in 'the perverted eroticism of Methodist imagery'. *The Making of the English Working Class* is a true work of historical revisionism, bringing into proper perspective the aspirations and conscious efforts of working people, too often treated by other historians as an inert and faceless mass, passive to the central forces in history. Its shape is interesting: 'a group of studies, on related themes, rather than a consecutive narrative'. Much of the important work of Kitson Clark, Trevor-Roper and Christopher Hill, discussed above, could be similarly described. So could the great works of Sir Lewis Namier. The insistence, shared by great amateurs and great professionals, that history must in all circumstances be narrative, is nothing but a red herring.

Younger historians for whom, often, there is little meaning in the label 'Marxist' have shared in the movement towards a more purposeful, a less destructively sceptical history. Professor J. P. Kenyon has recently written that although a few years ago it was considered a 'crippling disadvantage to share the opinions of any historical figure you wrote about', such days, 'mercifully', are passing. There has even been a revived interest in Toynbee: at least, the feeling is, his writing has breadth, vision and purpose. Some historians have begun to talk of the need for a new approach to universal history as a world-wide synthesis. The only successful efforts in this direction so far have been Maurice Crouzot's *L'Époque Contemporaine* (1957), volume seven in the *Histoire Générale des Civilisations*, and, on a vastly different and more ambitious time-scale, William H. McNeill's *Rise of the West* (1963). Two new English-language journals, both launched in the 1950s, represent well some of the newer trends in historiography: *Comparative Studies in Society and History* (founded in the U.S.A. by a pioneer sponsor of sociological history, Sylvia Thrupp) and *Past and Present* (founded in the U.K. by a group of historians, most of them Marxist). Among others, the editorial board of *Past and Present*, when it was inaugurated in 1952, included Professor Geoffrey Barraclough, a medievalist who has given a public lead in discussing the present crisis in historical study and in suggesting remedies – see especially his *History in a Changing World* (1955) – R. R. Betts, Professor of Central European History at London, V. Gordon Childe, Professor of Prehistoric European Archaeology at London, A. H. M. Jones, Professor of Ancient History, and Maurice Dobb, the Marxist economic historian, both from Cambridge, and Christopher Hill; E. J. Hobsbawm was assistant editor. The avowed aim of *Past and Present* was a demonstration that the 'methods of reason and science' are applicable to the study of history. While insisting upon a 'firm foundation of scholarly research', they would not publish 'articles which merely bring the results of a piece of detailed research'.[29] For nearly two decades *Past and Present* has convincingly testified to the contemporary belief that history can be scholarly and yet more than a mere academic exercise; can indeed fulfil that social function which, as argued throughout this book, lies in its very essence.

Notes

1. Carl Bridenbaugh, 'The Great Mutation', *American Historical Review*, LXVIII (1963).
2. C. E. Carrington, *The British Overseas*, preface to second edition (1968).
3. J. H. Hexter, *Reappraisals in History* (1961) p. 200.
4. Higham, *History*, pp. 132ff.
5. Denys Hay, *Europe in the Fourteenth and Fifteenth Centuries* (1966) p. x.
6. S. T. Bindoff, 'Political History' in Finberg, *Approaches to History*.
7. See Kitson Clark, *The Making of Victorian England* (paperback ed., 1965) p. 7.
8. Ibid., p. 4.
9. G. Kitson Clark, *The Critical Historian* (1967) p. 195.
10. See the critical discussion of the Elton thesis by Penry Williams and G. L. Harris, in *Past and Present*, xxv (July 1963).
11. Carr, *What is History?*, p. 37; Elton, *The Practice of History*, pp. 14, 21–2.
12. Not, to my mind, a persuasive comparison: see below, p. 243.
13. *Observer*, 5 May and 8 December 1968.
14. *Rumours of Wars* (1952) p. 8.
15. Introduction to Karl Marx and Friedrich Engels, *The Communist Manifesto*, p. 11.
16. *Past and Present*, xxx (1965) 113.
17. H. R. Trevor-Roper, *Religion, the Reformation and Social Change* (1967) p. xiii.
18. H. R. Trevor-Roper, *The Rise of Christian Europe* (1965) p. 9.
19. See above, p. 120, and below, p. 223.
20. *Social Geography of British Elections* (1967) p. 2.
21. Asa Briggs, in H. J. Dyos (ed.), *The Study of Urban History* (1968) pp. v–xi.
22. See A. C. Crombie and M. A. Hoskin, 'A Note on History of Science as an Academic Discipline', and Henry Guerlac, 'Some Historical Assumptions of the History of Science' in A. C. Crombie (ed.), *Scientific Change* (1963).
23. See G. C. Gillispie, *Genesis and Geology* (1951) and *The Edge of Objectivity* (1960).
24. See, e.g., J. D. Hargreaves, 'Towards a History of the Partition of Africa' in *Journal of African History* 1 (1960); and G. Shepperson and T. Price, *Independent African* (1958).
25. Arnaldo Momigliano, *Studies in Historiography* (1966) p. 91.
26. *History Today* (1952).
27. 'Recent Interpretations of the Civil War' in *History* (1956).
28. *Past and Present*, 5, 6 (1954).
29. *Past and Present*, 1 (Feb 1952).

7 Problems in History

∽∽

1 THE SIGNIFICANCE OF HISTORICAL CONTROVERSY

IT is easy sometimes to suspect that historians keep themselves in employment by continually revising each other's versions of past events. For the newcomer to historical study there may be something off-putting about a book such as Lawrence Stone's *Social Change and Revolution in England 1540–1640* (1965), a judicious selection of excerpts from the writings of leading historians illustrating the controversies surrounding the origins of the English Civil War: with historians ferociously tearing into each other and flatly contradicting each other's facts and conclusions he may well wonder whom he can believe. One of the purposes of this book has been to establish some of the criteria whereby a piece of historical writing can be deemed worthy of attention or not. Of course it is always open to a self-advancing extrovert, or a misguided crank, to offer the world a startling new interpretation of certain historical events: should his work not be based on thorough scholarship, should it not be offered in good faith, the ever-ready police battalions of the historical guild will soon club his pretensions into jelly. Yet historians with the highest scholarly qualifications do disagree (so, of course, do scientists from time to time). History, we have said more than once, is based on 'imperfect evidence': the more imperfect the evidence, the more room for disagreement over its interpretation. In the wider perspective, disagreement is a function of history as dialogue between present and past: succeeding ages produce new reconstructions of the past. Within the same age different historians give greater or less weight to ideal as against material factors; some strive hard to bring out some underlying pattern of events; others reject the very idea of the existence of such a pattern. Disagreement as between one generation and another is so obvious that one can have little sympathy with the student who complains about *that*: he simply cannot expect a book written in 1965 to concur with one written in 1905 – it would be a poor look-out for the advancement of historical study if it did. As for disagreements among historians of the same generation, it should be remembered that these are usually aired in the pages of the learned journals, from whence in fact most of Lawrence Stone's excerpts are culled. In such a context there is a tendency for areas of disagreement to seem larger than they really are: in a legitimate desire to make their theories stand forth as clearly as possible, historians naturally emphasise where they disagree with predecessors and colleagues. Again the inquirer can complain only if there are no good textbooks to which he can refer for guidance through the turbulence of historical controversy: quite often in practice the most embattled controversialists are able at the same time to provide lucid straightforward textbooks which indicate the main areas of controversy.

Not that a true understanding of history can be derived from textbooks. Indeed no one can grasp the nature of history without some grasp of the nature of historical controversy. That is why one welcomes the many admirable series on 'problems in history' in which the Americans have excelled for some years, and to which British historians (as, for instance, Stone – though at present he is Dodge Professor at Princeton) are increasingly turning. With regard to the value of historical controversy, two incidental points, and one fundamental one emerge. First, historical controversy illuminates the dialogue aspects of history: interpretations do change, usually, I believe, in the direction of getting closer to the objective reality of what happened in the past; it is important that the inquirer, layman or student, should understand that history is not a monolithic hunk of received truth; although his 'opinions' of course are in no sense equal in value to those of the historical expert who has steeped himself in the sources and in all aspects of a particular controversy (wise fools are often to be found asserting that their opinions do have this value), he should be encouraged to exercise his own mind in entering the dialogue between historian and reader. Second, historical controversy brings into sharp focus the nature of historical sources and historical methodology and shows the basic agreed criteria upon which the historian operates. One opinion is not as good as another: the would-be historian who lunges in with a specious scheme based on inadequate source material and faulty methodology will very soon be exposed in the clash of battle. Again and again the appeal will be made to the texts, or to a certain statistical analysis, or, sometimes, to a notion of how, in a particular age or particular context, things were *likely* (and unlikely) to happen. When a controversy has run its course, which may well take many generations, it will usually be seen that the final differences, save in problems where the surviving evidence really is so fragmentary that only imaginative guesses are possible, are those of emphasis and definition rather than of fact or fundamental interpretation: some historians, like some scientists, will remain unconquerably extrovert rather than introvert, or optimistic rather than pessimistic in their assessment of human aspirations. Actually it is wrong to talk of controversy 'running its course': even if a consensus among informed authorities seems to have been reached, that consensus is always open to the challenge of the discovery of new sources or the application of new methodologies, as well as to the changing perspectives drawn by succeeding generations from their own immediate historical experience (that is, it is open to the perennial influence of the present–past dialogue).

But the really important point about historical controversy is the manner in which it furthers the development of a more *truthful* account of the past. The historian delving ever deeper into some great corpus of source material, surfacing it may be every now and again to classify his quantities and have his little cards run through a computer, can very easily and understandably fall into the belief that the picture of events and their interconnections which he has so painstakingly put together is the only one consistent with the known evidence (and who knows the evidence better than he himself?). So deeply is he involved in his own researches that he may well fail to see relationships and perspectives which are evident to another scholar approaching matters from a different angle. Or, on the other hand, if his talents lie in a different direction, he may have formulated some striking high-level thesis or series of interrelated generalisations. We all fall in love with our own theories, repeating them, pushing them ever harder, in seminar after seminar, in conference, in learned articles, to our students, to our friends, to our colleagues, to the wider public if it will listen. It is in controversy that the wild hypothesis is exposed to discussion and criticism, just as it is in controversy that the blinkered account is opened to the stimulus of fellow historians' 'bright ideas'. As Trevor-Roper has remarked, there are times 'when a new error is more life-giving than an old truth, a fertile error than a sterile accuracy'. It is out of the clash of differing interpretations and conflicting hypotheses that a new, profounder, more rounded version of some historical problem finally emerges.

It is not my purpose in this chapter to repeat work which has been better done by the distinguished editors of the various 'problems in history' books already referred to. Indeed I would hope that certain of these books might be used in conjunction with this chapter, which seeks simply to relate some of the broader issues raised in the course of the present book to specific historical controversies. I have tried to choose historiographical 'problems' (another dangerous word, but let it stand) which illuminate 'the development of historical studies' as I have described it, as well as the main technical and conceptual matters discussed in this book: they are the significance of Magna Carta – sometimes held to be the foundation-stone of liberty throughout the English-speaking world (there is an excellent edition by G. R. C. Davis, published in paperback by the British Museum); the causes of the English Civil War (Lawrence Stone's excellent volume in Longmans 'Problems and Perspectives' series has already been mentioned); the causes of the American Revolution (there is a volume with this title, edited by John C. Wahlke, in D. C. Heath's 'Problems in American Civilization' series, which should be studied along with chapter 4 of the more up-to-date *Interpretations of*

American History, volume one, edited by Gerald N. Grob and George
A. Billias, and published by the Free Press, New York); the many controversies surrounding the Industrial Revolution (of many selections the
most illuminating is M. W. Flinn's *Origins of the Industrial Revolution*
in the 'Problems and Perspectives' series); imperialism, which involves us
in problems of historical semantics (abstractions, labelling generalisations,
and all that) as well as of fact and causation (two excellent collections
here are: George H. Nadel and Perry Curtis, *Imperialism and Colonialism* (1964) in the 'Main Themes of European History' series published by
the Macmillan Company of New York; and Robin W. Winks, *British
Imperialism: Gold, God, Glory* (1965) in the 'European Problems' series
published by Holt, Rinehart & Winston); and the origins of the Second
World War (Taylor's famous work is available in a Penguin paperback;
it should be read in conjunction with Alan Bullock's Raleigh Lecture,
Hitler and the Origins of the Second World War, published in paperback
by the British Academy).

Two cautions must be stated. Historians are not exclusively concerned
with wars and revolutions: equally vigorous and important controversies
exist over the nature of the manorial economy, over the significance of
medieval parliaments, over the relations between science and industrial
development, and so on; I have simply chosen topics which lend themselves most easily to the elaboration of the essentially simple points I wish
to make. Secondly, although every student of history should understand
the scope and significance of historical controversy, the excitement of
battle should not obscure the real purpose of the historian: a deepened
understanding of the past. The true concern of the historian is history,
not historiography.

2 MAGNA CARTA

Stated in its most extreme form, the question raised by Magna Carta is
this: is it the fundamental constitutional defence of English liberties, or
is it merely a 'feudal document', reactionary in tone, by which a baronial
clique extracted certain concessions beneficial only to themselves? Because
the source material is so patchy it has not been possible to establish an
exact account of the events leading to the drawing up and sealing of
Magna Carta in June 1215. The Charter itself is in medieval Latin: much
of the debate centres upon the particular shade of meaning the scholar
attaches to certain difficult passages. The bare outline of events is not,
however, in dispute. As a king, John does not seem to have been much
more arbitrary than his two immediate predecessors, but his manner was
such as to make him always seem even shabbier than he was. What

counted anyway was the series of disasters which bedevilled his reign. Philip of France waged successful war against the once-great English Empire in France while John became embroiled in a dangerous quarrel with the Pope. In 1214 John made his last desperate bid to recover Normandy: he failed, and in doing so bankrupted himself completely.

As a feudal ruler John was entitled to certain 'incidents', which could be a valuable source of income, due to him on certain occasions: when a tenant-in-chief died the king could exact a substantial 'relief' from the succeeding heir; if the heir was under age, the king had right of 'wardship' of his lands, which meant that he could himself pocket all the revenues they yielded; the king had the right to dispose of heirs and heiresses in marriage; the king was also entitled to certain 'aids' due on specified occasions, as for example, when his eldest daughter got married. This system of rights and dues extended through the social structure: tenants-in-chief (the great feudal barons) exacting similar payments from their tenants (the knights) and so on. By 1215 the older obligation of barons and knights to furnish the king with military service had been commuted to yet another financial payment, scutage. John certainly squeezed the last drop and more out of these customary rights, raising the cry that he was in fact going far beyond what was customary and right; the dismal failure of his policies greatly strengthened the position of the protesters. As early as 1213 the barons began to discuss proposals for exacting some guarantee from John that he would rule in conformity with the customs of the kingdom. In the past, kings had often made promises of this sort on their coronation: the barons lighted upon the comparatively elaborate Coronation Charter of Henry I which itemised the abuses which Henry swore to renounce; this the barons took as their model.

The collapse of 1214 opened the way to the baronial revolt of 1215: John quickly conceded defeat (suggesting that the barons had managed to secure quite wide support) and in June 1215, on the Thames-side meadow of Runnymede, he agreed to put his seal to Magna Carta. The essential shape of Magna Carta derives directly from the demands known as the 'Articles of the Barons', modified and rephrased by the officials of the great royal office of Chancery. The two great men who stood somewhat apart from the conflict, William, the Earl Marshal, and Stephen Langton, Archbishop of Canterbury, may or may not have played an important part in formulating the final draft. This is one of the minor controversies associated with Magna Carta, which in turn is bound up with the major controversy. Many of the historians who have argued that Magna Carta does indeed have significance in the wider story of English liberties have attributed this element to the good offices of the saintly Langton, who is said to have transmuted the purely selfish claims of the barons into a statement of universal significance. Circumstantial evidence and the known facts about the character of Stephen Langton make this argument entirely reasonable, but it does not rest on any sufficient direct evidence.

The sealing of Magna Carta did not restore civil peace. Having little faith in John's word, the barons wrote into the Charter (clause 61) an elaborate provision whereby a special committee of twenty-five barons would be responsible for seeing that the other provisions were in fact carried out. John however proceeded at once to try to overthrow the charter, now enlisting the support of the Pope, who declared it to be null and void; open rebellion broke out again, and Louis, son of the French king Philip Augustus, came over from France in the hope of profiting from English divisions. It may well be that at this point Magna Carta would have sunk without trace had not John suddenly died in October 1216 at the age of forty-nine. The supporters of John's nine-year-old son Henry seem to have seen at once that Magna Carta could be used as a rallying call for unity behind the young king. On 12 November 1216 a pruned and revised version was issued on behalf of the newly crowned Henry III. By the autumn of 1217 Louis had been defeated, and Magna Carta, further revised, was again reissued (that is, copies, or 'exemplifications', were sent out to various parts of the country, there to be publicly announced). In 1225 Magna Carta was issued once more in what proved to be its final form, the king securing in return the right to levy a special tax on movable goods. This version was confirmed three times by Henry III (1237, 1253 and 1265), once by Edward I (1297), and on various occasions by later kings. It was Edward I's confirmation which was placed on the newly established Great Roll of Statutes.

Magna Carta was appealed to by seventeenth-century lawyers at the time of the gathering conflict with the Stuarts: in it they found the legal basis for such fundamental rights as parliamentary control of taxation, trial by jury, habeas corpus, equality before the law and freedom from arbitrary arrest. 'The Great Commoner', William Pitt, Earl of Chatham, in 1770 included Magna Carta with the Petition of Right (the statement of parliamentary rights in 1629 which opened the first round in the conflict which led to the Civil War) and the Bill of Rights (the statement of 1689 which embodied the permanent results of the Civil War) as the 'Bible of the English Constitution'. References to Magna Carta figured prominently in the claims of the American colonists, and it has continued ever since to play an important role in American concepts of basic justice.

As with many big issues in history, it is very difficult to disentangle the history from the historiography. It should however be possible to make distinctions between the significance of Magna Carta in 1215; its significance throughout the thirteenth century; and its significance in the subsequent development of constitutional theory and practice. Seventeenth-century lawyers, American colonists or William Pitt were no more making objective historical judgements than is an American Democrat when he invokes the memory of F.D.R. or a British Prime Minister when he appeals to 'the spirit of Dunkirk'. The trouble came when nineteenth-century 'Whig' historians combined their zealous researches among the primary sources with a too ready acceptance of the mythology of Magna Carta. A minor, but typical, legal historian, Sir Edward Creasy, expressed a common view in 1853 when he described Magna Carta as 'a solemn instrument deliberately agreed on by the King, the prelates, the great barons, the gentry, the burghers, the yeomanry, and all the freemen of the realm'. Creasy had few doubts about the import of the famous clause 39 which, in Davis's translation, reads:

> No free man shall be seized or imprisoned, or stripped of his rights or possessions, or outlawed or exiled, or deprived of his standing in any other way, nor will we proceed with force against him or send others to do so, except by the lawful judgement of his equals or by the law of the land.

'I believe', said Creasy, 'that the trial by peers here spoken of means trial by jury.' Nineteenth-century historians put great weight, too, on clause 61 mentioned above, seeing it as a sign of wide acceptance of the *representative* principle, and on clause 12 which stated that 'no "scutage" or "aid" [apart from the customary 'incidents'] may be levied in our kingdom without its general consent.' Even the great Bishop Stubbs could not free himself of the romanticised, Whig view of Magna Carta: the 'scientific' onslaught had to await the arrival of a younger Scottish contemporary of J. B. Bury, W. S. McKechnie. In his *Magna Carta* (1905), which is still a standard authority, McKechnie presented the forceful definition, and delimitation, of the Great Charter as 'a feudal document'. Clause by clause McKechnie elucidated the technicalities and explained the demands of the barons by reference to the early thirteenth-century feudal context. As he clearly demonstrated, a great part of the Charter is indeed concerned to set firm limits upon the demands which the king can make of the barons. Clauses 17 and 18 simply attempt to stabilise the legal procedures which had been developed in the reign of Henry II. Not only are clauses 12 and 61 (the 'general consent' and the 'representative' ones) vague and ambiguous, but in any case they are omitted from all subsequent reissues. Whatever the intentions of clause 39, trial by jury did not, as a matter of actual fact, become firmly established in the immediately succeeding years.

McKechnie's great work establishes very clearly the significance of Magna Carta in its immediate temporal context, though, as a lawyer, McKechnie was primarily concerned with its implications for the history of law. For historians today Magna Carta is of greatest interest as a priceless revelation of the preoccupations and prejudices of the leaders of early

thirteenth-century English society: J. C. Holt's *Magna Carta* (1965) aimed
at presenting 'the Charter in the context of the politics, administration
and political thought of England and Europe in the twelfth and thirteenth centuries'. Since McKechnie, too, historians have stressed the
symbolic importance that Magna Carta came to have for later generations; and they have emphasised that the reissues of the thirteenth century imply a recognition that good government depends upon co-operation
between the king and his principal subjects. Historians have also
examined those parts of the Charter which relate to men of lesser social
status than the great barons. Clause 60 calls upon all men (albeit somewhat vaguely) to behave towards their own tenants as the king is undertaking to behave towards his; the rights of the city of London (clause 13),
the free movement of merchants (clause 41), and the interests of con-
sumers (clause 35) are to be protected. More important is the basic theme
which seems to underlie the somewhat diffuse phraseology of the whole
document: that there *is* a body of law covering political and personal
relationships throughout the kingdom, and that there are accepted and
acceptable processes for implementing this law: the last few words of
clause 39, referring to 'the law of the land', now emerge as the important
ones. To have orderly rather than arbitrary government was, historians
have maintained, in the interests of the entire community. Rather than
attribute this generalising of the Charter to the vision of Stephen Langton or William Marshal, some historians, Namier-wise, have attributed
it simply to the need of the barons to win allies from all walks of life.

Much about Magna Carta necessarily remains obscure. Perhaps an
agreed version would run like this: Magna Carta in 1215 was a political
bargain struck between a desperate king and his rebellious magnates; the
men who put their seals to it lived in a type of society which later generations have termed 'feudal' – clearly these men could no more escape
from the accepted concepts of that society than we can escape from the
accepted concepts of twentieth-century society; yet Magna Carta does
contain clauses which suggest that it went beyond mere service of the
self-interests of a selfish clique. But for the accident of John's early death
little more might have become of it; but in the minority of Henry III
Magna Carta became established as an earnest of the community of
interests between king and subjects, and a guarantee that the king would
not violate that community of interests. In much later centuries Magna
Carta became a potent symbol for radicals and revolutionaries. Without
Magna Carta other symbols would doubtless have been found; but historians, at any rate, have learned to place due weight upon the importance in human history of the image and the symbol.

3 THE 'GREAT REBELLION' ALIAS THE 'GREAT CIVIL WAR'
   ALIAS THE 'PURITAN REVOLUTION'

In the later years of the reign (1558–1603) of Queen Elizabeth there were
rumblings of discontent from some members of parliament over the
Queen's insistence that certain topics, such as foreign policy and the
religious settlement, were matters for royal decision alone and inappropriate for parliamentary discussion. Careful management of parliament
had clearly become necessary; Elizabeth was not so successful in this in
her last years as she had been in her earlier and middle years. Under
James I (1603–20) there were signs that the discontent was intensifying.
His successor, Charles I, was autocratic by nature and totally incapable of
comprehending parliamentary demands: in 1629, after the boldest statement so far of such demands, the Petition of Right, Charles dispensed
altogether with parliament. The so-called eleven years' tyranny ended
when in 1640 Charles had become so embroiled in financial and religious
difficulties that he sought escape in the summoning of parliament. The
demands made by the 'Long Parliament' in 1640, and the events
attending them, are usually taken as marking the beginning of the revolutionary crisis. In 1642 open civil war broke out; in 1648 after the King
had been captured, had escaped and had been captured again, a group
usually known to history as the 'Independents' (and distinguished from
the politically more moderate 'Presbyterians') seized power. In 1649
Charles I was executed. From then till the Restoration of 1660 England
had no king: Oliver Cromwell, leader of the 'Independents', ruled as
Lord Protector from 1653 to 1658.

Without doubt great social, economic and cultural changes took place
in the century 1540 to 1640. The inflationary trend, caused in part by
population growth and by repeated debasement of the coinage, had a
highly disruptive effect on existing social and economic relations; in certain spheres important advances were being made in trade and industry;
scholars and intellectuals were developing a new faith in empirical science
and the possibilities of human reason; the Elizabethan church settlement
did not please the more extreme Protestants, the 'Puritans', whose successors were to find themselves in sharp conflict with Charles I, whom they
suspected of undue tenderness towards Roman Catholicism; some individuals and groups were growing more prosperous and found that the
existing political structure did not give them the power they felt was their
due; others were doing badly and developed a dangerous sense of in-
security; the central monarchy was growing in prestige – those upon
whom the King looked with favour prospered, those out of favour became embittered. The controversy among historians has been over the

exact nature of these changes, their relative importance, and their relationship to the political events of the 1640s.

Seventeenth-century commentators on the Civil War – men who lived through it – came out remarkably strongly for an interpretation based on a simple clash of economic and social interests: Winstanley, Harrington, Hobbes, Baxter and Clarendon can all be read in this sense. Richard Baxter (1615–91), a Presbyterian minister, listed on the King's side lords, knights, gentlemen 'and most of the tenants of these gentlemen, and also most of the poorest of the people'. On Parliament's side were

> the smaller part (as some thought) of the gentry in most of the counties, and the greatest part of the tradesmen and freeholders and the middle sort of men, especially in those corporations and counties which depend on clothing and such manufactures. . . .[1]

Edward Hyde, Earl of Clarendon (1609–74), the Royalist historian, presented a similar view: support for Parliament in 1642 was to be found 'in those corporations and by those inferior people who were notorious for faction and schism in religion'. In the county of Somerset Parliamentary leaders were

> for the most part clothiers, and men who, though they were rich, had not been before of power or reputation there. . . . Though the gentlemen of ancient families and estates in that country were for the most part well affected to the King, . . . yet there were a people of an inferior degree who by good husbandry, clothing and other thriving arts had gotten very great fortunes, and by degrees getting themselves into the gentlemen's estates, were angry that they found not themselves in the same esteem and reputation with those whose estates they had. . . . These from the beginning were fast friends to the Parliament. . . .[2]

In crude essentials these analyses were strikingly like the materialist interpretation put forward in the nineteenth century by Karl Marx and his disciples. Friedrich Engels, Marx's celebrated collaborator, explained that Calvinism (or Puritanism) was the doctrine of 'the bourgeoisie', and maintained that it was the bourgeoisie which 'brought Charles I to the scaffold'.[3]

However, as we have noted, Marxism played little part in the nineteenth-century revolution in British historical studies. That monument of detailed scholarship, S. R. Gardiner's eighteen-volume *History* covering the years 1603 to 1656, presented the Civil War quite distinctly as 'the Puritan Revolution', a war fought to secure religious and constitutional liberty. This interpretation triumphantly held the field till the First World War: as R. G. Usher noted in 1913, the enigma of the Civil War was to be solved 'by repeating the Grand Remonstrance' – the Long Parliament's statement of its political and religious grievances. Then came the new interest in economic history (see above, pp. 60–7). R. H.

Tawney had already explored *The Agrarian Problem of the Sixteenth Century*, and his studies were taken further by Joan Thirsk; A. P. Newton showed, in his *Colonizing Activities of the Early Puritans* (1914), that Pym and other Long Parliament leaders had important trading connections; the detailed researches of John U. Nef, Peter Ramsey, Maurice Dobb, W. H. Court and others suggested, as Christopher Hill puts it in his excellent summary, that there had been 'something like an industrial revolution in the century before 1640'.[4] There was in the inter-war years no satisfactory synthesis of these valuable contributions towards an economic rather than a religious and constitutional interpretation of the Civil War. But R. H. Tawney added a further important element when in *Religion and the Rise of Capitalism* he elaborated the various subtle interconnections between Puritanism and capitalism. For historians to go on speaking simply of a 'Puritan Revolution' seemed to beg the question of the great variety of other interests which Puritanism might mask.

From Tawney, too, came the first attempt at synthesis: a learned article entitled 'The Rise of the Gentry, 1558–1640' published in the *Economic History Review* in 1941. Tawney postulated a changing social and economic balance resulting from a decline in the wealth and influence of the old-fashioned landowners and a rise in a new class of gentry made up primarily of 'agricultural capitalists', but also including merchants and industrialists. These men fought the Civil War in order to establish a political position commensurate with their economic and social one. In keeping with the growing fashion of the time, Tawney provided impressive-looking statistical evidence which seemed to show first, that the number of manors held by the aristocracy was declining compared with those held by the gentry, and second, that the number of large holdings was declining, while the number of medium-sized ones was increasing. Support for this thesis came from another statistic-laden article which took further the idea of a declining Elizabethan aristocracy, published in 1948 by Lawrence Stone. It was now that H. R. Trevor-Roper launched his devastating counter-attack, exposing the grave deficiencies in the statistical methods adopted by Tawney and Stone. In 1953 Trevor-Roper presented his own synthesis, *The Gentry, 1540–1640*, published as an *Economic History Review Supplement*. The 'mere gentry' – those who had no access to the gifts and patronage of the Court or to the spoils of law and trade – were in fact declining: they were the 'Country' who finally rose in anger against the corrupt, centralising 'Court'. The gentry could not in any event be regarded as an entirely separate social class from the 'aristocracy': thus the Civil War, essentially, was fought by two factions of the same ruling class, the luxurious, free-spending courtiers on the one side, and the jealous, puritanical country party on the other. There are shades of Namier in this essentially Tory conception of the mighty struggling over immediate material interests. And the application to *Members of the Long Parliament* (1954) of overtly Namierite 'multiple biography' methods by D. Brunton and D. H. Pennington seemed to bolster the view that no broad social classification of the contestants in the Civil War into aristocracy on one side, and gentry or bourgeoisie on the other, was feasible: gentlemen, lawyers and merchants were to be found among M.P.s on both sides.

In the late fifties important criticisms were made of the Trevor-Roper–Namierite synthesis. First of all new sources – always of critical moment in the development of historical inquiry – had been studied, since the taxation policies of the postwar Labour Government had provoked the release of a whole flood of private family papers. Furthermore a number of historians had got down to the necessary task of fundamental research at the local level, resulting in such important publications as *The Committee at Stafford 1643–5* (1957), edited by D. H. Pennington and I. A. Roots, *The County Committee of Kent in the Civil War* by A. M. Everitt, and *Essays in Leicestershire History* by W. G. Hoskins. Just as the new material was becoming available, three established historians, J. H. Hexter, Perez Zagorin and Christopher Hill, moved into the attack. Hexter drew attention away from the 'gentry', whether 'rising' or 'declining', to the aristocracy, whose critical weaknesses, he argued, could be seen in the collapse of their military power. The result was

> a power vacuum in England during the very years when a concurrence of fiscal, constitutional, political and religious grievances evoked widespread opposition to the Crown and made it necessary for that opposition to achieve some measure of co-ordinated action. Into that vacuum created by the temporary incapacity of the magnates poured the country gentry – not the brisk hard-bitten small gentry of Professor Tawney, nor yet the mouldy flea-bitten mere gentry of Professor Trevor-Roper – but the rich, well-educated knights and squires who sat in the Parliaments of James I and Charles I. . . .[5]

This particular theory was developed and put on a solid base by the extensive researches in the family archives, backed by an updated and sophisticated statistical expertise, which issued in Lawrence Stone's *Crisis of the Aristocracy* (1965). Zagorin meanwhile pointed out that the Revolution must be considered in two stages: the first, 1640–2, was indeed a mere struggle between different factions within the ruling class; thereafter, however, there developed a true social revolution, aiming at the establishment of a democratic republic.

Christopher Hill began his attack by pointing out that Namierite methods, pioneered to deal with the stable British political structure of 1760, were less suited to a time of crisis and revolution. He showed that Brunton and Pennington had failed to take account of the special reasons which would make *some* merchants support the Crown and thus distort the analysis. More positively Hill stressed the geographical aspect of socio-economic classification:

> The Parliamentary areas were the South and the East, both economically advanced, while the strength of the royalists lay in the still half-feudal North and West. All the big towns were parliamentarian; though often (as in London) their ruling oligarchies were for the King. . . . Only one or two cathedral towns, such as Oxford and Chester, were royalist. The ports were all for Parliament.[6]

Having reasserted the need to give due attention to the broader socio-economic conflicts underlying the Civil War, Hill then, as we have noted, reaffirmed the importance of ideas, religious and non-religious, in shaping the Revolution. Our understanding of the intellectual roots of the Revolution, too, has been greatly furthered by C. H. and K. George's study of *The Protestant Mind of the English Reformation 1570–1640* (1961). Though it would be wrong to suggest that historians are all now in happy agreement with each other, it can be said that the rather narrow theses which in the forties and fifties stood out in sharp conflict with each other have now given place to a much more complex analysis more in conformity with the nature of historical reality; the remaining differences between individual historians are now more clearly revealed as matters of emphasis. Some of the most recent research, as is brought out in Ivan Roots's excellent general study *The Great Rebellion 1642–1660* (1966), has begun to restore emphasis on the personal defects of Charles I as an immediate cause of the Revolution. It does seem too that the subtle multi-causal explanation, blending ideas and material factors with the unique and personal, which in one form or another now holds the field, can be integrated with the broader thesis of a 'general crisis' in the seventeenth century. There is even the suggestion in Lawrence Stone's stimulating introduction to his collection of readings that historians are now near to a satisfactory theory about the causation of revolutions in general.

4 THE AMERICAN REVOLUTION

Two interrelated problems are involved in the study of the American Revolution: what caused it? and what sort of revolution was it anyway? In a curious way the historiography of the American Revolution echoes that of the English one. The first commentators, writing with the live experience still throbbing in their minds, put forward a common-sense proto-sociological explanation, involving social, economic and cultural factors. The *History of the American Revolution* (Philadelphia, 1789) by David Ramsay is in many respects worthy of being ranked with the leading works by the contemporary Scottish historical school (Ramsay, who lived from 1749–1815, was born in Pennsylvania of Scottish Presbyterian parents). Ramsay stressed such circumstances as 'the distance of America from Great Britain' which, combined with the essentially tolerant policies of the mother country, encouraged both the growth of attitudes favourable to liberty and the establishment of local legislatures which implemented these ideas; liberal ideas were in any case promoted by the Puritan ideology of a large number of the colonists. The social composition of the colonies, Ramsay argued, fostered egalitarianism and democracy – the vast majority of the colonists being independent farmers. At the same time he accepted that the handful of rich colonial merchants were motivated by their own special economic interests when in the later stages of the crisis they gave a lead to the agitation against Britain. To Ramsay the specific event which converted background preconditions into an immediate state of crisis was the British Government's imposition upon the colonies of the Stamp Act (the attempt made in 1765, two years after the ending of the Seven Years War, to recoup some of the expenses of that war, which had once and for all provided the colonists with security from the French). Although the Stamp Act was immediately repealed, the vigorous cry of 'No taxation without representation' had already gone up: this constitutional principle, derived of course from socio-economic and cultural circumstances, was, Ramsay contended, 'the very hinge of the controversy'. Ramsay was moderate in his assessment of the responsibilities of British ministers: he could see that in an extraordinarily complex situation there were indeed two points of view:

> From the unity of empire it was necessary, that some acts should extend over the whole. From the local situation of the Colonies it was equally reasonable that their legislatures should at least in some matters be independent. Where the supremacy of the first ended and the independency of the last began, was to the best informed a puzzling question.

Finally Ramsay stated quite clearly that the colonists were far from united in their opposition to Britain: but he explained that because of 'the resentment of the people' the opponents of revolutionary action tended to hold their peace.

The balanced sociological account of Ramsay and his contemporaries (the others are listed by Professor Page Smith in his brilliant article 'David Ramsay and the Causes of the American Revolution' in the collection of readings edited by John C. Wahlke, from which I have borrowed extensively) quickly gave place to the wildly Whig (or 'democratic' as Ranke termed it) account of George Bancroft, which conjured up the twin images of the wicked tyranny of George III and the selfish evil of 'mercantilism' as basic causes of the Revolution: images which

proved extraordinarily durable. This interpretation, born in the period of
strong American nationalism and Jacksonian democracy, is of course
almost an exact counterpart of the Whiggish interpretation of Magna
Carta noted above, or of the 'Puritan Revolution' interpretation of events
in seventeenth-century England.

American historiographers are generally agreed that in the period of
the Rankean revolution and the 'new history' reaction, that is, from
around 1890 to the Second World War, two broad schools of historical
inquiry can be identified (which indeed coincide roughly with the Rankean, straight-line professional approach on the one hand, and the 'new'
approach on the other). Professors Grob and Billias describe these respectively as the 'imperial' school and the 'progressive' school, the former
school stressing 'constitutional' issues, the latter social and economic
ones; Professor Wahlke, with all necessary qualifications and reservations, suggests a distinction between those historians who, *in the last
analysis*, hold to a political interpretation and those who, in similar case,
hold to an economic one. Actually, so subtle and intricate are the arguments in the leading books in both schools that the result was not, save
in the minds of inferior polemicists, to produce a sharp polarisation of
views, but rather to produce a broad consensus which directed attention
away from the alleged villainies and heroisms of individuals towards
examination of broader forces and circumstances. This movement was
reinforced, appropriately enough given Namier's own original bent towards the American Revolution, by the Namierite revision of British
eighteenth-century political studies. The 'imperial' school – headed by
George L. Beer, Charles M. Andrews and Lawrence H. Gipson – brought
new light to bear on the question by setting it within the wider perspective of the problems of the British Empire. All presented sympathetic
portrayals of Britain's imperial and economic policies towards the
colonies. Andrews stressed that at the heart of the Revolution lay the fact
that a new nation had grown up in North America, a fact which simply
could not be accommodated to existing imperial ideas (this, it may be
noted, has been very much the line taken by British historians such as
Vincent Harlow and Esmond Wright). Gipson stressed the strategic difficulties which faced the British Empire and argued that it was reasonable
for the British Government to expect the colonists to contribute to the
costs of their own defence. These historians emphasise constitutional and
political issues only in the sense of seeing such issues as the offspring of
much deeper conflicts of interest. Leaders in the other school were
Charles A. Beard, Arthur Schlesinger Sr and Louis M. Hacker. Arguably,
these historians fell into the error later repeated in Britain by the violent
protagonists in the Tawney–Trevor-Roper controversy, an exaggeration
of the dominance and autonomy of economic motivation.

As in the controversy over the English Revolution, the freshest work accomplished since the Second World War has been in the direction of restressing the importance of ideas: it is not, I think, fanciful to note a parallel between Bernard Bailyn's *Ideological Origins of the American Revolution* (1967), and the book by Christopher Hill which bears a remarkably similar title. Earlier Edmund S. and Helen M. Morgan in their *The Stamp Act Crisis: Prologue to Revolution* (1953) had redirected attention to the wave of popular resistance, based apparently on constitutional principle, aroused by the Stamp Act. Here we have a reminder (which again can be compared with the re-emphasis in British historiography upon the character and actions of Charles I) that amid all the talk of broader forces the historian should not neglect the specific, unique event. One final historiographical parallel: to set beside the 'general crisis of the seventeenth century' hypothesis, we have of course Palmer's thesis of the Atlantic-wide 'Democratic Revolution' (see above, p. 160).

What sort of Revolution was it anyway? As early as 1910 Carl M. Becker identified two revolutions: the colonial rebellion, and the internal socio-economic clash over who should rule in independent America. There was, as Becker put it with characteristic elegance, the 'question of home rule' and the 'question . . . of who should rule at home'. Schlesinger reckoned that in the struggle for power which followed the colonial rebellion the rich merchants finally reasserted control, whereas J. Franklin Jameson in *The American Revolution Considered as a Social Movement* (1926) argued that during the war sweeping reforms in the direction of economic and social democracy did in fact take place. Historians writing after the Second World War, following through on the sociological-cultural interpretation which stresses the growing sense of identity of an American *nation*, have seen the Revolution as essentially a conservative one, fought to maintain the existing liberal-democratic *status quo* against the threatened encroachments of British imperial power: such have been the arguments of Robert E. Brown in *Middle-Class Democracy and the Revolution in Massachusetts 1691–1780* (1955), a depth study of social structure in one colony (again comparison is invited with the recent local studies of the English Revolution) and of Daniel J. Boorstin in his brilliant work of original synthesis *The Genius of American Politics* (1953). These interpretations, needless to say, have not stood unchallenged.

5 THE INDUSTRIAL REVOLUTION

The Industrial Revolution will be treated here as essentially a problem in British history; the fact that other countries subsequently went through similar revolutions and that some countries are at present going through such a revolution, in any case, gives the topic a wider significance to both historians and social scientists. Of all the wide variety of controversies this simple two-word phrase conjures up, perhaps the least important is that of whether there was an Industrial Revolution at all. We shall simply glance briefly at that one in passing. Accepting that there was a 'revolution' the question then arises, when did it begin? More important is the very complex question of *how* did it begin? – involved here are all sorts of sub-controversies over population growth, the 'stages of economic growth', the relationship of technology to economic demand and to intellectual progress, and so on. But before we turn to that and these, we shall take what for many historians and laymen is *the* issue, involving the entire nature of the Industrial Revolution and the changes which it brought to the whole of society: were these changes for better or for worse?

As with the seventeenth-century English Revolution and the American Revolution, there was no shortage of contemporary comment on the Industrial Revolution. Much of this was summarised and given his own peculiar gloss by Friedrich Engels in the opening chapter of his *Condition of the Working Class in England* (1845): here in its pristine freshness is the tale of the sturdy independent yeomen driven off their land into a squalid existence in the industrial slums, a tale with which many of us were regaled at school. A sense of outrage over the social evils attending upon the process of industrialisation, too, lay at the core of Arnold Toynbee's *Lectures on the Industrial Revolution* (1884), the book which did more than any other to popularise the concept of an Industrial Revolution. Toynbee's concern for the exploited poor was developed further by the Hammonds in their studies of *The Village Labourer* (1911), *The Town Labourer* (1917) and *The Skilled Labourer* (1919) (see above, p. 64). Until the recent book by Hobsbawm and Rudé, the Hammonds were the last historians to study the peasant risings of 1830. Then, as we saw in chapter 3, came the tough-minded school of economic historians led by Sir John Clapham, who declared that their statistics controverted earlier soft-hearted accounts of the declining living standards of the poor, and that, anyway, the greater good of general economic growth far outweighed any temporary sufferings on the part of the poor. Recent work by Peter Laslett and others has certainly demonstrated very conclusively that the story of idyllic pre-industrial conditions shattered by industrialisation is quite without foundation: children performed sweated labour within the confines of their own homes; women worked in primitive mines; whole families trembled year in year out on the verge of starvation; rural slums were often just as noxious as those later to be found in the industrial towns. On the apparently quantifiable issues aroused by the great 'standard-of-living controversy', the statistics adduced on either side have simply highlighted the grave imperfections of the evidence. It does seem likely that, for many, living standards were going down in the early decades of the nineteenth century: for them the fact that subsequently their children and grandchildren enjoyed some of the fruits of economic growth cannot have been much consolation. However, in recent years the area of dispute has moved away from the quantitative aspects (which in fact have not been successfully quantified) to the qualitative changes brought about in the lives of the many by the Industrial Revolution. E. P. Thompson has been to the fore in stressing how the new factory discipline, the new omnipresent sense of time, the new master-operative relationship affected the quality of life. In the end few historians today would deny the long-term booms of the Industrial Revolution; it is scarcely to be argued anyway that the Revolution could somehow have been 'stopped'. But within that wider, slightly complacent framework historians are now, with the help of modern social psychology, looking more closely at the human implications of industrialisation. As Thompson has put it:

> What needs to be said is not that one way of life is better than the other, but that this is a place of the most far-reaching conflict; that the historical record is not a simple one of neutral and inevitable technological change, but is also one of exploitation and of resistance to exploitation; and that values stood to be lost as well as gained.[7]

Toynbee, naturally, was clear that there had been an Industrial Revolution: the social implications which he saw all around him were too great to be ignored. Yet the economic historians of the inter-war years came close to denying any validity to the term: they were in fact the victims of tunnel history (and indeed perhaps of ball-of-string history as well); examining only economic development in the narrowest sense, they saw steady evolution stretching far into the past, and missed the really important phenomena: the rapid urbanisation and the social and cultural upheavals of the late eighteenth and early nineteenth centuries. Toynbee had thought the Revolution began somewhere around 1760; curiously the cataclysmic view (which still holds the field in many textbooks) was given its most forceful expression by the young Charles A. Beard, who saw it as coming to what was 'virtually a medieval England . . . almost like a thunderbolt from a clear sky'. As early as 1908 an important study postulated that the Revolution had a much broader chronological base in the eighteenth century; but that book was in French, and did not become generally available to the insular British till 1928 (E. Mantoux, *The Industrial Revolution of the Eighteenth Century*). Historians are now inclined, thanks in particular to the quantitative (in the Marczewski sense – see above, p. 116) studies by Phyllis Deane and W. A. Cole, to distinguish two phases in the Industrial Revolution: a slight intensification of economic activity from the 1740s, followed by a more 'revolutionary' upturn in the 1780s; the traditional attribution of the 'beginning' of the Revolution to 1760 (accession of George III) has been pretty thoroughly discredited.

Now to the question of the 'causes' of the Industrial Revolution. Toynbee and his generation produced a somewhat simple list of 'causes' which again has embedded itself deeply in the textbooks: the list included the alleged replacement of mercantilism by *laissez-faire*, the growth of population, enclosures, a collection of inventions, and the substitution of the factory for the domestic system. The great achievement of the interwar economic historians was, through thorough investigation of individual industries, to lay the basis for a more complex analysis. However, the really important advances towards a convincing synthesis only came after the Second World War: partly this derived from more efficient detailed studies into particular areas long dominated by specious generalisation, such as historical demography, the sources of finance for industrialisation, the availability of new markets, and the complicated relationship between culture, education and the willingness to innovate, as seen in technological inventiveness or (something recent historians have greatly stressed) entrepreneurship; partly it derived from the enlistment not just of the more refined statistical methods, but also of the modes of analytical conceptualisation more usually found in the social sciences. These developments are admirably summarised in M. W Flinn's *Origins of the Industrial Revolution* (1966).

The first important general advance after the Second World War was made by T. S. Ashton's deceptively textbookish *The Industrial Revolution 1760–1830* (1948). Ashton laid particular stress on the lowering of interest rates in the early eighteenth century as a reason for the quickening pace of economic development. Scarcely less important, Flinn argues, was his emphasis on the connection between nonconformity and business enterprise, which Ashton thought could be most readily explained through reference to the high level of education nonconformists received in their own academies. In 1960 W. W. Rostow published a full version of his famous theory of *The Stages of Economic Growth*. Rostow's five stages are: the traditional society, the preconditions for take-off, the take-off into self-sustained growth, the drive to maturity, and the age of high mass consumption. Relevant to the study of the Industrial Revolution, obviously, are the 'preconditions for take-off' and, of course, the 'take-off' itself. Rostow laid down conditions which must apply to any 'take-off', which at one level are extremely precise and at another are totally vague. They have been subjected in detail to some devastating criticism. Nonetheless this model has proved an appealing one; that this is so demonstrates the turning away in recent years from the concept of history as simply 'one damn thing after another'. In his concluding chapter Flinn himself offers an interesting and flexible three-tier model. First he places 'the accumulation of a set of necessary prerequisites', which he lists (in a much more elaborate fashion than can be represented in this blunt summary) as 'improvement in agriculture', efficient means of transport, a 'sophisticated monetary system', making in particular for 'increased availability of capital', and 'an educational system suitable for the new orientation of society'. On the second tier Flinn places the emergence of 'a group of sectors of steady expansion' – industrial and regional. These sectors, as it were, set the pace, making for the diffusion of a 'growth mentality' among businessmen, and for technological innovation. Flinn's third element, the one which is 'concerned with the timing of the beginning of rapid economic development', is the least satisfactory. In it he runs together, in ascending order of importance, 'population growth', 'the expansion of home and overseas markets' and 'technology'. Yet one cannot leave this topic without commenting on how well Flinn's balanced yet immensely stimulating textbook sums up the advances that have been made in twentieth-century historical study: compare it with works of similar scale by Toynbee, Unwin, Lipson, or even Ashton, and the point is made.

6 IMPERIALISM

With imperialism we encounter again the problem of historical semantics. Beyond that we have problems of motivation: what makes men and nations imperialistic? We have problems of periodisation: was there a particular era when, say, Great Britain pursued imperialist policies, which can be contrasted with other periods when she did nothing of the sort? What, finally, were the consequences of imperialism? We shall see that as in the other controversies we have studied, historians have gradually abandoned monocausal, instrumental explanations for more complicated ones which take account of the irrational in man and of the appeal to him of apparently abstract ideals.

Richard Koebner has shown that the word 'imperialism' first came into general use in Britain to describe the aggressive policies pursued by Napoleon III in the 1850s. It remained a term of abuse when Radicals and Liberals used it of Disraeli's policies in the 1870s. However, by a not unfamiliar process ('Whig' and 'Tory' both began life as terms of abuse) the word became respectable in the 1880s and a number of politicians and publicists were proud to announce themselves as imperialists. But the South African War at the turn of the century again knocked most of the burnish off the word. The epoch-making study *Imperialism*, published in 1902 by the self-styled 'economic heretic' J. A. Hobson, presented a most disenchanted view which attributed imperialism to the

pressure of selfish economic and financial interests, unable to find profitable outlets for investment at home. Lenin's *Imperialism, the Highest
Stage of Capitalism* (1916) borrowed heavily from Hobson. Marxists and
others denounced the First World War as an imperialist war, the final
and logical outcome of the struggle of rival capitalisms for world markets. If one could go by the history of the word alone, one might deduce
that British imperialism as a historical phenomenon lasted only from the
1880s to the early twentieth century. In fact the activities and relationships which the word was coined to describe have a much longer history.
(The fact that Hobson and Lenin *thought* the phenomenon they were
describing was intimately bound up with economic causes does not mean
that it necessarily was so.) Professors Nadel and Curtis, in the introduction to their valuable collection of readings, offer a useful definition:
imperialism is 'the extension of sovereignty or control, whether direct or
indirect, political or economic, by one government, nation or society over
another together with the ideas justifying or opposing this process.
Imperialism is essentially about power both as end and means.'[8] Behind
the slogans and the symbols of the imperial power, they continue, lies the
reality of its superior military, economic, political and moral power. In
fact the imperial power always has a conscious sense of its own
superiority. Imperialism involves the collision of two or more cultures
and a subsequent relationship of 'unequal exchange'.

Hobson believed that a new age of imperialism began in the 1870s –
and it is indeed fairly usual for the history textbooks to describe the last
decades of the nineteenth century as the age of the 'new imperialism'. At
heart Hobson was really concerned with domestic social problems: he saw
'underconsumption' as the basic evil – the masses were not paid high
enough wages so they could not afford to buy the goods they themselves were helping to manufacture, which in turn meant that the manufacturers in Britain and elsewhere were in effect overproducing:

> Overproduction in the sense of an excessive manufacturing plant, and
> surplus capital which could not find sound investments within the
> country, forced Great Britain, Germany, Holland, France to place
> larger and larger portions of their economic resources outside the area
> of their present political domain, and then stimulate a political expan-
> sion so as to take in the new areas.

Lenin specifically associated imperialism with the growth of large-scale
monopoly capitalism, which again, he argued, cut down investment
opportunities at home.

The Hobson–Leninist thesis has been subject to attack from four
angles. First of all it has been criticised for its epochal, discontinuous
view of events: it implies that since imperialism only began in the 1870s,
the period from the end of the Napoleonic Wars (1815) till then had been

a time of peace and hostility to imperial ventures. In the pages of the *American Historical Review*[9] J. H. Galbraith attacked what he called 'The Myths of the Little England Era', arguing that at no time did the vociferous Manchester school of 'anti-imperialists' in practice influence government policy. This was the view also of J. Gallagher, R. Robinson and Alice Denny, who in a famous book, *Africa and the Victorians: The Official Mind of Imperialism* (1961), introduced the term 'informal empire' to cover British overseas activities and attitudes in the mid-Victorian period. The argument here then is that there was no such sharp break in the 1870s as Hobson maintained, or indeed as other utterly non-Leninist historians maintained through taking Disraeli's speeches of that decade at their face value. Secondly, overseas trade statistics have been cited to confute Hobson. Without any doubt the figures quoted by Hobson do not prove his case; but there has been a certain amount of confusion on the other side as well – although it can be shown that Britain *as a whole* did not make much of a profit out of the Empire that does not necessarily mean that certain influential individuals were not doing well and so might still be strong protagonists of imperial expansion. Thirdly, a single glance at the record demonstrates that the great burst of imperial activity, on the part of all European countries, not just Britain, came in the 1880s, not the 1870s. Finally, accepting that there was indeed a 'scramble for Africa' in the 1880s, though generally arguing that no sharp break with the past could be posited, historians have offered various alternative explanations to the Hobson–Lenin 'economic' one.

Some of these possibilities are expressed pungently in the subtitle to Professor Winks's collection of readings, *British Imperialism: Gold, God, Glory*. Hobson had admitted the important part played by missionary idealists, but dismissed them as the tools of economic interests. Historians nowadays are less happy about this kind of facile dismissal, and Galbraith has been one among several to stress the reality of the missionary motive in the period of informal empire. The new factor provoking the great burst of formal expansion is no longer thought to lie exclusively (if at all) in the development of large-scale capitalism in the European countries (such a development is not, for instance, awfully noticeable in Italy, who nonetheless had her imperial adventures). Robinson and Gallagher find the starting-point in a series of nationalist crises *within* Africa (this emphasis is in itself very much in the modern idiom, see above, p. 201) which provoked the aggressive and insecure powers of Europe into violent response. Ultimately, then, we are back to a question of European power politics (which, of course, could still be determined by economic rivalries). Certain historians, including D. K. Fieldhouse, have identified the new factor as the sudden entry in 1884–5 of Germany into the 'bid for colonies'. Such experts on Bismarckian Germany as Erich Eyck, or on

German colonialism as Mary E. Townsend (writing in 1921) have explained Bismarck's switch in policy as due to pressure from, or a desire to win the support of, German commercial interests. A. J. P. Taylor, as we noted, provided an important link in the 'power politics' argument by suggesting that Bismarck's main motive was to stir up rivalry between France and Britain. The *immediate* impelling motive for the new imperialist expansion, then, is the exigencies of the European diplomatic scene: imperialism is the projection into the wider world of the power struggle in Europe.

This helps to explain specific events. But it does not satisfactorily explain the wider phenomenon which affected Italy and the United States as well as France, Britain and Germany, which affected entire peoples as well as statesmen. Hence the search for 'sociological' explanations. Joseph A. Schumpeter (1883–1950), one of the great 'sociological' economic historians in the tradition of Sombart (above, p. 61), had suggested, in an essay on the Sociology of Imperialism, published in English translation in *'Imperialism' and 'Social Classes'* (1951), that the new imperialism involved a kind of atavism among the masses, a throwback to ancient glories. Research on the psychology of imperialism has not yet got very far (see O. Mannoni's case study of Madagascar, *Prospero and Caliban: The Psychology of Colonization* (1950), and Bruce Mazlish's discussion of it in the *Journal of Contemporary History*)[10] but some thought has been given to such Freudian suggestions as that dominion over another society reconciles Western man to the disciplines of his own society, especially if he can be reassured that the subject peoples are inferior to himself; or perhaps the great colonisers have simply re-enacted their childhood fantasies and fears in the colonial environment. The latter notion will probably not prove helpful in explaining the responses of whole sectors of society to the imperial idea. For the moment the state of contemporary professional opinion can best be summed up in two quotations, one from D. K. Fieldhouse, one from Nadel and Curtis. 'It is clear', says Fieldhouse,

> that imperialism cannot be explained in simple terms of economic theory and the nature of finance capitalism. In its mature form it can best be described as a sociological phenomenon with roots in political facts: it can properly be understood only in terms of the same social hysteria which has since given birth to other and more disastrous forms of aggressive nationalism.[11]

Nadel and Curtis point out that 'anyone who believes in the diversity of human behavior and who rejects cosmic solutions or single causes in history will not hesitate to point out the inconsistencies, mysteries, and even absurdities of imperialism'.

To assess the effects of imperialism one must take the wider context and the universal meaning. Karl Marx, who was of course on the side of the 'march of history', noted the modernising effects, as well as the evident exploitation, inherent in imperial rule. Many of the English Fabian Socialists also approved of imperialism as a civilising influence. As with the study of the Industrial Revolution, it is important not to make blanket assertions one way or the other: again to echo E. P. Thompson, there is no record of neutral and inevitable change, but of exploitation and resistance, values lost and values gained. Herbert Luethy, the distinguished Swiss scholar (the Swiss incidentally were never colonisers), has seen imperial and colonial expansion as part of the development of civilisation: 'The history of colonisation is the history of humanity itself.'[12] Victor Kiernan, a leading Marxist in the contemporary school, has shown in scholarly style just how evil in practice this 'history of humanity' could be.[13]

7 The Origins of the Second World War

There is a link between the present section and the previous one in Professor W. N. Medlicott's heart-felt but hopeless cry of 1963 that 'Appeasement should now be added to Imperialism on the list of words no scholar uses.' The mention of appeasement is a reminder that really there are two major controversies over the origins of the Second World War – interrelated certainly, but not necessarily interdependent: the big question, presumably, is 'Was it *Hitler*'s war?' but a much larger amount of ink, blood, and synthetic emotion has been lavished over the 'appeasement' policies of British governments in the thirties which failed to 'stop' Hitler when they could and should have done so – thus the 'appeasers' were said to hold a particular responsibility for the war. In a brilliant and indispensable article Donald Watt maintains that the condemnation of the appeasers rests upon the acceptance of the 'Hitler's war' thesis.[14] This is not absolutely true: it is possible to attribute more diffuse and less clear-cut ambitions to Hitler, to accept that there are deeper economic, social and ideological causes of war, and yet still to maintain that appeasement had the unfortunate effect of encouraging rather than deterring such aggressive impulses as Hitler was subject to. Still it is true that until the publication of Taylor's *Origins* in 1961 the accepted versions of events conflated the idea of a war carefully planned in advance by Hitler with a blind and craven policy on the part of the British which failed to prevent this plan from running its course: the fundamental point was repeated again and again that the Second World War was, in Churchill's phrase, an 'unnecessary' war, that by simply following an obvious set of alternative choices the British Government could have averted the war. The breathtaking naïvety of this thesis would be un-believable were it not for the fact that honest souls (mostly American) go on serving it up to this day.

Taylor's *Origins* cuts across both controversies. In the opening chapter of the first edition he explains his intention of re-examining the simple accepted explanation that Hitler's will alone caused the war; but in the 'Second Thoughts' he explains that the 'vital question' concerns Great Britain and France – the 'appeasing nations'. My own belief, which I would not like to defend in a court of law but which I derive from my readings in various ephemera Taylor was throwing off in the period when he was planning the *Origins*, is that Taylor was in process of changing his own mind, and that this explains certain unsatisfactory features of his book. At one stage Taylor seems to have wished to defend the appeasers against the wilder denunciations which had been fashion-able from the time of the polemical tract *Guilty Men* (1940) through J. W. Wheeler-Bennett's magisterial *Munich: Prologue to Tragedy* (1948) and on to the then unpublished *Appeasers* (1963) by Martin Gilbert and Richard Gott: yet in the end the arguments of the book, while removing from Hitler a peculiar and special responsibility for the war, seem to rivet responsibility all the more heavily on the appeasers; he has removed, as again he announces in the first chapter, the basis for the 'claim that appeasement was a wise, and would have been a successful policy if it had not been for the unpredictable fact that Germany was in the grip of a madman'. (This argument, with refinements, lies at the base of what might be called the contemporary 'pacifist' defence of appeasement.)

The importance of Taylor's book was that it threw open again what had seemed likely to become a closed subject – though it should not be forgotten that in a number of earlier scholarly works Medlicott and Watt had already pointed the road towards revisionism. An important study, already completed though at that time not yet published, Esmonde Robertson's *Hitler's Pre-War Policy and Military Plans* (1964), brought out forcefully that from 1937 onwards Hitler simply rushed from one hasty improvisation to another, and that when war came in 1939 it was two or three years earlier than expected. Two general works took matters rather further through a deliberate renunciation of old-style narrative diplomatic history. An important essay in F. H. Hinsley's *Power and the Pursuit of Peace* (1963) argued that the root cause of war in 1939 was an imbalance in the European power structure: apparently defeated in 1918, Germany was in fact potentially in a relatively more overwhelmingly strong position than ever before – for the time being the Russian Empire was out, the Austrian Empire was gone for good, and France, though nominally a victor, had been gravely weakened by the long war of attri-tion fought largely on her own soil. Hinsley clearly saw himself as an opponent of the Taylor thesis, but the differences are more apparent than real; Taylor, in less abstract fashion, had covered much the same ground in his second and third chapters. In 1966 F. S. Northedge published his masterly *The Troubled Giant: Great Britain Among the Powers 1916–1939*. Northedge's title was carefully chosen: his theme was that of a Great Power, still ruling over a nineteenth-century Empire yet, through political sluggishness and economic weakness brought on by the sacrifices of the previous war, unable to come to terms with the problems and the new ideologies of the twentieth century. Northedge suggested that British policies in the later thirties were not uniquely immoral or uniquely craven. Britain's rulers then, as in the nineteenth century, really wanted nothing more than to be allowed to carry on peaceful trading policies: Britain in the nineteenth century had cut no very noble figure over the Schleswig–Holstein crisis; but when serious jeopardy threatened, Britain always had in reserve the possibility of intervention with overwhelming effect, as in 1914. In the thirties, Northedge argued, Britain had neither the power nor the *will* for such intervention (though in the end she did just that).

Historians have steadily mopped up various myths surrounding the appeasement issue. It used to be argued that Hitler could have been 'stopped' at the time of the invasion of the Rhineland in 1936 for he would have 'climbed down': Dr Watt has shown that this is by no means certain. There was much talk about how the Czechs ought to have been 'saved' in 1938; given the geographical and strategic factors involved, it is hard to visualise this 'saving' – unless again Hitler was expected to 'back down'. Northedge singled out the British Foreign Secretary's clear-sighted appraisal of the situation at the time of Munich:

> To fight a European war for something that you could not in fact protect and did not expect to restore was a course which must deserve serious consideration before it was undertaken.

Much was once made of 'pacifist' British public opinion which is supposed to have deterred Britain's Conservative Government from taking the action it really believed to be desirable: the labours of D. C. Watt and some early work of my own have, I hope, done something to dispel this nonsense – 'public opinion' and government policy formed a confused continuum in which pacifism was one element, but never a dominant one. Conservative defenders of the appeasers (see, for example, Iain Macleod's *Neville Chamberlain* (1962)) like to stress that Chamberlain recognised Russia as the greater long-term threat than Germany: left-wing critics make this a further item in the indictment. The record does not show any consciously worked-out policy of this sort on the part of Chamberlain, but there can be no doubt about the general distrust of Russia which informed his moves. Most recently the contemporary 'pacifist' school, exemplified by Keith Robbins, *Munich 1938* (1967), have argued that after all appeasement is the highest and best policy for any statesman to follow: in this case it failed only because of most exceptionally bad luck.

To sum up: on balance the appeasers still do not come out very well, but they are now seen in the wider context of the deeper weaknesses of the British political structure in the inter-war years; their mistakes were the counterpart of the economic miscalculations which brought depression and unemployment – unhappily the stakes in modern war are immeasurably higher. To return to the Hitler controversy: Taylor does not in this case carry the day, though he has rendered the old simple formulations completely obsolete. The clearest and most convincing short analysis is to be found in Alan Bullock's Raleigh Lecture. Bullock points out that Hitler was neither crazy fanatic (the traditional view) nor cynical opportunist (the Taylor view): he was each in turn; his foreign policy 'combined consistency of aim with complete opportunism in method and tactics'. Hitler's consistency of aim, Bullock continues, with obvious reference to Taylor,

> has been confused with a time-table, blueprint, or plan of action fixed in advance, as if it were pinned up on the wall of the General Staff Offices and ticked off as one item succeeded another. Nothing of the sort. Hitler frequently improvised, kept his options open to the last possible moment, and was never sure until he got there which of several courses of action he would choose. But this does not alter the fact that his moves followed a logical (though not a predetermined) course. . . .

But in restoring the traditional, and surely correct, interpretation of Hitler, Bullock is not accepting the thesis of the 'unnecessary war'. After summarising Hitler's consistency of purpose, as shown in his aims – restoration of German military power and a new German Empire in the east – his full recognition from the first that such aims would involve war, and the strength of will which enabled him to run ever more dangerous risks, Bullock concludes:

> Given such an attitude on the part of a man who controlled one of the most powerful nations in the world, the majority of whose people were prepared to believe what he told them about their racial superiority and to greet his satisfaction of their nationalist ambitions with enthusiasm – given this, I cannot see how a clash between Germany and the other Powers could have been avoided. Except on the assumption that Britain and France were prepared to disinterest themselves in what happened east of the Rhine and accept the risk of seeing him create a German hegemony over the rest of Europe. . . .
>
> If the Western Powers had recognised the threat earlier and shown greater resolution in resisting Hitler's (and Mussolini's) demands, it is

possible that the clash might not have led to war, or at any rate not to a war on the scale on which it had finally to be fought. The longer they hesitated, the higher the price of resistance. This is their share of the responsibility for the war: that they were reluctant to recognise what was happening, reluctant to give a lead in opposing it, reluctant to act in time. Hitler understood their state of mind perfectly and played on it with skill. None of the Great Powers comes well out of the history of the 1930s, but this sort of responsibility even when it runs to appeasement, as in the case of Britain and France, or complicity as in the case of Russia, is still recognisably different from that of a government which deliberately creates the threat of war and sets out to exploit it.

This is a gloomy view, perhaps too gloomy. But then history, in many ways, is a gloomy subject. History teaches that there are no easy solutions. At best, some historians would argue, different policies from Versailles onwards would have put Europe in less dangerous straits – there will always be danger – in the 1930s.

Notes

1. Quoted in Lawrence Stone, *Social Change and Revolution in England* (1965) p. 164.
2. Quoted in Stone, p. 166.
3. Ibid., p. 4.
4. *History* (1956).
5. Quoted in Stone, *Social Change and Revolution in England*, p. 43.
6. Ibid., p. 61.
7. E. P. Thompson, 'Time and Work-Discipline' in *Past and Present* (Dec 1967) 93–4.
8. G. H. Nadel and P. Curtis, *Imperialism and Colonialism* (1964) p. 1.
9. LXVIII (Oct 1961).
10. III 2 (1968) 174–5.
11. D. K. Fieldhouse, 'Imperialism', *Economic History Review*, second series, XIV 209.
12. Quoted in Nadel and Curtis, p. 29.
13. V. G. Kiernan, *The Lords of Human Kind* (1969).
14. D. C. Watt, 'Appeasement: the rise of a revisionist school' in *Political Quarterly* (1965). See also W. N. Medlicott's Historical Association pamphlet *The Coming of War in 1939* (1963).

8 *Conclusion: The Industry of History*

WE cannot escape from history. Our lives are governed by what happened in the past, our decisions by what we believe to have happened. Without a knowledge of history, man and society would run adrift, rudderless craft on the uncharted sea of time. The intelligent layman makes formal contact with history at school (where he may form lasting prejudices against academic history), in books, reviews, articles in newspapers (which very often are written by history graduates); more informally he makes contact with history in the speeches of politicians and in the asides of colleagues, family and friends. Having no skill in, only immense respect for, modern educational psychology, I have not attempted to deal in this book with history teaching in schools (at the levels affecting the ordinary layman, that is; history teaching in the later years is now often conducted with more of the true historical imagination than it is at some universities). If, however, there are corridors of power in the industry of history they are to be found in the universities: graduates are the teachers, journalists, politicians, raconteurs of the future. In this last brief chapter I propose to look more closely at the implications of the main points made in this book for the teaching of history in the universities. Research and writing, and teaching, in fact, are indissolubly associated with each other: the worst teacher may well be the scholarly pedant, interested only in the minutiae of his own area of research; the best is certainly the man who because he is working on the frontiers of knowledge can both convey the significance and excitement of such work, and communicate his understanding of the wider perspective.

Over the last generation changes in university history teaching have been taking place in the leading American universities. More recently change has come to the British universities and is specially apparent in the new universities built since the Second World War. In some instances the British, as has happened in the case of the construction of urban motorways, have been happy to copy the mistakes of the Americans, though on the whole the different structure of British universities has enabled genuine and valuable experimentation to take place. The 'crisis in historical studies' is clearly reflected in a recent controversy in the pages of the British journal *History*, when an enthusiastic celebration of recent innovations by Dr Brian Harrison was subjected to cold-eyed appraisal by Professor Elton.[1] With telling effect Harrison has quoted from a Fabian tract on the British Civil Service which criticised the standard method of history teaching at the older universities, where the subject is 'learnt by writing essays which marshal existing views and doctrine into a balanced summary and judgement'. Rather than interven directly in this controversy, I should prefer to suggest that whatever is taught in the way of period or geographical area, a history degree, or the history component of a wider degree, ought to contain four elements. First, the nature and methodology of history, its relation to other disciplines, the relevance of quantification and other techniques drawn from the social sciences: in other words, 'historiography' in the broad sense in which I have tried to present it in this book. Secondly, the writing of essays which are invaluable as exercises both in marshalling evidence and in *communication*: in modest fashion they exemplify the historian at work. Essays, preferably, should be discussed in seminar-style tutorials: if possible they should be circulated in advance so that time is not wasted on the boring non-exercise of having them read aloud; failing that, it is sometimes worth while to have two students prepare essays on the same topic, so that one can act as critic of the other; at all events all members of the seminar should have done advance preparation on the subject under review. Even if the essay has been read aloud, and the matter thoroughly discussed in seminar, the tutor should not then dodge the duty of carefully reading and annotating the essay: only thus can faults of form and presentation be properly corrected. The third element, which I am afraid many of my colleagues will find terribly old-fashioned, should be the detailed study of a relatively limited range of documentary materials: trade statistics and poems, perhaps, as well as the more traditional charters and official papers. Here the student learns the basic techniques and methodology of his subject, learns how the historian develops that special gift of 'squeezing the last drop' out of the text in front of him. Detailed work on sources is best examined, not through short gobbets, or 'context questions', but by setting whole passages, paragraph-length or more, and asking for a full commentary which will be as long as the traditional essay answer. Finally, any decent history degree should involve a piece of private research on a topic chosen by the student: given that the other elements have been mastered, it is only here that a student can develop true originality, develop that talent for asking the right questions which must appertain to any good historian (not to mention the putative civil servant). Much is made of the problems of examining such research. The answer actually is breathtakingly simple (and was successfully practised by me for several years at the University of Edinburgh). The student delivers one or more progress reports to his seminar, receives encouragement, criticism, guidance as to the pattern and shape to give his labours. These do not ever have to be written up in the form of a dissertation: instead one final examination paper (or substantial part thereof) is set aside for the student to present a coherent summary of his researches, stressing what is new about his work, and what its broader significance is. This can then be assessed in the normal way along with his other papers.

This is to leave entirely aside the problem of content in university history courses. Clearly these must keep in step with the broader changes in historical fashion; it is patently absurd that a man who is doing original work on Indian civilisation should be expected to devote all of his time to teaching modern European diplomatic history. This in turn raises the vexed question of the nature of 'special subjects': should these be confined to a certain limited range of central topics which any reasonably qualified professional could be expected to handle, or should they arise directly from the special concerns of one particular teacher? The latter presents great administrative difficulties, since when the teacher leaves the special subject necessarily folds up. Nonetheless, since the research topic mentioned above will usually be associated with the special subject, and since the contact between a maturing student and a teacher who is himself deeply involved in the subject he is teaching is one of the most fruitful possible in the entire university environment, I would myself think there to be a strong case for special subjects of this type.

What of the current emphasis on 'contemporary history'? It is as absurd at the one extreme to refuse to teach any history before the Industrial Revolution as it is at the other to insist that there is something peculiar (and perhaps rather dangerous) about 'contemporary history'. 'Contemporary' is simply a convenient label like 'medieval' or 'Victorian'. Essentially the contemporary historian employs the same concepts and the same methodology as any other historian: one or two of today's most distinguished contemporary historians in fact received their early training in the field of ancient history. Certainly contemporary history has some peculiarly difficult problems of its own (for example, often one simply does not know 'what happened next', and one finds difficulty in suppressing the influence of personal recollection); but, as we saw, the study of Magna Carta was not exactly without difficult problems either. To go all modern and deny any value to the study of earlier history is in fact to deny the value of history altogether: an understanding of man based only on the last two hundred years of his history is no understanding at all.

The truly vexed topic is that of what are called 'inter-disciplinary studies'. The trouble with too many such ventures, as experience in a number of universities has shown, is similar to that which afflicted the projects of the 'new' historians: superb in intention, but in practice a bit wet round the bottom. One hears dreadful stories of inter-disciplinary courses in which a lecture by, say, an English literature specialist is followed by one by a philosopher in which the previous lecture is torn to shreds as being philosophically untenable. Controversy, the clash of opinion, is of course a vital part of the pursuit of knowledge; but no academic course can be anything but a ragbag if it lacks internal cohesion and coherence. The justification for the inter-disciplinary approach – and it is an unanswerable one – is that a full understanding of the complexities of man's experience cannot be attained through the medium of one academic discipline, and that academic disciplines do, in fact, in that great continuum which we envisaged on pp. 106–7, shade imperceptibly into each other; or, more accurately, they overlap. We have already discussed both co-operative inter-disciplinary research projects, and the borrowings made by historians from other disciplines. The point remains, of course: given that all this is relevant to the professional historian operating on the frontiers of knowledge, is it relevant to the undergraduate? The answer is: yes – by the same token by which it is relevant for an undergraduate to study methodology and historiography, textual criticism, and to undertake a private research project. But as in all of these instances the purpose behind the operation must be clearly enunciated. The purpose is the better understanding of some problem of importance in human experience; the nature of revolution, the processes of industrialisation, the social effects of war – something like that. For an understanding of revolution the literary critic can contribute an analysis of revolutionary imagery, the philosopher an analysis of revolutionary thought; the sociologist, the political scientist, the historian all make their own specific contributions. The coherence is in the problem itself; the cohesion lies in the understanding among the teachers of exactly what they are trying to do. An academic course is not the mere presentation of a mass of miscellaneous information: it is particularly important that an inter-disciplinary course should have a clear exposition of the nature, techniques and basic concepts of the various disciplines, and the manner in which they differ from each other. It will be recalled that I began this book with the suggestion that first-year history courses should take the form of an introduction to history as a discipline. Arguably there should, at a still earlier level, be foundation courses which would involve a brief introduction to each of the main arts and social science disciplines.

But this diversion into inter-disciplinary matters must not soften the special objective of this book, which is to illuminate the purposes of history and the social needs which it has to meet. I have tried to show that the great historians share in these purposes and in practice meet these needs, even if, like great artists, they prefer simply to say that they do what they do because they like doing it. History is not in the end analogous to music or poetry or painting. My former colleague, the gifted musician Mr Edward Harper, reads my books and discusses them intelligently with me; I go and listen to his string quartets, but like most historians I am not capable of discussing them intelligently with him. History does belong to everyman: that is a strength, not a weakness.

NOTE

1. *History*, LIII (Oct 1968) and LIV (Feb 1969).

Appendix: Some Aphorisms

All men are born and live and die in the same way and therefore resemble each other (Machiavelli).

When one is too curious about the practices of past centuries, one ordinarily remains very ignorant of the practices of this one (Descartes).

History is but a pack of tricks we play on the dead (Voltaire).

History is the most popular species of writing, since it can adapt itself to the highest or lowest capacity (Gibbon).

History is little more than the crimes, follies and misfortunes of mankind (Gibbon).

The mutual relations between the two sexes seem to us to be at least as important as the mutual relations of any two governments in the world (Macaulay).

History is as much an art as a science (Renan).

The dignity of an historical epoch depends not upon what proceeds therefrom, but is contained in its very existence . . . each epoch has its own dignity in itself (Ranke).

General tendencies do not decide alone; great personalities are always necessary to make them effective (Ranke).

Men make their own history, but they do not know that they are making it (Marx).

There will always be a connection between the way in which men contemplate the past and the way in which they contemplate the present (Buckle).

We get our ethics from our history and judge our history by our ethics (Troeltsch).

It is a reproach of historians that they have too often turned *history* into a mere record of the butchery of men by their fellow men (Green).

Such is the unity of history that anyone who endeavours to tell a piece of it must feel that his first sentence tears a seamless web (Maitland).

In its amplest meaning history includes every trace and every vestige of everything that man has done or thought since he first appeared on the earth (J. Harvey Robinson).

History is the story of the deeds and achievements of men living in societies (Pirenne).

The quickest and the surest way of finding the present in the past, but hardly the soundest, is to put it there first (McIlwain).

History is the sextant and compass of states, which, tossed by wind and current, would be lost in confusion if they could not fix their position (Nevins).

The historians are the guardians of tradition, the priests of the cult of nationality, the prophets of social reform, the exponents and upholders of national virtue and glory (Bagby).

The study of history is a personal matter, in which the activity is generally more valuable than the result (V. H. Galbraith).

A society sure of its values had needed history only to celebrate the glories of the past, but a society of changing values and consequent confusions also needed history as a utilitarian guide (Cochran).

Man generally is entangled in insoluble problems; history is consequently a tragedy in which we are all involved, whose keynote is anxiety and frustration, not progress and fulfilment (Arthur Schlesinger Jr).

The task of the historian is to understand the peoples of the past better than they understood themselves (Butterfield).

History fulfils a social need, and that is its essential function (Renier).

Political and social history are in my view two aspects of the same process. Social life loses half its interest and political movements lose most of their meaning if they are considered separately (Powicke).

The aim of the historian, like that of the artist, is to enlarge our picture of the world, to give us a new way of looking at things (James Joll).

History free of all values cannot be written. Indeed, it is a concept almost impossible to understand, for men will scarcely take the trouble to inquire laboriously into something which they set no value upon (W. H. B. Court).

What better preparation for a history which seeks to bring societies to life and to understand that life than to have really lived, commanded men, suffered with them and shared their joys (Febvre on Marc Bloch).

A mere collector of supposed facts is as useful as a collector of matchboxes (Febvre).

Consciousness of the past alone can make us understand the present (Herbert Luethy).

The justification of all historical study must ultimately be that it enhances our self-consciousness, enables us to see ourselves in perspective, and helps us towards that greater freedom which comes from self-knowledge (Keith Thomas).

History is not a succession of events, it is the links between them (Evans-Pritchard).

It is a mark of *civilised* man that he seeks to understand his traditions, and to criticise them, not to swallow them whole (M. I. Finley).

Sociology is history with the hard work left out; history is sociology with the brains left out (D. G. MacRae).

Periodization is indispensable to historical understanding of any kind (Gordon Leff).

Bibliography

~~~~~~

THERE is an excellent classified bibliography by Martin Klein in Louis Gottschalk (ed.), *Generalization in the Writing of History* (Chicago, 1963) pp. 231–47. The present bibliography is more selective, but includes the main works published since 1963. It does not include the historical (as distinct from historiographical) works mentioned in the text or footnotes.

A. HISTORY OF HISTORY

Carlo Antoni, *From History to Sociology: the Transition in German Historical Thought* (Detroit, 1959).

M. F. Ashley-Montagu (ed.), *Toynbee and History* (Boston, Mass., 1956).

Herman Ausubel, *Historians and their Craft: a Study of Presidential Addresses to the American Historical Association 1884–1945* (New York, 1950).

Herman Ausubel *et al.* (eds.), *Some Modern Historians of Britain* (New York, 1952).

H. Elmer Barnes, *A History of Historical Writing* (Norman, Okla, 1936; revised paperback ed., New York, 1962): encyclopedic; too often reads like an encyclopedia.

W. G. Beasley and Edwin Pulleybank, *Historians of China and Japan* (London and New York, 1961).

Henry E. Bell, *Maitland: a critical Examination and Assessment* (London, 1965).

H. Hale Bellot, *American History and American Historians* (Norman, Okla, and London, 1952).

Reinhard Bendix, *Max Weber: an Intellectual Portrait* (Garden City, N.Y., and London, 1960).

J. B. Black, *The Art of History* (London, 1926): a study of the Enlightenment historians.

T. B. Bottomore and M. Rubel, *Karl Marx: Selected Writings in Sociology and Social Philosophy* (London, 1956; paperback ed. 1967).

J. H. Brumfitt, *Voltaire: Historian* (London, 1958).

J. B. Bury, *Selected Essays* (London, 1930).

Herbert Butterfield, *Man on his Past: The Study of the History of Historical Writing* (Cambridge, 1955; Boston, Mass., 1960); *The Whig Interpretation of History* (London, 1931).

G. N. Clark, *Sir John Harold Clapham, 1873–1946* (London, 1947).

François Drion de Chapois, *Henri Pirenne* (Brussels, 1964).

M. I. Finley, *The Greek Historians: the Essence of Herodotus, Thucydides, Xenophon, Polybius* (New York, 1959; London, 1960).

H. A. L. Fisher, *Frederick William Maitland* (London, 1910): interesting for what it tells about Fisher and his generation, as well as for what it says about Maitland.

M. A. Fitzsimons, A. C. Pundt and C. E. Nowell, *The Development of Historiography* (Harrisburg, Pa, 1954): brief, useful, dull.

F. Smith Fussner, *The Historical Revolution: English Historical Writing and Thought, 1580–1640* (London and New York, 1962).

V. H. Galbraith, *Historical Research in Medieval England* (London, 1951).

H. H. Gerth and C. Wright Mills (eds.), *From Max Weber: Essays in Sociology* (London, 1948).

Pieter Geyl, *Debates with Historians* (Cleveland, Ohio, 1958).

G. P. Gooch, *History and Historians of the Nineteenth Century* (New York, 1949; London, 1952).

J. R. Hale, *The Evolution of British Historiography: From Bacon to Namier* (London and New York, 1967).

S. William Halperin, *Some 20th Century Historians* (Chicago, 1961): contains illuminating essays by James L. Cate on Pirenne, Henry R. Winkler on Trevelyan, Gordon H. McNeil on Lefebvre, S. William Halperin on Renouvin, and Palmer A. Throop on Febvre.

John Higham, with Leonard Krieger and Felix Gilbert, *History* (Englewood Cliffs, N.J., 1965): a classic account covering American and some leading European historians.

Richard Hofstadter, *The Progressive Historians: Turner, Beard, Parrington* (New York, 1968; London, 1969).

H. Stuart Hughes, *Consciousness and Society: the Reorientation of European Social Thought 1890–1930* (New York, 1958; London, 1959): intellectual history at its finest, specially relevant here for Chapter 6 on Croce and Meinecke.

M. David Knowles, *Great Historical Enterprises: Problems in Monastic History* (Cambridge, 1963).

Joseph T. Lambie (ed.), *Architects and Craftsmen in History* (Tübingen, 1956): includes valuable essays by F. C. Lane (on Schmoller, Sombart and Schumpeter), Edgar Salin (on Sombart), C. B. Welles (on Rostovtzeff), Lucien Febvre (on Bloch) and Charles Verlinden (on Pirenne), with a stimulating introduction by W. N. Parker.

A. D. Momigliano, *Studies in Historiography* (London, 1966): mainly concentrates on ancient history, with a particularly valuable study of Rostovtzeff.

F. M. Powicke, *Historical Study in Oxford* (London, 1929).

Arthur Schlesinger Sr, *In Retrospect: the History of a Historian* (New York, 1963).

R. L. Schuyler (ed.), *Frederick William Maitland, Historian: Selections from his writings . . . with an introduction . . .* (Berkeley, Calif., 1960).

Page Smith, *The Historian and History* (New York, 1966).

P. L. Snyder (ed.), *Carl L. Becker: Detachment and the Writing of History* (New York, 1958).

Fritz Stern (ed.), *The Varieties of History: Voltaire to the Present* (Cleveland, Ohio, 1956): the justly famous and indispensable collection of readings.

Ronald Syme, *Tacitus* (Oxford, 1958).

Trygve R. Tholfsen, *Historical Thinking* (New York, 1967).

G. M. Thompson, *Gibbon* (London, 1948).

James Westfall Thompson, *A History of Historical Writing*, 2 vols (New York, 1942): still an important work of reference, though there are many inaccuracies, and the judgements are trite.

E. W. F. Tomlin, *R. G. Collingwood* (London and New York, 1953).

Edmund Wilson, *To the Finland Station: A Study in the Writing and Acting of History* (London 1940; paperback ed. 1960).

Harvey Wish, *American Historians* (New York, 1962); *The American Historian* (New York, 1960).

B. THEORY AND METHOD OF HISTORY

Raymon Aron, *Introduction to the Philosophy of History* (London, 1961).

M. P. Ashley, *Is History Bunk?* (London, 1958).

Philip Bagby, *Culture and History* (London, 1958; Berkeley, Calif., 1959).

Geoffrey Barraclough, *History in a Changing World* (Oxford, 1955; Norman, Okla, 1956).

Jacques Barzun and Henry F. Graff, *The Modern Researcher* (New York, 1957; paperback ed., 1962).

Howard K. Beale, 'The Professional Historian: his Theory and his Practice' in *Pacific History Review*, XXII (1953).

M. W. Beresford and J. K. S. St Joseph, *Medieval England: an Aerial Survey* (Cambridge, 1958).

Isaiah Berlin, *Historical Inevitability* (London, 1954; New York, 1955); *The Hedgehog and the Fox* (London and New York, 1953): a study of Toynbee, but containing material of wider general importance.

G. F. A. Best, 'History, Politics, and Universities', in *Philosophical Journal*, vi (July 1969).

Marc Bloch, *The Historian's Craft* (Manchester and New York, 1954): one of the rare classics in this genre.

British Universities Film Council, *Film and the Historian* (1968).

C. N. L. Brooke, *The Dullness of the Past* (Liverpool, 1957).

W. H. Burston and D. Thompson (eds.), *Studies in the Nature and Teaching of History* (London, 1967): contains some very important articles by S. W. F. Holloway, W. H. Walsh and others.

Herbert Butterfield, *History and Human Relations* (London, 1951).

Werner J. Cahnman and A. Boskoff (eds.), *Sociology and History: Theory and Research* (New York, 1964).

Norman Cantor and R. Schneider, *How to Study History* (New York, 1967).

E. H. Carr, *What is History?* (London, 1961; New York, 1962; paperback ed., 1964): one of the best introductions.

V. Gordon Childe, *What is History?* (New York, 1953).

G. Kitson Clark, *The Critical Historian* (London, 1967); *Guide for Research Students working in Historical Subjects* (Cambridge, 1960).

Thomas C. Cochran, *The Inner Revolution: Essays on the Social Sciences in American History* (New York, 1964).

R. G. Collingwood, *An Autobiography* (London, 1939); *The Idea of History* (London, 1946); *The Philosophy of History* (London, 1930): much less subtle than *The Idea of History*, this last pamphlet forms a useful introduction to Collingwood's thought.

H. S. Commager, *The Nature and the Study of History* (Columbus, Ohio, 1965).

A. C. Crombie (ed.), *Scientific Change* (New York, 1963): contains important essays on history of science by A. C. Crombie and M. A. Hoskin, and by Henry Guerlac.

C. G. Crump, *History and Historical Research* (London, 1928): useful for British professional orthodoxy in the 1920s.

Robert V. Daniels, *Studying History: How and Why* (Englewood Cliffs, N.J., 1966): useful, but rather elementary.

Alan and Barbara Donagan, *Philosophy of History* (New York, 1965): brief excerpts from Augustine, Vico, Hegel, Dilthey, etc.

Folke Dovring, *History as a Social Science* (The Hague, 1960).

W. H. Dray, *Philosophy of History* (Englewood Cliffs, N.J., 1964).

H. J. Dyos (ed.), *The Study of Urban History* (London, 1968).

G. R. Elton, *The Practice of History* (London, 1967): an up-to-date statement of the 'straight-line professional' position.

E. E. Evans-Pritchard, *Anthropology and History* (Manchester, 1961).

H. P. R. Finberg (ed.), *Approaches to History* (London and Toronto

1962): contains important essays by S. T. Bindoff, David Talbot Rice, Harold Perkin and many others.

V. H. Galbraith, *An Introduction to the Study of History* (London, 1964); *The Historian at Work* (London, 1962).

Patrick Gardiner (ed.), *Theories of History* (Glencoe, Ill., 1959): a useful collection of readings.

D. V. Glass and D. E. C. Eversley, *Population in History* (London, 1965).

Louis Gottschalk (ed.), *Generalization in the Writing of History* (Chicago, 1963).

Louis Gottschalk, *Understanding History: A Primer of Historical Method* (New York, 1951).

Oscar Handlin, *et al.*, *The Harvard Guide to American History* (Cambridge, Mass., 1954): part 1 is an admirable introduction to the Nature and Methods of History.

J. H. Hexter, *Reappraisals in History* (Evanston, Ill., and London, 1961).

'History and Social Science', in *International Social Science Journal*, XVII 4 (1965).

Homer C. Hockett, *The Critical Method in Historical Research and Writing* (New York, 1955).

W. G. Hoskins, *Field Work in Local History* (London, 1967).

H. Stuart Hughes, *History as Art and as Science* (New York, 1964); 'The Historian and the Social Scientist' in *American Historical Review*, LXVI (Oct 1960).

George Iggers, 'The Image of Ranke in American and German Historical Thought' in *History and Theory*, II (1962).

Irish Committee of Historical Sciences, *Historical Studies*, I, II and III (1958–60): important papers by Alfred Cobban, Denys Hay, W. H. Walsh and others.

M. D. Knowles, *The Historian and Character* (Cambridge, 1963).

Richard Koebner, 'Semantics and Historiography' in *Cambridge Journal*, VII (1953).

Hans Kohn (ed.), *German History: Some new German Views* (Boston, Mass., and London, 1954).

Mirra Komarovsky, *Common Frontiers of the Social Sciences* (Glencoe, Ill., 1957).

J. B. Krieger, 'The Historical Value of Motion Pictures' in *The American Archivist*, XXXI, 4 (Oct 1968).

Sir Henry C. M. Lambert, *The Nature of History* (London, 1933): a rather slim essay.

C. V. Langlois and C. Seignobos, *Introduction to the Study of History* (London, 1898; new ed., London and New York, 1966).

Dwight E. Lee and Robert N. Beck, 'The Meaning of "Historicism"' in *American Historical Review*, LIX, 3 (April 1954).

Gordon Leff, *History and Social Theory* (London, 1969): a wonderful book, the sort of thing one wishes one could write oneself.

I. M. Lewis (ed.), *History and Social Anthropology* (London, 1968).

May MacKisack, *History as Education* (London, 1958).

Bruce Mazlish, *The Riddle of History* (New York, 1966).

Robert K. Merton, *Social Theory and Social Structure* (Glencoe, Ill., 1961)

Hans Meyerhoff (ed.), *The Philosophy of History in Our Time* (New York, 1959): interesting collection of readings.

S. E. Morison, *Vistas of History* (New York, 1964).

L. B. Namier, *Avenues of History* (London, 1952): includes in the essay on 'History' a condensed statement of Namier's views on historical writing.

Emery Neff, *The Poetry of History* (London, 1947).

Allan Nevins, *The Gateway to History* (New York, 1938; revised paperback ed., 1962).

'New Ways in History', *Times Literary Supplement*, 7 April, 28 July and 8 September 1966: stimulating articles by Keith Thomas, M. I. Finley, Peter Temin, Bruce Mazlish and many others.

M. J. Oakeshott, *Rationalism in Politics* (London, 1962).

Richard Pares, *The Historian's Business* (Oxford, 1961).

J. H. Plumb, *The Death of the Past* (London, 1969): a characteristically rich and life-enhancing affirmation of purpose in history.

J. H. Plumb (ed.), *Crisis in the Humanities* (London, 1964).

'Reappraisals: A New Look at History; the Social Sciences and History', *Journal of Contemporary History*, III, 2 (1968): papers by Herbert Luethy, Charles Morazé, C. Vann Woodward, Jean Marczewski and others.

Gustav J. Renier, *History: Its Purpose and Method* (London, 1950).

C. H. Roads, 'Film as Historical Evidence' in *Journal of Society of Archivists*, III (1966).

A. L. Rowse, *The Use of History* (London, 1946; New York, 1963).

Bernadotte Schmitt, *The Fashion and Future of History* (Cleveland, Ohio, 1960).

John Snell and Dexter Perkins, *The Education of Historians in the United States* (New York, 1962).

R. W. Southern, *The Shape and Substance of Academic History* (Oxford, 1961).

'The Uses and Abuses of History', *Encounter*, XXXIII 4 (October 1969): essays by Max Beloff, Asa Briggs, Denis Brogan and others.

Keith Thomas, 'History and Anthropology' in *Past and Present*, no. 24 (April 1963).

David Thomson, *The Aims of History* (London, 1969).

Sylvia Thrupp, 'History and Sociology: New Opportunities for Co operation', in *American Journal of Sociology*, LXIII 1 (July 1959).

A. J. Toynbee, *The New Opportunity for Historians* (London, 1956).

H. R. Trevor-Roper, *History, Professional and Lay* (Oxford, 1957); *Men and Events* (London, 1957).

United States Social Science Research Council, *Bulletin 54: Theory and Practice in Historical Study* (Washington, 1946); *Bulletin 64: The Social Sciences in Historical Study* (Washington, 1954).

W. H. Walsh, *Introduction to the Philosophy of History* (London and New York, 1951; revised paperback ed. 1967).

Alban Gregory Widgery, *Interpretations of History: Confucius to Toynbee* (London, 1950); *The Meanings in History* (London, 1967): both of these books are philosophical rather than historiographical in character.

Index

The main treatment of subjects is indicated by bold type page references